Saudi Arabia

THE COMING STORM

Saudi Arabia

THE COMING STORM

Peter W. Wilson and
Douglas F. Graham

M.E. Sharpe
80 Business Park Drive
Armonk, New York 10504

Library of Congress Cataloging-in-Publication Data

Wilson, Peter W.
Saudi Arabia: the coming storm / Peter W. Wilson, Douglas F. Graham.
p.   cm.
Includes bibliographical references and index.
ISBN 1-56324-394-6 (c)—ISBN 1-56324-395-4 (p)
1. Saudi Arabia. I. Graham, Douglas, 1955–   . II. Title.
DS244.63.W55   1994
953.8—dc20
94-16412
CIP

Printed in the United States of America

The paper used in this publication meets the minimum requirements of
American National Standard for Information Sciences—
Permanence of Paper for Printed Library Materials,
ANSI Z 39.48-1984.

⧈

MV (c)   10   9   8   7   6   5   4   3   2   1
MV (p)   10   9   8   7   6   5   4   3   2   1

For Our Parents

CONTENTS

LIST OF TABLES

ACKNOWLEDGMENTS

Writing this book has left us indebted to a number of people. Many cannot be thanked by name, either because they remain in the Kingdom or because they specifically requested anonymity. Therefore, certain sources remain anonymous.

Note

All Hejirah (Islamic calendar) dates appear in the Gregorian equivalent to avoid complications. Most sums are also given in Saudi riyals, or SR. As of February 1994, U.S. $1 = SR 3.75. The wire service transliteration system has been used for Arabic terms and names.

Saudi Arabia

THE COMING STORM

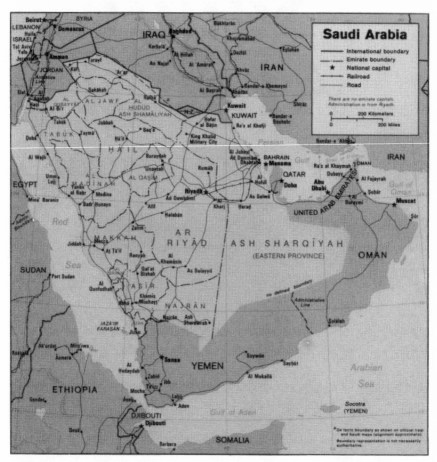

Source: U.S. Department of State. Some spellings differ from those used in the text of this book.

INTRODUCTION: STORM CLOUDS

When Iraqi armored units rumbled across Kuwait's borders at 2:00 A.M. on August 2, 1990, Saudi Arabia's leaders were so paralyzed by the invasion that they refused to inform their people about Saddam Hussein's actions for twenty-four hours. In the smoking wreckage of their neighbor, the Saudi elite saw the destruction of their own cautious strategies. Multibillion-dollar arms purchases, the carefully crafted Gulf Cooperation Council (GCC), and the constant promotion of pan-Islamic causes did not spare the Saudis the indignity of having to call on the United States to save them from a brother Arab country.

The Iraqi invasion of Kuwait did more than just alter the geopolitical landscape. Saddam Hussein's actions also signaled the end of the Saudi old order. The arrival of hundreds of thousands of Allied troops, hundreds of journalists, and an unfettered flow of information spurred an unprecedented introspection in Saudi society, with particular emphasis on the country's policies and its leadership. Today, Saudi Arabia is at the crossroads of its development as a nation-state.

Perils abound. The war with Iraq and the decision to leave Saddam Hussein in power has left the Kingdom in a dangerous position. Saudi foreign considerations now revolve around the powerful and intractable foe on its northern borders which the technically advanced but small and divided Saudi armed forces cannot hope to contain by themselves. But Iraq is not the only danger. To the east lies an equally hostile Iran, which has made new claims in the Gulf. A unified and populous Yemen poses a threat to the Kingdom's southern flank while Jordan and Iranian ally Sudan provoke additional worries. For the first time in its history, Saudi Arabia is surrounded by foes. To ensure its survival, the House of Saud has entered into an uncomfortable de facto alliance with the United States, an eager suitor who has unsuccessfully courted the standoffish Saudis for years.

The Gulf conflict and its aftermath have also had economic and financial repercussions. The Saudi economy is again growing, finally rebounding from a deep recession that saw GDP decrease by more than 50 percent during 1981–1987. Increased government expenditures, especially in defense, and the crucial oil and petrochemical industries have fueled expansion. Construction cranes again tower over many of the country's cities and industrial complexes.

However, the boom is largely illusory and belies the inherent weaknesses in the Kingdom's economy, especially the government's growing indebtedness. Although Saudi Arabia released its first balanced budget in nine years in 1994, adherence to it may prove difficult given fluctuating oil revenues coupled with increased military purchases and the domestic subsidies needed to keep a restive population content. Instead, the Kingdom's ruling dynasty, the al-Saud, are expected to keep to their old spending ways while waiting for a recovery in oil prices.

Such a course may prove dangerous. From 1983 to 1993, the al-Saud recorded eleven consecutive years of deficit budgetary spending, nearly exhausting the country's U.S. $115 billion in liquid foreign reserves in the process.[1] To cover the shortfall, the al-Saud reversed a twenty-five-year policy in 1988 that prohibited borrowing. The Kingdom's debt load has subsequently soared from nearly zero to more than $70 billion, or more than one-half the country's annual GDP.

The Gulf War further worsened the country's financial situation with war-related expenditures estimated at more than U.S. $55 billion. When Iraqi crude returns to the world market in 1994 or 1995 as expected, the results for the Kingdom's economy—already shaken by falling oil prices in 1993—could be disastrous. Saudi oil revenues could again plummet, throwing the economy into recession. And unlike the previous drop in 1981, when the Kingdom had financial reserves to soften the impact, the option of cushioning a current financial blow no longer exists.

The House of Saud faces one additional challenge: how to maintain its grip on power in the face of the greatest concerted *domestic* unrest and opposition in more than sixty years. The Gulf conflict unleashed new social forces whose aim is to change the existing political order. The struggle between those who would make the Saudi state more democratic and secular, and those who want to continue and strengthen the Saudi theocracy has rent the Kingdom's fragile social fabric and placed the government in an increasingly difficult position. Within weeks of the arrival of Allied troops, Saudi women staged an impromptu drive-through in Riyadh, protesting the ban on their driving. Their cause was subsequently taken up by the country's small progressive clique who called for greater freedoms. Not surprisingly, liberals have pressured the al-Saud for greater power sharing, more freedoms, and the free admittance of women in what is now a strictly segregated workplace. They have also pushed for curbing the power of the religious community.

Fundamentalists have been active as well. In groups such as Islamic Awakening, conservatives have launched an unprecedented and increasingly aggressive campaign against liberal ideas via fax machine, cassette, the mosques, and street protests. Fundamentalists have questioned the American link and the al-Saud's mistakes during development and have ominously demanded answers about corruption, "immorality," and policies that appear to pander to Western non-Muslim interests. By their very questions, these fundamentalists—many of whom are funded, ironically, by the same Saudi state they attack—have struck a responsive chord among the growing thousands of young, unemployed Saudis as well and strike at the legitimacy of the al-Saud. The threat of a fundamentalist takeover is a real one.

The al-Saud have moved slowly to contain the danger posed by their fundamentalists, leery about antagonizing any segment of an increasingly polarized Saudi society. In March 1992, King Fahd bin Abdulaziz finally fulfilled decades of al-Saud promises by creating a Consultative Assembly, as well as guaranteeing certain human rights. Fahd also moved to blunt fundamentalist pressure by arresting leaders of Islamic Awakening and reshuffling the Saudi religious establishment, or *ulema*. These moves, however, have done little to address the country's deep-rooted problems.

How the House of Saud deals with its foreign and domestic challenges will shape Saudi Arabia's future for decades. The regime's failure to handle these problems adeptly could have far-reaching consequences, not only for the future of the al-Saud, but for an energy-dependent world as well.

Note

1. "Country Report: Saudi Arabia," *Economist Intelligence Unit,* no. 1, 1993.

1 LAND AND PEOPLE

Gulf states

It has often been said that Saudi Arabia is the only family-owned business recognized by the United Nations. Of the nearly two hundred countries in the world today, only one is named after its rulers. The name Saudi Arabia, literally Arabia of the al-Saud, was adopted in 1932, less than a decade after the country was united by dynasty founder King Abdulaziz bin Saud.[1]

The al-Saud's presumption can be forgiven as their country occupies some of the harshest land in the world. As late as eighteen thousand years ago, the Arabian peninsula was a grassy savannah blessed with ample rainfall, vegetation, and wildlife. But the retreat of the glaciers at the end of the Ice Age led to a prolonged drought. Over time, the rivers evaporated and the once fertile land turned to desert, leaving behind only fossils and dried up riverbeds, or wadis, as reminders of a more fertile period.

There have been some compensations. Through another quirk of nature, the peninsula was covered by shallow seas several million years ago. As the abundant mollusks, brachiopods, and other creatures died, they slowly sank into the seafloor. When the sea receded, the floor was subsequently compressed at high temperatures under layers of sedimentary rock to form oil and natural gas. Today, the Kingdom's oil reserves are the largest in the world.[2]

Saudi Arabia's second blessing is just as important. At the start of the seventh century A.D., the Prophet Mohammed began preaching Islam in the small oasis town of Mecca where he was born. The new religion spread quickly and was centered around the Prophet's birthplace. Today, the world's devout Muslims pray facing Mecca five times daily. Saudi Arabia, by virtue of its guardianship of Mecca and the Prophet's burial place in Medina, is the spiritual home of Islam and one-fifth of the world's population.

Trade Center + Ka'ba

6

Location and Borders

Saudi Arabia covers 70 percent of the Arabian peninsula or an area of approximately 2.2 million square kilometers. It is roughly the size of Greenland, an area equal to the American states of Texas, Oklahoma, New Mexico, Arizona, Nevada, and California. Seas form two of the country's borders. To the west, the Kingdom is skirted by the Red Sea, an important world trade artery. To the east, the Kingdom's frontier is limited by the shallow Persian or Arabian Gulf, which serves to transport 60 percent of Japan's oil, 30 percent of Europe's, and 10 percent of the United States'. Saudi Arabia controls neither sea, an important strategic concern for the House of Saud. Iran, by its command of the Straits of Hormuz, controls the chokepoint of the Persian Gulf, while access to the Red Sea is controlled by Egypt at the north, and Yemen and Eritrea at the south.

The Kingdom's land boundaries are less clear. Its northern borders with Jordan, Iraq, and Kuwait are the best delineated. The frontier with Jordan was last adjusted in 1965 when the two countries exchanged small slivers of territory to give the Jordanians additional footage near their port of Aqaba. Saudi Arabia's border with Iraq was settled in 1922 when British officials representing Baghdad and Abdulaziz signed the Treaty of Mohammara. Ironically, one of the losers in that accord was Kuwait, which saw its southern border with the Kingdom shifted 160 miles northward as the al-Saud were compensated for territorial concessions to Iraq.[3] The Kingdom also shares two Neutral Zones with Kuwait and Iraq. The one with Kuwait was evenly divided *still* in 1966 with each country agreeing to share its oil resources. The one with Iraq was divided as well, following agreements reached in 1975 *disputed* and 1981.

Saudi Arabia's eastern and southern boundaries are more troublesome. The Kingdom's border with fellow Gulf Cooperation Council (GCC) member, Qatar, was the scene of clashes in November 1991 and again in the fall of 1992 when Saudi troops reportedly attacked the Qatari frontier outpost at al-Khofous. Two Qatari soldiers and one Saudi lost their lives in the latter incident. Peace was only restored three months later when an agreement was signed in Medina, following Egyptian mediation. Both sides promised to respect the existing 1965 border agreement, and Saudi Arabia recognized Qatari control of al-Khofous. In return, Qatar acknowledged Saudi sovereignty over the strip of territory which separates it from the United Arab Emirates (UAE).[4]

Saudi Arabia also has long-standing border differences with two other GCC members—Oman and the UAE. Borders between the two and the Kingdom remain fluid, the legacy of British control over Oman and the Trucial States, as well as centuries of conflicting tribal claims. Fighting broke out over the al-Buraiymi Oasis in the late 1940s and early 1950s between the Saudis and the British and their allies but proved inconclusive. Saudi Arabia and the UAE reached a settlement in 1974 when the latter received control of several villages in the oasis in return for a strip of territory along its Qatari border. Omani-Saudi conflicting border claims were resolved in a separate agreement in May 1990. Settlements notwithstanding, all sides continue to publish conflicting maps of the area, and the Kingdom continues to use border disputes, real and manufactured, as a means to pressure its smaller neighbors to comply with its wishes.

Saudi Arabia's southern border with the newly united Yemen remains the most unclear. The unification of Yemen in 1990, and that country's subsequent support of Iraq in the Kuwaiti conflict, only exacerbated deep-seated Saudi suspicions that Sanaa remains committed to regaining what it lost sixty years ago in the 1934 Asir War. That conflict cost Yemen the Asir region and Najran Oasis, and Yemenis have never been reconciled to their loss. In addition, the border from the Najran Oasis to Oman remains undelineated, and skirmishes are common. The boundary issue has grown in importance as large quantities of commercially exploitable oil have been discovered in the area, resulting in new claims and counterclaims, as well as isolated attacks (see Chapter 3).

Physical Characteristics

The Arabian peninsula is dominated by a plateau that rises from the Red Sea and falls gently to the Persian or Arabian Gulf. The plateau is centered on a great Precambrian shield of rock that is inching imperceptibly away from Africa, widening the Red Sea and slowly pinching shut the Persian Gulf at the Straits of Hormuz. The peninsula is also cut by two mountain ranges. The first runs along Saudi Arabia's ambiguous borders with Oman and Yemen while the second passes along the western spine of the peninsula, starting just north of Medina and continuing south into Yemen. Saudi Arabia is divided into four distinct and major regions, none of which has any year-round running streams or rivers.

The Hejaz

The coastal strip that runs along the Red Sea and the highlands that rise above it comprise the Hejaz, or "Barrier." Roughly corresponding to the Kingdom's Western Province, the Hejaz covers an area of 150,000 square kilometers and encompasses the port of Jeddah, the holy cities of Mecca and Medina, Taif, and the industrial city of Yanbu. Ranging in elevation from sea level to heights of more than 2,500 meters in the mountains south of Mecca, the Hejaz has traditionally been the most cosmopolitan section of Saudi Arabia, thanks to the holy cities and the annual influx of pilgrims fulfilling their religious duties.

The Hejaz's coastal strip, known as the Tihama, is characterized by oppressive heat and humidity and sparse rainfall. Prior to the oil boom, the majority of the Tihama's residents survived by herding, subsistence farming, or rudimentary commerce such as the pilgrim trade. Even today, the Tihama remains relatively undeveloped, and its inhabitants among the poorest in the country. The Tihama also is subject to earthquakes. The last one occurred in 1985, resulting in a few deaths and the destruction of several villages.[5]

Towering over the Tihama is the Hejaz's second zone, the Western Highlands. Containing some of the Kingdom's oldest and most developed cities, the Western Highlands are crisscrossed with trails dating from before Christ when camel caravans traveled to Yemen for frankincense, an aromatic resin especially beloved by the ancient Egyptians and Romans. Caravans often stopped in Mecca, which even before the founding of Islam was the peninsula's religious center. The highlands have long been favored by the Kingdom's elite as a summer resort, for daytime temperatures rarely climb above 113 F. (45 C.), and nighttime lows are cool and refreshing. The city of Taif, in fact, is the country's unofficial summer capital.

The Nejd

The Nejd, or "Highland," physically dominates the Kingdom. Corresponding to the country's Central Province, the Nejd encompasses the cities of Riyadh, Buraidah, Qassim, and Hail. Meeting the Western Highlands at elevations upward of 1,525 meters, the Nejd slowly slopes downward to an elevation of 600 meters near the Persian Gulf and al-Hasa. The Nejd is among the driest areas in the world and receives on average only 100 milliliters of rain per year, although wide fluctuations are normal. Temperatures are severe. During the summer, highs of more than 129.2 F. (54 C.) are not uncommon. Humidity, in contrast to the rest of the country, is pleasingly low. Winter temperatures occasionally dip below freezing, and snow and sleet occur.

The Nejd contains the Kingdom's three main deserts. To the extreme south is the largest, the Rhub al-Khali, which covers approximately 647,500 square kilometers and has the distinction of being the largest continuous sand area in the world. The Rhub al-Khali often goes for years without rain and is so inhospitable that its name literally means the "Empty Quarter." The Nejd's second largest desert is the al-Nafud, encompassing 57,000 square kilometers in an area just south of the Iraqi and Jordanian borders. The al-Nafud is the most striking of the Kingdom's deserts with its alternating red and white sands. The al-Dahna is the third Nejdi desert, and links the previous two in a wide arc of sand more than 1,300 kilometers in length but with a width narrowing to only 50 kilometers in some places.

 Containing roughly one-half of the Kingdom's population, the Nejd is the spiritual and cultural heart of the Kingdom. The ruling al-Saud dynasty has its roots in the Nejd as did Mohammed al-Wahhab, the preacher whose fundamentalist vision of Islam, known to outsiders as Wahhabism, is now followed by 85 percent to 90 percent of Saudis.

Al-Hasa

Conquered by Abdulaziz from the crumbling Ottoman Empire in 1913, al-Hasa, literally "Sandy Ground with Water," corresponds to the Kingdom's Eastern Province. Al-Hasa's topography is unspectacular as it drops from its juncture with the Nejd to sea level at the Persian Gulf. Al-Hasa's coastline is shallow and irregular, punctuated by salt marshes.

The region's chief population centers are al-Khobar, Dammam, Dhahran, and al-Hofuf, the latter being the site of the Kingdom's largest oasis with thousands of acres of date palms. Al-Hasa is also the home of the Kingdom's sizable Shiite minority. Estimates put the Shi-ite composition of the province's overall Saudi population at between 35 percent and 50 percent, or approximately 500,000 to 600,000.

Al-Hasa also houses the bulk of the Kingdom's oil and petrochemical facilities. The state oil concern, Saudi ARAMCO (the former Arabian-American Oil Company—ARAMCO) has its headquarters in Dhahran while the industrial city of Jubail has become the country's largest producer of petrochemicals.

The Asir

The fourth region of Saudi Arabia is the smallest and also the most densely populated. Taken from Yemen after the 1934 war, the Asir (or "Difficult") is the Kingdom's most geographically diverse region. It is also the most active geologically with frequent tremors. The Asir holds the country's highest mountains, with the tallest at over 3,000 meters located just north of Abha, the region's capital. The province also encompasses a small bit of the Tihama as well as the port of Jizan, Saudi Arabia's most "African" part, which is located just across from Eritrea. Many of Jizan's residents have definite Negroid features, and the outlying countryside is dotted with grass-thatched *kraal* huts. Other population centers in the region include Khamis Mushayt and Najran.

The Asir's rainfall is the most plentiful in the Kingdom. Located at the tip of the Indian Ocean monsoon system, the Asir averages 300 milliliters of rain per year, allowing the terraced farming of cotton, wheat, and other crops. To facilitate agriculture, the government has built several catchment dams, the largest of which is located at Najran. Farming is done by both men and women, and the Asir is perhaps the most relaxed of the Kingdom's regions as regards the restrictions placed on women.

The area is also the most fortified in the country, because of Saudi distrust of Yemeni irredentism. Smuggling continues to be a problem in the Asir, especially for weapons and *qat*, a woody shrub whose leaves produce a slight narcotic effect when chewed. A national pastime in Yemen, the use of *qat* is banned in the Kingdom.

People and Population

The Saudi government released the results of its third official census in late 1992. The Kingdom's population was put at 16.9 million, of whom 12.3 million were said to be Saudi. The remainder—4.6 million, or 27 percent—were said to be expatriates.[6] The government reported that the Kingdom's population was growing at an annual clip of between 3.5 percent and 3.8 percent. At that rate, the population will reach 19 million by the year 2000 and double by 2020, even though the Kingdom's infant mortality rate is among the highest in the region at approximately eighty deaths per one thousand live births.

Official statistics notwithstanding, Saudi population figures have always been suspect, and the 1992 figures are no different. The results of the country's first census, undertaken in 1962–1963, were never released and were later repudiated by the government. That ill-fated effort was followed by an estimate in 1974 conducted by the Saudi Central Department of Statistics, which declared the country's population to be 7,012,642. However, the department later admitted that the number had been chosen arbitrarily.[7] Two years later, the Kingdom undertook another census, but again the figures were never released.

Saudi census taking is complicated by the presence of large numbers of nomads who, despite being settled at an increasingly rapid pace, are still said to comprise upward of 10 percent of the Kingdom's population. Another problem is that many Saudi households are reluctant to answer questions regarding themselves or their nationality. A far greater obstacle is the government's anxiety about the country's relatively meager population, especially vis-à-vis the more numerous Yemenis to the south, as well as the Iraqis to the north. The Kingdom's elite have also been leery about having their per capita income appear lofty to their less fortunate neighbors. To that end and even before the Iraqi invasion of Kuwait, diplomats say the Saudis consistently released inflated population estimates to the United Nations and other international bodies.[8] So, while the Saudis claim that their official population is nearly 17 million, the U.S. embassy in Riyadh concluded in a less publicized 1988 study that the Kingdom's Saudi population ranged between 5 and 6 million.[9] Expatriate workers were diplomatically estimated at 3 million. The actual numbers, although unprovable, probably rest nearer the embassy's estimate.

If differences exist over the sum of the Kingdom's population, there is general agreement that it is a young one. The U.S. Bureau of the Census estimated in 1989 that more than one-third of the Kingdom's population was under the age of fourteen, and that segment of the population was expected to top 40 percent by the year 2000. Other estimates place the under-twenty population at roughly 50 percent to 60 percent.[10] The Kingdom's elderly are also increasing in number, thanks to better health care and nutrition. The U.S. Census Bureau estimated that only 1.9 percent of the 1989 population was age sixty-five or older; by the year 2000, the figure is expected to touch 2.7 percent as life expectancy has risen from a median of forty-eight years in the mid-1970s to its current level of sixty-four years for men and sixty-seven years for women.

Other population data remain sketchy. However, it is generally agreed that Saudi Arabia's population is increasingly urban with approximately 75 percent of the country's population residing in cities.[11] Jeddah and Riyadh are usually estimated to hold approximately 1.5 million residents apiece, with the latter usually said to be larger, if only for political reasons.[12] The Eastern Province conurbation of al-Khobar, Damman, and Dhahran is said to hold another million, while Mecca's population is put at 600,000, Medina's at 350,000, and Taif's at 250,000. Other large cities numbering more than 50,000 include Jizan, Tabuk, Hail, Khamis Mushayt, Abha, and Buraidah.

Like other Gulf states, the Kingdom employs vast numbers of expatriates, who continue to dominate the construction, retail, service, and technical sectors of the economy (see Chapter 6). It is difficult to estimate the exact number of expatriates in the country. Few embassies require their nationals to register on arrival. The expatriate population is also swollen by large numbers of illegal immigrants arriving from Eritrea, Ethiopia, and the Sudan via the Farasan Islands off the Saudi coast, as well as thousands of pilgrims who overstay their *hajj* visas to find work. Saudi labor officials, sensitive about the large number of non-nationals employed, also release no conclusive figures. A survey of fifteen embassies in the Kingdom in 1988 suggested a population of at least 3.9 million expatriate workers, excluding dependents (see Table 1.1). That number was seemingly confirmed by the Ministry of Planning in its Fifth Five-Year Report in 1990 when it gave the number of workers in the Kingdom at 5.771 million, of whom 3.848 million were said to be non-Saudi.[13] The report also conceded the failure of the government's Fourth Five-Year Plan, which had as one of its primary goals the reduction of the expatriate work force by 600,000. Instead, the ministry admitted that the expatriate population increased substantially during the plan's life span.

Table 1.1

Expatriate Labor Population, Selected Countries, 1985–1988

Country	Population (August 1985)	Population (August 1988)	% Change
North Yemen	1,600,000	1,500,000	−6.3
Egypt	600,000	500,000	−16.6
Pakistan	600,000	400,000	−33.3
Sudan	270,000	250,000	−7.4
Philippines	250,000	300,000	+20.0
India	240,000	385,000	+60.4
Thailand	100,000	145,000	+45.0
Turkey	100,000	130,000	+30.0
Sri Lanka	100,000	80,000	−20.0
United States	70,000	30,000	−57.2
Bangladesh	70,000	150,000	+114.3
South Korea	60,000	17,100	−71.6
United Kingdom	35,000	25,000	−28.6
West Germany	5,000	3,000	−40.0
Kenya	3,000	4,500	+50.0
Total	3,581,000	3,919,600	+9.5

Source: Embassies in the Kingdom.

The composition of the expatriate population also has changed. Prior to August 2, 1990, North Americans and Europeans were being replaced by cheaper Asians. Other nationalities, such as Lebanese, Iranians, and Syrians, were being eased out due to political considerations. The Iraqi invasion of Kuwait, however, further complicated the complexities of the Saudi expatriate population. Following the Yemeni government's support for Iraq and impromptu pro-Hussein demonstrations among Yemenis in Riyadh and Jeddah, the Saudi government changed labor regulations for Yemenis working in the Kingdom.[14] More than 1.5 million Yemenis were suddenly forced to find Saudi sponsors or leave the country.[15] The vast majority could not and summarily departed, their treatment raising questions about the Kingdom's human rights record.[16] Other nationalities affected were those whose governments supported the Iraqi incursion: many Palestinians, Jordanians, and Sudanese suddenly found their work visas not being renewed. Their places were largely filled by Egyptians, whose numbers have doubled to more than a million, as well as Indians, Pakistanis, and Filipinos.[17]

Ethnographic Divisions

Native Saudis are racially Arab Semites, with those in the Nejd regarded as having the purest bloodlines as the result of their traditional isolation. The Kingdom's other regions all have a greater mixture of races. The Hejaz is ethnographically the most diverse because of the thousands of pilgrims who have settled there to be close to Mecca and who subsequently intermarried. Another contributing factor was the area's relatively developed economy, which attracted traders and merchants from throughout the Arab world, especially Yemen. In the Asir, the Yemeni background of the population is undeniable: not only are the people smaller and thinner than their Saudi brethren but their complexions are darker as well. Many people in al-Hasa also bear Pakistani or Indian features, reflecting centuries of trade and interaction between the Gulf and South Asia. Negroid-featured Saudis predominate around the southwestern city of Jizan but are also found throughout the Kingdom as a result of miscegenation between native Saudis and their slaves. Slavery was only abolished in 1962, and even today, dark-skinned Saudis are frowned upon as having "slave blood" in their background.

Racial differences apart, there are other divisions—religious, regional, and social—confronting Saudi society, divisions that the al-Saud have had minimal success in blunting and in fact have often encouraged in order to maintain political power. These divisions have grown stronger in recent years. In fact, the royal family is often viewed as one of the few forces holding the country together. A secret study prepared by Western embassies in the Kingdom predicts that if the House of Saud were ever overthrown, the country would disintegrate into various tribal, sectarian, and ideological mini-states.[18]

Religious Differences

"Moral values bring us to Islam, which is, for good or evil, the central feature of Saudi Arabia," wrote the former British ambassador to the Kingdom, Sir James Craig, in his valedictory address about his host country.

> The ethics of Islam are not all that different from the ethics of Christianity: love your neighbor, keep your word, help the poor. But Islam is

everywhere and its ubiquity is inescapable and increasingly comprehensive. New mosques are in every street, the mention of God and his prophet in every sentence, even the King's budget speech. . . . Islam governs every detail of the believer's life. It tells him how to wash, how to urinate, how much of his estate to leave to his step-daughter.[19]

Islam, literally "submission to God," permeates Saudi life. The dominant Saudi brand of Islam is Wahhabism, or Unitarianism.[20] The peninsula's religious direction changed in 1703 with the birth of Mohammed al-Wahhab. Born in the Nejdi settlement of al-Uyayna, al-Wahhab was the son of a judge, or *qadi*, and subsequently underwent intensive religious training to follow his father. The young al-Wahhab memorized the Koran by age seven and later learned at the feet of renowned clerics in the Nejd and Hejaz. Al-Wahhab grew dismayed by what he saw: Islamic law was only laxly applied; the veneration of saints abounded, and many people worshipped stones, statues, and trees, believing them to harbor the souls of holy people. In 1720, al-Wahhab began his revivalist message, criticizing the Nejdi sheikhs for not enforcing the true Sharia, or Islamic law. Not content with cutting down holy trees and smashing idolatrous rocks and gravestones, al-Wahhab preached against the use of tobacco and said that dancing, music, and all outward signs of ostentatiousness hindered true believers from contemplating God.[21] Al-Wahhab also said that it was not enough for a true believer to purify his own life; he also had to reform those around him, this being the jihad or holy war.[22]

Central to al-Wahhab's teachings, which were to be called Wahhabism by outsiders and Unitarianism by Saudis, was the proscription against *bida,* or innovation. The young revivalist argued that any object or action not found in the Koran or Hadith (the deeds and sayings of the Prophet) was forbidden—although some exceptions such as guns were quietly made. Al-Wahhab's movement might never have succeeded except that he found an important ally in a local chieftain, Mohammed bin Saud, and together they succeeded in unifying the Arabian peninsula. One of the legacies of the union remains Unitarianism's place in modern Saudi Arabia.

It is tempting for scholars to portray the Kingdom as a religiously unified state, a Wahhabi monolith. Nothing could be further from the truth. Among Wahhabis, different interpretations abound. In the Hejaz, where the more liberal Hanafi and Shafii legal schools of Islamic thought hold sway, there is strong support for liberalizations along Islamic guidelines. Hejazi "progressives" support a more open society in which women would be allowed to drive and work without restrictions and where the judiciary would be freed from the mosque.

Nejdi fundamentalists, following the more puritanical Hanbali legal school, favor the creation of an orthodox and conservative Islamic state in which the dictates of Islam would be literally enforced and in which many reforms already enacted—education for women, television, the Western-style banking system—would be severely curtailed if not abolished. These fundamentalists blame the country's problems on "secularism" and further hint that the country and its rulers have been corrupted by un-Islamic influences.[23] The very real threat posed by fundamentalist Wahhabism was drawn home to the royal family in November 1979 when a group of zealots seized the Holy Mosque in Mecca. They justified their actions with vituperative attacks on royal corruption and the spread of Western influence in the country (see Chapter 2).

Related to the internal debate on Wahhabi Islam is the problem of the Kingdom's only official religious minority. Saudi Shiites, whose numbers are estimated to range from 500,000 to more than 600,000, are largely centered in al-Hasa, and especially in the city of Qatif. Long regarded as heretics by Wahhabi fundamentalists—in fact, Abdulaziz rejected several pleas from his cleric allies that the Shia be exterminated after al-Hasa was taken in 1913—the Kingdom's Shiites have traditionally been treated as second-class citizens and excluded from the government, armed services, and police.[24] An Amnesty International report found evidence of a systematic discrimination against Shiites and complained about their treatment in Saudi jails, noting that they "are usually in solitary confinement, routinely tortured or ill-treated, and denied access to family and legal counsel."[25] Saudi officials suppress public Shiite celebrations such as the self-flagellations and processions commemorating the martyrdom of Hussein during the Shiite holy month of Ashura. Since 1979 and 1980, when Shiite riots were bloodily suppressed with dozens of casualties, the Kingdom's largest minority has been treated better, especially following the appointment of the king's son, Prince Mohammed bin Fahd bin Abdulaziz, as governor of the Eastern Province.

Considering the restrictions the Saudis put on a sect of Islam, it is no surprise that all other public religious practices are banned.[26] The Saudis justify their action because the country is the birthplace of Islam. To avoid the prohibition on the holding of other religious services, many embassies and consulates hold ceremonies within their buildings. It had been hoped that a nondenominational church could be constructed in Riyadh's new Diplomatic Quarter. Although it was originally included in the quarter's blueprint, the church was never built.[27] There have also been repeated reports of Saudi police arresting and beating members of informal Christian groups who meet in private homes to worship.[28] Jews are regularly denied visas on the basis of their faith, although this has been changing since the end of the Gulf conflict.[29]

Regional Differences

Regional differences, an offshoot of the old tribal differences affecting the Kingdom in its first years, continue to be a serious problem for the House of Saud. The animosity among the Kingdom's four main regions, and in particular the Hejaz and Nejd, is deep-rooted and has grown rather than lessened in intensity.

The conquest of the Hejaz by the forces of Abdulaziz in 1925 brought the Hejazis into immediate conflict with the Central Arabian Nejdis. The Nejdis, whose homeland had never been colonized, considered themselves ethnically purer than the Hejazis, whom they called "driftwood" because their pilgrim forefathers "washed up" on the Red Sea shores. Although Islam is egalitarian, skin color and race still matter intensely in Saudi Arabia.[30] Many Nejdis also viewed the Hejazis as little better than heretics, because their form of Islam had been diluted by contact with foreigners.

The antipathy was reciprocated. The Hejazis, possessing telephones, cars, and relatively advanced legal and banking systems, viewed the Nejdis as ignorant and uncultured. That rivalry was worsened by the al-Saud, who initially staffed the Saudi bureaucracy with Hejazis by virtue of their better education, worldliness, and commercial experience. Although Riyadh was the new state's capital, certain institutions such as the Ministry of Foreign Affairs and the Saudi Arabian Monetary Agency (SAMA) were initially left in Jeddah. Anxiety over the possibility of problems due to conflicts with foreigners meant that all diplomatic missions were based in Jeddah as well.

The death of the late King Faisal bin Abdulaziz in 1975 signaled the end of the Hejazi domination of the Saudi civil service. Faisal's successors, first the late King Khalid bin Abdulaziz, and now Fahd bin Abdulaziz, have been much more inclined to favor Nejdis. The latter now make up a majority of the ministers, deputy ministers, and top government officials. In many ministries, Nedjization has occurred blatantly as hundreds of Hejazis have been pressured to leave; for other Hejazis the prospect of having to live in Riyadh, which now houses almost all ministries and agencies, is reason enough not to pursue a government career.[31] Regional differences have also been exacerbated by Fahd's policy of favoring people from Qassim in order to link his family to the tribespeople of that region.[32] Ironically, the appointment of thousands of Nejdis, who are more sympathetic to the Kingdom's fundamentalists and their conservative view of Islam, has confronted the ruling elite with the problem that now large sections of their bureaucracy are staffed by people opposed to their modernization policies.[33]

Other regional conflicts exist besides the Nedji-Hejazi rift. Residents of al-Hasa remain wary of the Nejdis and their attitudes, especially as the Eastern Province remains relatively liberal by virtue of being the headquarters of Saudi ARAMCO and its large number of expatriate employees. Another source of contention among people in the Eastern Province is the feeling that although their province supplies the bulk of the country's oil wealth, it is the Nejd that reaps the rewards. Finally, there is the Asir and its largely Yemeni population. The latter, although preferring the more affluent life-style of the Kingdom, nonetheless are tied by blood to their kinsmen across the border.

Social Stratification

Saudi Arabia's social divisions have traditionally been three in number: nomads or Bedouin, villagers, and townspeople. Prior to unification at the turn of the century, the difference between rulers and ruled was not very great within Bedouin tribes and somewhat greater among the townspeople. Today, the social equation is changing with the growth of the royal family, technocrats, and the religious establishment.

The Royal Family

It is difficult to make an accurate estimate of the size of the Saudi royal family. The first Saudi monarch, Abdulaziz, had forty-three sons and perhaps twenty daughters. His successor, the late King Saud bin Abdulaziz, was equally prolific. As a result, the Saudi royal family numbers well into the thousands, with estimates for both male and female members ranging from 15,000 to 25,000. However, membership in the royal family is not limited to Abdulaziz's descendants. Abdulaziz's uncle, Saud al-Kabeer, sired sons and daughters who are considered royal. Closely tied to the al-Saud are three other prominent families with whom they have intermarried: the al-Sheikhs descendants of Mohammed al-Wahhab; the al-Sudairi, the family of Abdulaziz's favorite wife; and the al-Thunayan.

Because of its great size, the royal family is not a tightly knit organization. Some Gulf ruling families share investments and business activities, but not the al-Saud. All members of the royal family are paid government stipends. Senior princes receive "salaries" of between $100,000 and $200,000 per year with cars. Second-tier princes receive $100,000, while minor princes are given $50,000, which is enough money to live on but hardly sufficient to make them wealthy.[34] Royal stipends are supplemented in a number of ways. Members of the royal house have business interests, and many benefit from business "commissions" and the proceeds from unofficial sales of crude oil. For example, in the early 1980s, Prince Mohammed bin Abdulaziz had more than half a million barrels of oil being credited to his personal account every day.[35] Another source of income has been the granting of land to members of the royal family who then resell it to the state for highways, government buildings, and other facilities.

Ambitious princes, and those governing the Kingdom's provinces, use the *majlis,* or council, to strengthen their constituencies and reward followers. While tribal sheikhs doled out gold and silver in their *majlis* to secure loyalty, princes today use their names or positions to provide favors, gifts, ministry contracts, or jobs. A word from a prince can get a roadway repaved, a government contract delivered, a telephone line installed, and can secure the admission of a family member into one of the Kingdom's specialist hospitals. Favors build a reputation for generosity and weave a web of obligation. This process also tends to create groups with similar political ideas, mirroring the divisions in Saudi society. Some princes, such as Prince Talal bin Abdulaziz, are identified with liberal, progressive elements in the Kingdom. The sons of the late King Faisal, the al-Faisal, are considered religiously conservative yet forward-looking. Crown Prince Abdullah bin Abdulaziz appeals to tribesmen and conservatives, while still other princes appeal to interest groups ranging from socialists (very rare) to hard-core Islamic fundamentalists.

The House of Saud is further divided among various blocks built around full brothers, a natural consequence in a society where blood relationships are so important. All of the sons of a particular mother tend to form cliques. The six full brothers of present King Fahd are known as the al-Fahd, and are the most powerful circle in the country, controlling several key ministries and governorships. Known as modernizers, the al-Fahd include Defense and Aviation Minister Prince Sultan bin Abdulaziz, Interior Minister Prince Naif bin Abdulaziz, Deputy Defense Minister Prince Abdulrahman bin Abdulaziz, Deputy Interior Minister Prince Ahmad bin Abdulaziz, Riyadh Governor Prince Salman bin Abdulaziz, and Prince Turki bin Abdulaziz, who holds no government portfolio due to the scandals surrounding his in-laws, the al-Fassi family. The al-Fahd are "opposed" by the cluster of princes surrounding Abdullah, who has the misfortune of having no full siblings. Other major blocks include the al-Faisal and the sons of former kings Saud and Khalid.

The family is controlled by the al-Fahd, Abdullah, and 200 other senior princes. Importance is generally determined by one's lineal proximity to Abdulaziz. For example, the sons of Abdulaziz come first (ranked by seniority), and they are then followed by the grandsons, and great-grandsons of the founding king. This arrangement, however, has been weakened by Fahd and his full brothers' assiduous promotion of their children. In some cases, the al-Fahds' sons have leapfrogged senior princes, a phenomenon that has caused growing familial tension. Distrust has grown with Fahd's proposal to change the succession sequence, part of his political reform package (see Chapter 2).

Like other Gulf monarchies, the House of Saud and its royal allies are increasingly monopolizing the upper echelons of the state and government bureaucracies. Its members serve as its own backup intelligence service and keep a close eye on potential subversives. To enhance security, each prince has an American-built mobile telephone that is part of a satellite network completely independent of the Kingdom's telephone system. This technology allows the royal family to unite on the one issue upon which every prince and princess agrees: survival.

Despite the rise in fundamentalism, antimonarchical sentiment in the Kingdom is muted. The Saudis, like the British, adore the trappings of the royal family. Although some groups might call for the abolition of the monarchy and the creation of an Islamic state—for example, those zealots taking over the Great Mosque in 1979—there is general agreement that the alternative to the House of Saud is chaos. This is not to say that most Saudis want to see the present system continued without changes. There is growing hope that the House of Saud can be induced to share power, as has occurred in neighboring Kuwait.

The Merchant Families

The merchant families have traditionally held a position of power in the Kingdom due to their financial clout. Many of these families, such as the Alireza, gained great influence and power by assisting Abdulaziz during the penurious early days of the Kingdom. These families occasionally intermarry with the al-Saud and benefit from social and familial contacts.

Ironically, few of the Kingdom's merchant families have Saudi backgrounds. Instead, most came from Yemen (and especially the Hadhramaut region of the former People's Republic of Yemen) or Bahrain. Most Saudis know the names of the fifty or so great merchant families—among them Kaki, Jamjoon, Kanoo, bin Mahfouz, Hafiz, al-Rajhi, Juffali, and al-Zamil—who dominate business in the Kingdom. Several members of these families have held ministerial posts.

The merchants are among the royal family's strongest supporters, fearing that its overthrow would result in a fundamentalist Wahhabi regime. However, some Jeddah merchants still support the idea of an independent Hejazi state, and in 1969 there was an unsuccessful attempt to overthrow the existing order. Hejazi merchants were also thought to have contributed to the rebels who seized the Mecca Mosque in 1979. Additionally, merchant support for the royal family is being tempered as the comity between the two groups has begun to fade. Harder economic times and an overabundance of young princes has created business competition.

"There are two things which do not mix," Abdulaziz was fond of saying to his children. "Running a government and making money. Do not compete with the merchants and they will not compete with you."[36] Those words of warning have been completely ignored by Abdulaziz's sons and grandsons as the al-Saud have begun penetrating the country's commercial sector to the dismay of the merchant class.

The problem is one of numbers. In the 1950s–1970s, most of the al-Saud contented themselves with positions in the state and government. Those few who entered business did so discreetly, and often in sectors where they were not competing directly with the more established merchant families. But as the family mushroomed, the state and government apparatus could no longer absorb them. As a result, many have had no choice but to enter business. "You have to understand one simple fact . . . ," noted Prince Saud bin Naif bin Abdulaziz, explaining the family's position on business. "Since it is a big family and we can't all have government jobs, some have to make a living. That's only fair."[37]

That may be true, but the awarding of government contracts to princely business ventures still causes resentment. Given the fact that the upper echelons of the government are filled with al-Saud, and that government expenditures remain the economy's chief mover, there are ample opportunities for conflicts of interest to emerge. Contracts have been given to princes with minimal business acumen solely on the basis of family connections. The future was made clear in 1989, when the son of the crown prince, Prince Miteb bin Abdullah bin Abdulaziz, won the Kingdom's Ford agency. Ford had just come off the Arab Boycott List, and most thought the agency would revert to its previous holders, Sulaiman Olayan in the Eastern and Central provinces, and Hajji Abdullah Alireza of the Western Province. Instead, the agency was granted to a prince who had no prior business experience.

The issue has become so sensitive that the ulema and their fundamentalist allies have repeatedly attacked the al-Saud's growing business rapaciousness in several petitions and memorandums to Fahd. Given the wealth Fahd's sons have amassed from government expenditures, it is no surprise that the king's response has never been published. The ulema's criticism did, however, have one effect. In the spring of 1992, Prince Saud bin Naif bin Abdulaziz, whose monopoly of the Kingdom's courier service had been particularly singled out by fundamentalists, was appointed deputy governor in the Eastern Province and supposedly had to give up his business interests.[38]

The Technocrats

When Abdulaziz was confronted by the revolt of the Ikhman, his religious warriors, in the late 1920s, one of the Ikhwan's bitterest complaints was that Abdulaziz was sending his sons abroad to non-Muslim schools and procuring them foreign educations. The religious conservatives were justly concerned, for the new educated technocrats have different aspirations than those of the ulema. The Saudi technocratic class is suspect in the eyes of both the Kingdom's religious conservatives and many members of the royal family because they have been traduced by foreign ideologies such as communism, Arab socialism, or Western democracy. During the 1950s and 1960s, the technocrats, whose ranks include military officers, were the biggest threat to the government. The change of heart has been the result of a number of factors, including fear that the deposition of the al-Saud would result in a theocratic state.

Some analysts say that the technocratic or middle class has now reached 8.1 percent of the labor force, a crucial percentage at which revolutions have occurred in other Arab monarchies.[39] However, the sobering results of Iran's Islamic Revolution have left the Kingdom's technocrats at a loss on how best to change the existing system. The technocrats have seen Islamic fundamentalists score heavily in Jordan, Algeria, and Iran, and the result has been less freedom, not more. In some cases, they find that the issue of democracy has been hijacked by antidemocractic forces and are confused on how best to respond. Many of their children are also in the fundamentalists' camp, which further complicates their position.

When the Americans entered the Kingdom during Operation Desert Shield, the technocratic class decided to press for more rights. Women staged their abortive driving protest, and intellectuals lobbied Fahd to fulfill his promises to establish a Consultative Assembly. Instead, Fahd cracked down on women and gave the religious police greater leeway.

Today, technocrats continue to staff a large percentage of the Kingdom's bureaucracy. However, their role is largely limited to implementation, rather than policymaking. Because of their backgrounds (i.e., nonroyal), their influence is circumscribed and subordinate to that of the royal family, which continues to place key members in each government ministry and agency, and selected para-statal concerns such as Saudi ARAMCO, the Saudi Basic Industries Corporation (SABIC), and SAMA, as well as the Saudi armed forces. As the House of Saud centralizes the government bureaucracy, the power of the technocrats is bound to decrease even further. The days when technocrats such as former Petroleum and Mineral Resources Minister Ahmad

Zaki Yamani could act with some independence ended with the death of King Faisal in 1975.

The composition of the technocratic class is changing as well. At one time, the class was largely comprised of Hejazis and people from al-Hasa. Today, there are increasing numbers of Nejdis in its ranks, many of whom support the growing fundamentalist movement in the country.

The Religious Establishment and Fundamentalists

Saudi Arabia's religious establishment has always been a powerful force in the Kingdom. Abdulaziz unified the Kingdom by coloring his crusade in religious terms, claiming to represent the true religion—Unitarianism. Today, religion continues today to give the ruling family legitimacy, and the al-Saud are careful to preserve the pretense if not the reality of the union fashioned between themselves and the first Wahhabis in the eighteenth century. The royal family has nonetheless attempted to loosen Unitarianism's grip on their country while fostering development. Such attempts have met limited success.

Saudi Arabia's religious establishment is topped by the Council of Senior Religious Scholars, a body often referred to as the ulema. However, the term ulema has broad usage and often refers to the hundreds of religious scholars who make up the country's religious establishment. The council's membership varies from ten to twenty members and acts as the Kingdom's "Supreme Court," approving the succession to the throne, deciding religious questions, and issuing *fatāwi,* or rulings on government policies, such as the al-Saud's decision to invite non-Muslim troops to the Kingdom to counter Iraq. The council came into existence in 1971; before its creation senior scholars met informally under the Grand Mufti, or head of Riyadh's religious establishment. The current head of the council is Abdulaziz bin Baz, a blind octogenarian who once attracted wide attention with his assertion that the earth is flat as per the dictates of the Koran. Despite his age, bin Baz continues to possess a quick mind and liberally sprinkles his pronouncements with quotations from the Koran and Hadith. Bin Baz is also a controversial figure; his role in the 1979 Mosque Uprising has never fully been explained, and it was he who advised the secret police to set the plotters free months before they seized the mosque. The cleric has also been suspected of having ties with both Saudi and foreign fundamentalist groups.[40]

The Saudi ulema are carefully controlled by the state. Unlike their Iranian counterparts, they have no set hierarchy and no income-generating lands of their own. Instead, the ulema, imams (preachers), and *muzzein* (prayer callers) are dependent on the al-Saud for their salaries, effectively making them civil servants. They also serve at the pleasure of the al-Saud. This point was amply illustrated in December 1992, when Fahd pushed seven members of his senior ulema into retirement after they declined or were unable to sign a letter condemning fundamentalist attacks on the al-Saud.[41]

Imams and *muzzein* serve to communicate the decisions of the ulema and the state when needed. As all official sermons must be approved, the al-Saud can use the religious establishment as a convenient device for making their wishes known. According to the former Ministry of Pilgrimages and Religious Endowments, there were more than 54,000 imams and *muzzein* in the Kingdom in 1991, and the ministry planned to hire an additional 7,200 in 1992.[42]

If the ulema make the country's religious decisions, and the imams communicate them, it is left to the Committee for Propagation of Virtue and Forbidding of Evil to enforce them. A committee member is known as a volunteer or *mutawa,* and in 1989 there were more than 20,000 *mutawaeen* in the Kingdom.[43] The committee functions as an independent and powerful government agency and is charged with ensuring that Islam's dictates are followed by both Muslims and non-Muslims. The *mutawaeen* trace their ancestry to a group of "Zealators" founded in 1855 by Imam Faisal. These twenty-two men carried canes for punishing those who wore silk or gold, those who smoked, sang, played musical instruments, or were lax in religious observances.[44] The first modern committees of *mutawaeen* were founded in 1903 to patrol the streets of Riyadh. The *mutawaeen* were empowered to arrest, bring to trial, imprison, and punish people who committed offenses. The committees were extended to the Hejaz in the late 1920s and were promoted through a *fatwa* issued by Meccan theologians. When Abdulaziz learned in 1930 that the *mutawaeen* were opposing some of his policies, he incorporated them into the Directorate General of the police. They were stripped of their powers of arrest and reduced to reporting crimes to the proper authorities. In 1960, civil service regulations were extended to the committees. They regained some of their powers during the reign of Saud, who bolstered them to refurbish his Islamic credentials. The national head of the committee was assigned ministerial status in 1975.

Strongest in the Nejd, today's *mutawaeen* ensure that shops and restaurants abide by prayer calls and shut their doors, and actively admonish people they consider improperly dressed (such people may be swatted with a cane for their transgressions). Offenders often have their names taken down and in extreme cases can be detained and imprisoned. In fact, many Westernized Saudis think the al-Saud keep the *mutawaeen* occupied with minutiae to prevent them from dealing with weightier issues. Their power also seems to wax when the government needs to improve its Islamic credentials.

Religious repression runs in cycles, usually getting stricter after upheavals, such as the Iranian riots in 1987, or the driving protest by women in Riyadh in 1990. This pattern of greater and lesser restrictions began long ago. For example, when Abdulaziz conquered the Hejaz, he allowed his followers to suppress many of the innovations they found in Jeddah and Mecca. A few months later, on the anniversary of Abdulaziz's accession to the throne of the Hejaz, celebrations

> were organized on an unprecedented scale for Arabia and were obviously intended to impress both foreigners and Arabs alike. . . . [T]hey may be said to mark a definite departure from the rigid precepts which the Ikhwan had succeeded temporarily in imposing. Photographs were taken freely; an official photographer had in fact come from Egypt and photographed the Emir on every possible occasion. Smoking was indulged in openly, or with only a pretense at concealment.

Then three months later,

> The regulations issued by these committees nineteen months ago had been allowed practically to become a dead letter, and the local citizens, who had been congratulating themselves on the gradual evanescence of these tiresome restrictions, were greatly annoyed to find them resuscitated by lictors or special police imported from the Nejd who carry out their duties with deplorable efficiency. . . . [S]mall boys playing mouth organs had been the first to receive attention. These diminutive miscreants are given a spate of cane and the offending instruments collected in baskets.[45]

Fahd moved to curb the excesses of the *mutawaeen* in December 1990 when a series of raids on private homes nabbed an aide, and created a diplomatic incident when a party being hosted by a member of the French diplomatic community was invaded by gun-toting committee members. A new director, Dr. Abdulaziz bin Abdelrahman al-Saeed, was appointed. Dr. al-Saeed later admitted that mistakes had been made but he blamed them on a lack of training and funds. The latter problem seemed remedied when Fahd earmarked $50 million for *mutawa* education, in a move intended to buy their grudging acceptance, if not loyalty. However, Dr. al-Saeed later said that the *mutawaeen* had legal rights to raid houses or apartments where they suspected drug or alcohol use. He further said they had a duty to ensure that Saudi males abided by prayer calls and that women dressed modestly.[46]

Since the Gulf conflict, the Saudi religious establishment has increasingly fractured between groups who support the al-Saud and those who back the country's growing fundamentalist movement. The latter is led by Islamic Awakening, a shadowy organization with roots in the old Ikhwan movement of the early 1900s. Calling for a religious revival and a cleansing of the Kingdom of all Western and secular influences, Islamic Awakening has drawn support from members of the ulema, many imams, *mutawaeen,* university professors, lawyers, and, most importantly, the growing numbers of unemployed Saudi youth (see Chapter 6).

Many of the latter are graduates of the country's universities where they have earned degrees in Islamic studies and Islamic law, disciplines already suffering from oversupply. In the past, these thousands were largely absorbed by the government bureaucracy, but since the recession, many ministries and agencies have stopped hiring. Rather than reducing the number of students in Islamic studies and steering them toward disciplines more needed by the economy, the government has done nothing. There are several reasons for this. Saudi students prefer Islamic studies to medicine or engineering because the former is easier and more "noble" according to Saudi cultural standards. The government has also been reluctant to cut back its support for Islamic studies because such backing helps bolster its Islamic legitimacy. This approach, however, is backfiring as the overproduction of Islamic studies graduates not only creates job market problems but also breeds difficulties since many Islamic students are radicalized by their professors and peers. As a result, the House of Saud is beginning to confront an increasingly large body of jobless young men who are diametrically opposed to its progressive policies and who question the regime's commitment to Islam.

The threat posed by these young men is a real one. Crown Prince Abdullah told his hosts during a 1988 visit to the United Kingdom that the greatest peril to the country was the rise of Islamic fundamentalism among Saudi youth.[47] Making matters worse is the fact that the Kingdom's present troubles have confirmed the direst predictions of the regime's critics that too much Westernization has already been introduced.

The Tribes

When Abdulaziz, the founder of the Saudi state, began consolidating his family's position in the central region of today's Kingdom, he encountered a centuries-old dilemma: how to build a state from dozens if not hundreds of small, local tribes of fractious Bedouin in the peninsula? The tribes were often at war with one another, and all were distrustful of city dwellers. In addition, their loyalty to anyone or anything beyond the family unit and clan was often slippery and shifting. "Draw the sword in their face and they will obey," Abdulaziz said of them to some British emissaries. "Sheathe the sword and they will ask for more pay."[48] Although Abdulaziz succeeded by the force of his will, strategic marriages, conquest, and hefty subsidies, he and his successors were less successful in fashioning a national psyche. That failure remains today. As well-known Saudi middleman Adnan Khashoggi told Pentagon officials in 1973, you should "recognize the fact that much of the culture of Saudi Arabia is based on a Bedouin philosophy. These people do not acknowledge a loyalty to anyone. They only recognize a loyalty based on material values."[49] This tribal element makes Saudi Arabia unique in geopolitical terms.

The tribes continue to enjoy a loose organization independent of the government and look to their sheikhs, or old men, for leadership. These tribal leaders are nominal employees of the Ministry of Interior, and are often guests at the *majlis* of local governors. Sheikhs handle local problems and, in a feudal custom, are sworn to supply the government a levy of men in times of trouble. They also help distribute governmental largess.

Saudi social life also remains organized around the extended family, clan, and tribe, and an individual's identity is linked to the tribe as well. It is also true to say that dynastic tensions within the ruling house have led to a resurgence in tribal power as princes and factions have sought allies. The issue came to a head in 1982 when Fahd and his full brothers attempted to have the tribes turn in their weapons in a move to limit the power of Crown Prince Abdullah, who is commander of the National Guard. When the tribes refused out of self-interest as well as support for Abdullah, the al-Fahd, whose support was limited to the cities, began cultivating their links to certain tribes in the Qassim region as a counterbalance. Tribal differences are manifested in many ways: low-ranking men of a noble tribe who serve in the military are sometimes known to disobey their superiors if the latter come from a less esteemed tribe.

Since the creation of the Kingdom, the House of Saud has employed several strategies to bring the tribes under control. Even though Abdulaziz is often portrayed as the desert king and a Bedouin himself, it was he, "perhaps more than anyone else, who set in motion the destruction of the traditional basis of their [the Bedouin] tribal life and began their incorporation into the Islamic-based Saudi state."[50] Abdulaziz initially tried to use Islam to weaken tribal ties, especially with the creation of the Ikhwan, or Brotherhood. The Ikhwan were tribes Abdulaziz settled in war villages, *hijar,* where they remained in constant combat readiness to aid the Saudi leader in his conquests.[51] As soon as the Kingdom was consolidated and the Ikhwan could no longer count on booty or soldiers' pay, they drifted off. They were eventually disbanded following their abortive attempt to overthrow the House of Saud.

Abdulaziz tried other tacts as well. In 1925, he deprived the tribes of their exclusive use and management of grazing areas. This cut down on intertribal conflict and also removed one of the key functions of tribal governments: the distribution of resources. Throughout Abdulaziz's reign, the Saudi state made repeated efforts to settle the tribes. In 1968, a new law stated that the Bedouin could gain land after farming it for three years, further eroding communal ownership and tribal solidarity. The government also tried to secure Bedouin loyalty through grants and jobs. A study in 1968–1970 showed that 80 percent of all Bedu had at least one family member in the Saudi National Guard whose salary was essential to the support of the family. Later studies showed that upward of one-third had government positions, while another one-third received government grants.[52]

Increasing urbanization, job opportunities, and the material benefits of settled life have put renewed pressures on the tribes, which are being settled at a rapid rate throughout the country. By the year 2000, Saudi planners predict all will be settled. However, their settlement has come at a cost, as one of the casualties has been the extended family unit. Not surprisingly, there has been a strong backlash, which has been manipulated by fundamentalists.

Expatriates

Saudi Arabia's expatriates form the lowest rung in the Kingdom's social ladder. Although they are very much second-class citizens, they constitute an important, if politically powerless group. Expatriates as an aggregate comprise anywhere from 27 percent to 45 percent of the Kingdom's population. Their labor is crucial to the Saudi economy. Further, their treatment could conceivably interest foreign governments in Saudi internal affairs. However, as unemployment among Saudis grows, resentment of foreigners increases, especially toward those employed in technical and managerial positions.

Relations between Saudis and expatriates have never been warm. Saudi xenophobia, coupled with linguistic and religious differences, always ensured a certain degree of separation. In addition, many Saudis resent expatriates for controlling large sectors of their economy. Relations have grown worse with increased job competition and growing labor abuse. The latter has occurred as unscrupulous Saudi employers have arbitrarily rewritten contracts and slashed salaries in violation of labor laws. Many also participate in an increasingly corrupt recruitment system in which foreigners pay bribes to secure work in the Kingdom. Saudis also want to avoid the situations found in Kuwait and the UAE where expatriates outnumber natives. The danger posed by too many expatriates was confirmed when many long-term Palestinian residents of Kuwait, some of whom had received Kuwaiti citizenship, turned on the government after the Iraqi invasion. To prevent the emergence of one strong expatriate group such as the Palestinians in Kuwait, the Kingdom has diversified its labor supply.

The level of Saudi antipathy toward expatriates is best illustrated by two incidents that took place in 1988. The first occurred when Fahd announced the resumption of an "expatriate-only" income tax. The plan was hastily withdrawn after thousands of expatriates in key industries, hospitals, and banks tendered their resignations. The incident irked many Saudis, who criticized expatriates as unwilling to make sacrifices for the good of the country.[53] The second incident took place a few months later when the Saudi national soccer team won its initial matches in the Asia Cup. Jubilant Saudis took to the streets to celebrate, but in some instances, impromptu celebrations turned into anti-foreigner protests as youths roughed up and threatened expatriates.

Expatriate workers pose little threat to the House of Saud or to Saudi society in general. First of all, the general population distrusts them, and second, the different groups of expatriates generally dislike each other too much to allow any concerted action. The Kingdom's elite have also shunned certain nationalities such as Lebanese, Syrians, and Jordanians who have shown an interest in Saudi domestic politics. Strikes are prohibited in the Kingdom, and, although they have occurred several times, they have always been suppressed by arresting and deporting the ringleaders. A graver danger to the country's stability is if the government were to reintroduce taxes for expatriates. Such a move would again result in mass resignations, creating huge logistical problems.

Saudi officials, however, are concerned not only about possible expatriate political opinions but about their effect on Saudi political attitudes. Saudi religious zealots find common ground with Arab traditionalists in harassing foreigners. Although the Saudi middle and upper classes insist on hiring foreign maids and drivers, they spend a great deal of time complaining about the deleterious effects these foreigners have on Saudi culture (see Chapter 6). In fact, one of the few areas of agreement within Saudi society as a whole is the need to keep foreigners in their place. Nonetheless, this foreign component of Saudi Arabia's population makes the resolution of problems more difficult.

Notes

1. Only Jordan comes close to being a country bearing its ruler's name. The Hashemite Kingdom was named for the country's founding dynasty who claim to be the descendants of Hashem, the prophet Mohammed's grandfather.

2. Proven Saudi ARAMCO reserves totaled more than 257 billion barrels in 1990, according to the annual report of the Saudi Arabian Monetary Agency (SAMA).

3. Jolyon Jenkins, "Shifting Sands: Why Kuwait Is So Small."

4. Qatari News Agency, December 21, 1992.

5. The earthquake, which occurred in April 1985, went unreported by the Saudi Press Agency but was confirmed to the authors by several residents of the region. Newspapers were instructed not to publish the story.

6. "Defining Market Strategies," *Middle East Executive Report (MEER)*, December 1992.

7. *The Economist*, February 8, 1986.

8. Staffers at both the Ministry of Planning and the Ministry of Finance and National Economy told the authors that they regularly used padded figures on the orders of their superiors.

9. *Saudi Arabian Investment Perspective*, United States Embassy, 1988.

10. Fouad al-Farsy, *Saudi Arabia: A Case Study in Development*, p. 42.

11. Richard Nyrop et al., *Saudi Arabia: A Country Study*, p. 74.

12. *MEED: Middle East Business Weekly*, July 17, 1992.

13. Ministry of Planning, "Fifth Five-Year Plan."

14. *New York Times*, October 22, 1990.

15. All expatriates employed in the Kingdom need a Saudi sponsor through whom a work document, or *daftir al iqama*, is issued. Prior to the Iraqi invasion of Kuwait, only Yemenis were exempt from this requirement, which was one of the provisions of the 1934 Treaty of Taif that ended the Yemeni War.

16. *New York Times*, November 2, 1990.

17. Ibid.

18. Said document was released to the authors by one of the embassies involved.

19. Sir James Craig, "Valedictory Number 2: The Saudi Arabians." Sir James's memo was leaked in November 1987, causing a minor diplomatic flap.

20. For an overview of Unitarianism, see Ayman al-Yassini, *Religion and State in the Kingdom of Saudi Arabia*.

21. David Holden and Richard Johns, *The House of Saud*, pp. 21–22.

22. The jihad was directed against both backsliding Muslims and unbelievers. Al-Wahhab's campaign against the former was novel.

23. *The Economist*, February 1, 1992.

24. As of 1993, there were no Shiite ministers and only two Shiite deputy ministers.

25. *Washington Post*, December 7, 1990.

26. Some authors say the ban is partially the result of the first American oilmen not asking Abdulaziz for religious privileges when they arrived to begin drilling in the mid-1930s. See D. van der Meulen, *The Wells of Ibn Sa'ud*.

27. The decision not to build the church was no doubt taken to avoid criticism by fundamentalists and thus bolster the regime's Islamic credentials. There were repercussions: Saudi plans to build a mosque in Geneva were subsequently rejected by the Swiss.

28. Minnesota Lawyers, *Shame in the House of Saud*, pp. 52–77.

29. *Washington Post*, January 23, 1992.

30. This point was repeated to the authors many times by Saudi contacts.

31. *Saudi Gazette*, July 17, 1986.

32. The al-Fahd's ties to Qassim is another one of the facts pointed out in the intelligence document entitled "Saudi Report" given to the authors.

33. One example is the Saudi Arabian Monetary Agency (SAMA), where up to 60 percent of the staffers are said to oppose interest-based banking. Peter Wilson, *A Question of Interest: The Paralysis of Saudi Banking*, p. 55.

34. Deborah Amos, "Sheik to Chic."

35. *Wall Street Journal,* May 1, 1981.

36. Robert Lacey, *The Kingdom,* p. 305.

37. *Washington Post,* March 27, 1992.

38. However, business sources told the authors that many princes, when appointed to government positions, only appear to give up their business interests. To circumvent restrictions, they set up bogus companies, which continue to service existing contracts.

39. *The Economist,* February 8, 1986.

40. Riyadh diplomats reported in 1988 that bin Baz was the target of a deranged knife-wielding Pakistani. Although the assassination attempt was checked, bin Baz was forced to accept twenty-four-hour police protection. Some diplomats theorized that the attack was bogus, staged by the Ministry of Interior as a pretense to put guards around the elderly cleric in order to see whom he was meeting. Up until the attack, bin Baz had refused police protection and/or surveillance.

41. *New York Times,* December 14, 1992.

42. "Country Report: Saudi Arabia," *Economist Intelligence Unit (EIU),* no. 3, 1992.

43. *Arab News,* November 12, 1988.

44. Christine Helms, *The Cohesion of Saudi Arabia: Evolution of Political Identity,* p. 129.

45. Taken from the Jeddah report, January 1930, from the British Consulate of Jeddah, quoted by Derek Hopwood, "The Ideological Basis: Ibn Abd al-Wahhab's Muslim Revivalism" in *State, Society and Economy in Saudi Arabia,* edited by Tim Niblock, p. 41.

46. "Country Report: Saudi Arabia," *EIU,* no. 4, 1991.

47. This was relayed to the authors by a member of the British Embassy who accompanied the crown prince to London in 1988.

48. Helms, *The Cohesion of Saudi Arabia,* p. 112.

49. Michael Field, "Merchants and Rulers of Arabia," *Euromoney,* July 1981, p. 30.

50. Donald P. Cole, *Nomad of the Nomads: The al-Murrah Bedouin of the Empty Quarter.*

51. *Hijra* literally means migration; the first Ikhwan believed they were moving from secular lives to holy ones.

52. Donald P. Cole, "Bedouin and Social Change in Saudi Arabia," pp. 128–49.

53. Saudi nationals also refused to accept proposed user fees.

2 THE POLITICAL SYSTEM

Saudi Arabia's political system has changed remarkably little since 1902, when Abdulaziz bin Saud captured Riyadh with forty followers and began his family's reconquest of the Arabian peninsula. Abdulaziz and his successor sons have continued the traditional autocracy, a fusion of tribal and state institutions. Today, the Kingdom has all the outward trappings of a modern state and government—a Council of Ministers, modern armed forces, a bureaucracy, courts, and a new Consultative Assembly—but this superstructure was erected on the simple political foundation of a traditional desert sheikhdom.

Abdulaziz used the Arab tribal tradition to establish his Kingdom. Like traditional sheikhs, he shrewdly pitted external and internal enemies against each other, and influenced friends and foes by disbursing generous gifts. He made strategic marriage alliances, and conferred with his subjects at the *majlis,* or council, in which his subjects could speak their minds, ask for favors or judgments, or simply partake in his generosity.

The Kingdom of Saudi Arabia still exists because Abdulaziz established it with far greater sagacity than the average sheikh, and because he benefited from the discovery of massive oil reserves. The latter in turn allowed Abdulaziz to excel in generosity, an important Arab tradition that is, for the most part, a naked appeal to the self-interest of the recipient. But whereas Abdulaziz threw gold coins to the populace to win their affections, his sons have disbursed oil wealth and built a generous welfare state to secure their subjects' support. Today, the government grants low-cost loans for homes, rental property, farms, and factories. University students receive free tuition, housing, and stipends while they attend classes. Saudis consume subsidized gasoline, electricity, water, and up until recently, subsidized staple foods.

All medical care is free. Further, Saudis are not conscripted into the military and pay no income tax.

Arab traditionalism is one of the two roots of the al-Saud's legitimacy. The other is Islam, specifically the al-Saud's vow to protect it and the two holy cities of Mecca and Medina. The Kingdom of Saudi Arabia remains a theocracy with little distinction made between religion and politics. The country's constitution is the Sharia, or Islamic law, and the al-Saud take care to couch all political decisions in religious terms. The al-Saud also have the ulema sanction especially controversial or weighty decisions including the invitation extended to non-Muslim troops in August 1990. The al-Saud have entwined their rule so closely with Islam that criticism of them is seen as being a threat to Unitarianism.[1]

This reliance on Arab tribalism and Islam means that a Saudi king, besides being the head of state, is also viewed as the leader of the tribe, as well as the imam or religious leader of the Kingdom's faithful. Interestingly, the al-Saud's two links to legitimacy may complement each other but they can also conflict. The Arab tribal link demands obedience and loyalty to the family and tribe above all else. Pre-Islamic Arabs had no other compass than kinship and tradition by which to navigate. Islam, being a universal religion, erases the importance of kith and kin, and sets up an ideal of brotherhood and unity that is alien to the tribalism of the Arabian peninsula. The two factors of tribal fractiousness and Islamic universalism provide two different tactics used by the royal family. Fractiousness allows the al-Saud to appeal to the self-interest of small groups, while Islam permits the royal family to appeal to all these groups on a different and higher level. This enables the royal family to distribute favors to different regions and groups in order to weaken opposition to themselves, while at the same time using Islamic calls for unity to weaken the individual groups whose favor they have been currying.

Background and History

Saudi Arabia's political development was always conditioned by the desert and the vast stretches of space that separated the few scattered settlements and tribes. In such a precarious environment, the creation of a central political authority was nearly impossible. Instead, family and tribal ties remained paramount. Bedouin tribes were governed by emirs or sheikhs, wise men who functioned more as consensus builders rather than as rulers. Tribal decisions were rendered in the *majlis* where the emir consulted his kinsmen before making any decisions. Concurrence was essential before any action was taken. The tribal system promoted egalitarianism, and divisions based on wealth were practically nonexistent.[2] Given the desert's capriciousness, wealth was transitory in any case, and used to "buy" a good name or influence others through generosity.

Few sheikhs attempted to subjugate other tribes, although it was common for sheep-herding tribes to pay protection money or tribute to their camel-raising counterparts. For the most part, Arabia's tribes co-existed with each other and the towns in an uneasy state of nonpeace, nonwar, in which tribes extorted money, fought blood feuds, or raided camels when possible. The shared hardship, equality of possessions, and love of independence meant that the Bedouin shared an informal agreement to avoid upsetting the traditional patterns of life. There were exceptions to this rule: from time to time one clan would attempt to expand its power in a bid to unify the peninsula, but it seemed Arabia's tribes were more adept at building rather than maintaining conquests, and such efforts always ended in failure.

Foreign powers also tried with no more success: conquerors would briefly master parts of the peninsula and try to establish some sort of permanent outpost before admitting failure and withdrawing. Perseverance was additionally tempered by the peninsula's meager resources, which made its conquest a low priority for most empire builders.

The only successful challenge to the peninsula's Arab traditionalism occurred in the seventh century A.D., when the Prophet Mohammed received his visions from God. Mohammed subsequently laid the foundations for a theocratic state by substituting Islam for tribal ties. Mohammed's vision led to a novel political interpretation: the state's sole function was to enforce the Islamic legal code, Sharia, thereby allowing (or coercing) believers to lead good Muslim lives.[3] As a result, the Islamic polity that emerged under the Prophet was theocratic in nature, with its leaders assuming both political and religious functions. This fusion was to have significant ramifications in the future, but the peninsula soon slipped back into its old ways as the center of the rapidly expanding Islamic Empire shifted first to Damascus and then to Baghdad. Arabia's brief moment of splendor was lost, and for the next thousand years, the old tribal system held sway.

The Rise of the Saudi-Wahhabi State

The peninsula's political backwardness changed with the rise of Mohammed al-Wahhab in the 1700s (see Chapter 1). Al-Wahhab's orthodox approach to Islam was bound to create controversy, and although
he initially met success in his town and surrounding settlements, he
later had to flee for his life when he made inflammatory statements
against the local governor.[4] Al-Wahhab turned for refuge to Mohammed bin Saud, the emir of Diriyah, a village a short distance from
today's Riyadh. It was a propitious choice. Although bin Saud was
initially wary of his guest, he was persuaded by his brothers and wife
to protect the preacher.[5] The two men quickly discovered that they
held one goal in common: the conquest of the Arabian peninsula.
Al-Wahhab wanted to purify the home of Islam, while the ambitious
bin Saud was motivated by power. The two purposes neatly dovetailed,
and an agreement was quickly reached. Bin Saud committed himself to
undertaking a cleansing jihad against all nonbelievers while al-Wahhab
recognized the chieftain as the lay leader of the movement.[6]

Religious zeal and military prowess proved an irresistible combination as the new state quickly grew in area and power. In the emerging
polity, al-Wahhab's importance was undeniable. Besides receiving 20
percent of all the booty bin Saud's forces seized, the preacher held a
seat of honor in the emir's *majlis* and approved all moves made by his
secular partner.[7] In newly conquered settlements, new emirs and
qudiāh (judges) were appointed, the latter to indoctrinate the people in
the new religion and to oversee the collection of the religious tax or
zakat.[8] For Arabia, this attention to bureaucratic detail was unique, and
aided the Saudi-Wahhabi state to solidify its gains. The union survived
bin Saud's death in 1765 when the emir's heir, Abdulaziz, married the
preacher's daughter. Military successes continued, and in 1803, the
Unitarian armies took Mecca and subjected it to a thorough cleansing.
Shrines were destroyed, holy trees were uprooted, and domes on
mosques demolished.[9] The zealots also cut off access to the holy city
by foreign pilgrims because of their deviation from true Islam. Four
years later, Medina fell and underwent a similar cleansing. The Unitarian empire now stretched from the Arabian Gulf to the Red Sea, and
from today's Jordan to Yemen.

Success was short-lived, however. The Ottoman Empire, which
claimed nominal guardianship over Mecca and Medina, decided to

crush the heterodox Wahhabi upstarts. Egypt's Mohammed Ali, at the urging of the Sublime Porte, sent his son against the al-Saud. With the help of tribes bribed from the Saudi-Wahhabi state, the Ottomans reconquered the holy cities and disposed of the first Unitarian state after several years of ruthless fighting. The capital of Diriyah was razed and its date palms cut down, while the chief leaders of the movement were carted off to Constantinople for execution or imprisonment.

Later attempts to resurrect the Saudi-Wahhabi alliance fell prey to dynastic squabbles. Following two decades of civil war, the Nejd and Riyadh came under the control of a rival clan, the al-Rashid, and the al-Saud fled to Kuwait for asylum. The descendants of al-Wahhab (who were now called the al-Sheikh) deserted their one-time allies and made an alliance with the al-Rashid in order to preserve Unitarianism, as well as their own positions.[10] The al-Sheikh even participated in the defense of Riyadh in 1901 when the al-Saud unsuccessfully attempted to regain it.

Abdulaziz and the Founding of the Modern Saudi State

The foundations for the present Saudi state were laid the next year when Abdulaziz bin Saud (the great-great-great-grandson of Mohammed bin Saud) retook Riyadh from its Rashidi governor. Abdulaziz resurrected his family's traditional alliance with the al-Sheikh by marrying the daughter of Riyadh's chief imam.[11] The religious community, however, remained hostile to the new ruler. Riyadh's ulema, who at this time were coalescing into a body of ten to fifteen senior judges and scholars under the leadership of the city's Grand Mufti, were suspicious of Abdulaziz's religious qualifications. Their skepticism was centered on bin Saud's relative youth and his stay in Kuwait, which had a reputation as the region's local fleshpot.[12] The ulema only relented after Abdulaziz agreed that his father should retain the title of imam, and conceded jurisdiction over the city's moral and legal development to the clerics.[13]

Abdulaziz found the first years of empire building slow and difficult. The outcome of the struggle with the al-Rashid seemed in doubt for nearly two decades, and was finished to the al-Saud's satisfaction only after World War I. Although Abdulaziz benefited from his conjugal alliances and the occasional use of foreign weaponry and tactics, it was the religious link that proved most useful. Abdulaziz stressed that he was the protector of true Islam, and that adherence to Unitarianism superseded tribal and other secular allegiances. Abdulaziz's use of religion was the masterstroke in his bid to unify Arabia.

This religious tie-in was strengthened by Abdulaziz's adoption of a group of men called the Ikhwan, or Brotherhood.[14] The exact origins of the Ikhwan are unknown. Some authors claim they were Abdulaziz's invention while others suggest that they were discovered by the king. Whatever their roots, the Ikhwan were religious reformers of al-Wahhab's ilk who supplanted tribal ties with Islam. They preached and lived an austere form of Islam, which they eagerly imposed on others. Unlike al-Wahhab, who was a townsman, the Ikhwan were nomadic Bedouin who settled in religious-military-agricultural communes called *hijar* where dancing, music, smoking, and all signs of ostentation were prohibited. The fanatical Ikhwan believed that there was no higher glory than dying in battle for the cause of Islam. Rejecting the advice of some of his family members who felt the Ikhwan were a threat, Abdulaziz instead encouraged them, calculating that his efforts at building a Saudi state could not succeed until the tribes were settled in villages from which they could be more easily controlled (see Chapter 1). To show his solidarity with his new allies, Abdulaziz even destroyed his prize possession, a gramophone he had carted over the desert from Kuwait.[15]

The number of *hijar* grew quickly to more than two hundred, and at their peak, they could field more than sixty thousand fighting men. Although all settlements engaged in agriculture, their chief purpose was to supply Abdulaziz with a constant stream of soldiers and supplies. To ensure loyalty, Abdulaziz provided each *hijra* with an imam, who indoctrinated the settlers in the major tenets of Unitarianism, including jihad, and the al-Saud's support of it. Membership in *hijar* was made mandatory for all Bedouin in 1916, and they were forced to pay *zakat* as well.[16] From this time onward, the nascent Saudi state was based on three pillars: the al-Saud, the ulema, and the Ikhwan, a triad that was to have dangerous implications in the future.

Abdulaziz introduced few innovations in government during the first years of his reign. He ruled as his forefathers did, using his *majlis* to build coalitions or disburse presents and cash to emirs and followers to maintain their loyalty. The Saudi leader also attended to local administration, appointing emirs, *qudiāh,* and financial officers for each of his towns and villages. The emir was in charge of local administrative details, and enforced bin Saud's will. The *qadi* provided the people with religious instruction and settled religious disputes. The financial officer oversaw the collection of *zakat* and other duties.

With the defeat of the al-Rashid in 1921, Abdulaziz's domains spread from today's Iraqi-Jordanian border in the north to Asir in the south. The only area outside his control was the Hashemite Kingdom of the Hejaz, encompassing the two holy cities of Mecca and Medina, as well as the port of Jeddah. Under the venal rule of the mentally unstable Shareef Husain, the Hejazi Kingdom seemed impregnable, given Britain's considerable support to the Shareef. However, the Shareef blundered badly in 1924 when he proclaimed the resurrection of the caliphate and himself as caliph.[17] Such religious posturing by the Shareef infuriated the international Islamic community, and drove the Ikhwan to a fever pitch; they took little persuading to invade the Hejaz. They seized the mountain city of Taif in their first battle, and slaughtered hundreds of its inhabitants. Mecca surrendered a few days later in December 1924, and the Ikhwan entered the holy city unopposed.[18]

Early Political Institutions

The conquest of Mecca confronted Abdulaziz with a number of dilemmas. He wanted to avoid a repeat of the events of 1803, when Wahhabi excesses had led to foreign intervention. This was guaranteed to happen again if there was a repeat of the Taif massacre. Abdulaziz sought a moderate course, and sent conciliatory letters to most of the world's Muslim organizations, calling for an international conference to discuss a pan-Islamic administration of the holy city. He also prohibited his followers from cleansing Mecca of its "ungodliness," much to the Ikhwan's discomfort. The conqueror also showed a marked readiness to accept his new dominion's existing institutions, which were far more advanced than anything found in the Nejd. Against the wishes of his more fundamentalist followers, Abdulaziz left most of the city's administration intact and created a Consultative Council, or *al-Majlis al-Ahli,* to help him rule.[19] The council was initially comprised of representatives from the city's three leading classes: the ulema, merchants, and nobles. Each representative was elected by his peers. The council had broad local powers, leaving only foreign and military matters in the hands of Abdulaziz. Its formation was a masterstroke. Not only did Abdulaziz's moderate approach to government allay the concerns of the international Muslim community, but it also underlined his recognition that the primitive tribal councils of the Nejd were unsuitable for his new possessions.

Abdulaziz disbanded Mecca's Consultative Council six months later and replaced it with a new body with even broader representation. The new council had fifteen elected members, of whom two were from the ulema, one from the merchants, and one each from Mecca's twelve districts. Rounding out the body were three nobles appointed by the king. The new body's powers were broad. Besides overseeing municipal services and security, the council was also given responsibility for religious education and organizing the Sharia courts.[20] The success of the Mecca council was repeated in other cities of the Hejaz, whose conquest was completed in 1925 with the fall of Jeddah. Similar councils were subsequently put in place in Medina, Jeddah, Taif, and Yanbu. Each council was headed by a chairman appointed by the king, but other representatives were elected by leading citizens from the ulema, merchants, notables, and the heads of leading professions. Each body then forwarded a set number of representatives for the Hejaz's General Consultative Council.[21]

The conquest of the Hejaz rounded out Abdulaziz's empire building, save for the absorption of the Asir in the 1934 war with Yemen. Additional conquests were unlikely as the Kingdom was now hemmed in by British protectorates and mandates. Once outlets for war and plunder were closed, the Ikhwan not only became superfluous, they became a liability. Abdulaziz tried, in good desert sheikh fashion, to reconcile his allies with his new priority of laying the foundations for his Kingdom, but placating the Ikhwan proved difficult. Abdulaziz was only barely able to restrain his followers from purging the Hejaz of all ungodly "innovations" they found, including telephone wires, mirrors, and automobiles. Another vexing issue was tobacco, which the Ikhwan opposed, but which many in the Hejaz used. Abdulaziz pragmatically permitted tobacco sales but only after Hejazi merchants agreed to pay a tax on it to their financially strapped conqueror.[22] Abdulaziz finally removed the Ikhwan from the Hejaz after they precipitated an international incident when they fired on Egyptian pilgrims bringing a new Mahmal, or ornate panoply, to cover the Kaaba, a black monument inside Mecca's Grand Mosque.[23] The Ikhwan had outlived their usefulness, and a day of reckoning was nearing.

While his erstwhile allies brooded in their *hijar,* Abdulaziz remained in the Hejaz, overseeing its incorporation into his state. The Saudi leader was motivated by several reasons, and especially by the fact that pilgrims to the Hejaz paid a head tax that increased royal income severalfold.[24] To ensure an uninterrupted flow of money, Abdulaziz had to find some way to incorporate the province's more advanced institutions into his state. Failure to do so would have risked rebellion; on the other hand, if he had left these structures to stand unaltered the Hejaz would have never been absorbed. To this end, the king was willing to make some concessions, and hit upon a near perfect solution: he decided to allow the Hejaz most of its laws and institutions but also appointed his son, Prince Faisal bin Abdulaziz, as viceroy to make sure the royal prerogative was kept intact.[25] This compromise was codified in the constitution Abdulaziz gave his new province in September 1926.

The constitution, which held sway only in the Hejaz, did not create a constitutional monarchy, and Abdulaziz's power remained absolute. Divided into nine sections, the constitution's first articles restated truisms about the state: it was Islamic; its capital was Mecca; and the king was the chief administrator. It also provided for the appointment of a viceroy. Of particular interest was Section Four, which created several councils. First among them was the General Consultative Council or *al-Majlis al-Shura*. Comprised of the viceroy, his advisors, and six appointees, the council was empowered to discuss all issues brought to the viceroy, and then vote on them. However, all decisions had to be approved by Abdulaziz. Similar bodies were instituted for each administrative section, city, district, and village.[26] The constitution restricted who could run for office for the new councils; only those approved by the king could be candidates.

One year later, in 1927, the king made several adjustments. Among the most important was the dissolution of the existing General Consultative Council and its replacement with a new body of eight men who were to advise Faisal in his administration of the Hejaz. Of the octet, four were to be appointed by the government after consultation with "people of integrity and experience," while the other four were to be appointed by the government at its own discretion. Two members had to be Nejdis as well.[27] Abdulaziz defended his decision to limit his choices by selection, noting that "we looked into the matter of the Consultative Council on which the people depend and we wanted to leave the question of electing its members to the people and we wished all the people would participate." However, the king then explained that due to time limitations, such elections were impossible, and consultation would have to suffice.[28] Ensuring further cooperation was the fact that the council's chairman was none other than Viceroy Faisal.

The constitution created one other body as well. A Council of Deputies, whose sole purpose was to assist the viceroy in executive matters, was initiated in 1932. The council was comprised of the deputy of foreign affairs, the deputy of financial affairs, and the deputy of the General Consultative Council. Heading the new body was the viceroy, who was responsible for enacting its decisions when the king was out of the Hejaz. All decisions rendered by the council still had to go to the king for approval, but Article Seven gave the council the power to make and enforce its own decisions when the matter was sufficiently urgent. The Council of Deputies functioned sporadically until 1953 when the Council of Ministers was formed.

The Constitution of the Hejaz was a first step in the broadening of the political process in the Kingdom. Theoretically, it was a breakthrough as its creation admitted the need for man-made laws to supplement, if not actually supplant, the Sharia. Although it can be said that its promulgation was largely geared to calming international fears about the fate of the holy cities following their takeover by Abdulaziz and the Ikhwan, the constitution also served to incorporate the Hejaz's more advanced institutions into the Saudi state. However, once these institutions were brought under Abdulaziz's control, he often let them atrophy from neglect or emasculated them by failing to appoint members, ensuring that these political entities were in no position to challenge him. This pattern has been repeated by all subsequent Saudi monarchs, who have systematically undermined any institution that could threaten their absolute power.

The Fall of the Ikhwan

While Abdulaziz planted new institutions in the Hejaz, a crop of troubles was blossoming in the Nejd as ties between the Saudi leader and some of his religious backers were quickly deteriorating. Despite his assumption of the title of "imam" in the early 1920s, Abdulaziz's relations with the ulema were cordial but distant. Although the latter had come to depend on him for financial support, they often greeted the king with faintly disguised condescension, and some refused to speak to the Saudi leader.[29] The king's relations with the Ikhwan were even worse. The latter, along with some members of the clerics, faulted the king for allowing the Shia of al-Hasa to continue their religious ceremonies after the province's conquest in 1913, and for tolerating Hejazi practices. Abdulaziz's suspension of the jihad infuriated other true believers, who in defiance of the king's edicts continued their raiding in Iraq and Transjordan, where they came close to provoking international incidents with the British several times. The king attempted to reason with his followers, but the idea of international relations was a difficult concept to grasp, especially among the Ikhwan, whose narrow-minded religiosity the king had previously stoked when it had suited his purpose.

Abdulaziz first tried persuasion. The imams from each *hijra* were recalled and instructed to preach that the pursuit of material goods and earthly riches was good, and that Islam was a religion of toleration.[30] Abdulaziz's hope that the Ikhwan could be moderated was unrealistic, and the result was hardly unexpected. In late 1926, several thousand Ikhwan met at the first *hijra* at al-Artiwaya, where they restated their criticisms of Abdulaziz. The charges were so serious that the Riyadh ulema were brought in to mediate. At this critical juncture when the ulema could have sided with the Ikhwan and perhaps altered the country's power equation, the scholars adopted a middle position. Confining themselves to criticizing the decision to allow the Shia their ceremonies, the ulema refused to take a stand on the telephone, telegraph, and automobile, and more importantly, said the issue of jihad rested with the imam or king.[31] Their cautious ruling satisfied no one, and tensions continued.

Seeking a compromise, Abdulaziz assembled his nobles and the ulema in November 1928 and offered to abdicate, but only to a member of his own family. Abdulaziz's offer had the intended effect; it was roundly rejected by the assembly, many of whom had been feted and given gold and silver for several days prior to the vote. When in the following year the Ikhwan continued to pillage Iraqi and even Saudi settlements and caravans, Abdulaziz had no choice but to destroy them. He assembled an army of townspeople and loyal tribesmen, and equipped them with armored cars and machine guns. The deciding battle was fought at Sabillah, and the Ikhwan, outnumbered and outgunned, were crushed in less than thirty minutes.[32] The Ikhwan rebellion, which nearly succeeded, left a lasting impression on Abdulaziz and his sons. Never again would the al-Saud create any institution or group that could challenge their power.

After Sabillah, only the religious scholars posed a threat to Abdulaziz. Not surprisingly, they remained loyal, largely because they were fearful that open opposition risked a further erosion of their power and endangered Unitarianism's position within the Saudi state. The ulema had other reasons as well: al-Wahhab had preached obedience to earthly rulers unless they stopped following Islam's dictates. For his part, Abdulaziz sought to avoid open confrontation with his clerics and strove to maintain the pretense of the old alliance in which the ulema were the moral arbiters of the state—and which gave him legitimacy. He continued to have daily consultations with his scholars following sunset prayers.[33] He also sought to co-opt them, and paid their salaries, effectively making them civil servants. In addition, he tried to alter the composition of the ulema by lessening the influence of the al-Sheikh and promoting families more dependent on the al-Saud.[34] Abdulaziz also allowed them their small victories, especially in the fields of religion and education, and listened to their complaints about some of his innovations. But as H.C. Armstrong wrote in 1934, "in matters of religion, bin Saud submitted to the wishes of the ulema, but when they rendered him advice on political and military matters, with which he disagreed, he sent them back to their books."[35] The difference was a subtle one: although the Saudi ruler did not accept the ulema's traditional right to rule on his policies, he did seek their approval on selected issues. This struggle would continue throughout Abdulaziz's reign and those of his successors. The discovery of oil and the subsequent arrival of thousands of non-Muslims, the introduction of army uniforms and bugles, and the growth of schools would all create tension between the al-Saud and the ulema, but the latter never seriously challenged the ruling family.

The Last Years of Abdulaziz

The crushing of the Ikhwan gave Abdulaziz the opportunity to tinker further with his government. In 1932, he changed the name of his country from the unwieldy Kingdom of the Nejd, Hejaz, Asir, Hassa, and Dependencies to Saudi Arabia, or Arabia of the al-Saud. The change was indicative of how Abdulaziz viewed his domain: it was his possession. Not surprisingly, no distinction was made between state and personal revenues. Outside the king's *majlis*, there were no government bodies or institutions. The Saudi "civil service," save for the Hejaz, consisted of the king's retinue and advisors. This continued to be a small group of men, most of whom were foreigners. The military had been disbanded after the Yemeni War, and Abdulaziz's palace force consisted of fifty to sixty black bodyguards and whatever levies his tribal emirs could raise for him at his command. The ulema's independence had been countered as well. As David Holden and Richard Johns pointed out in *The House of Saud*, Abdulaziz was "the state because no other focus of loyalty or tribute existed beyond his person —and the ever present threat remained that if his person should be removed or his reputation stained, the state he had created would disappear as well."[36] Abdulaziz delegated little authority to his sons, preferring to involve himself in all of the issues besetting his country, from the most pressing to the most trivial. Not only did this jealous guarding of the royal prerogative preserve the traditional tribal mechanisms but it also served to stunt development of more modern institutions.

The discovery of oil in 1938, and the tremendous inflow of petrodollars after World War II, initially had minimal impact on the Saudi political system. To administer the new wealth, the aging Abdulaziz oversaw the creation of several new ministries. The Ministry of Defense was formed in 1944, joining the existing Finance and Foreign Affairs ministries, and the Ministry of Interior was created in 1951. Several other ministries, including Communications, Education, Agriculture, Commerce, and Health, were created two years later. What motivated the increasingly feeble Abdulaziz to begin the bureaucratization of his administration is open to conjecture. Equally perplexing was the king's decision to create a Council of Ministers, signing the decree just a few weeks before his death at the end of 1953. The decree stated:

> A Council of Ministers is to be formed under the presidency of our son Saud, Crown Prince of the Kingdom and Commander-in-Chief of the Armed Forces. It shall be composed of all those Ministers of State charged by Royal decree with the conduct of the affairs of ministries entrusted to them so that they may look into all the affairs of the nation whether foreign or domestic, and it shall decide what corresponds to the interests of the country in these matters in order to refer them to us.[37]

It is possible that Abdulaziz sensed the inadequacy of his son, Crown Prince Saud bin Abdulaziz, and established the council as a sort of weak regency to assist him. If that was the intent, it failed, for in practice, the Council of Ministers wielded less power than its Hejazi precursors. Unlike the latter, all decisions reached by the Council of Ministers had to be approved by both the president of the council and the king. The decree also gave Saud the power to determine the role of the council, as he was empowered to draw up each ministry's role and functions. The edict further stated that the council was to meet at least once a month, and that some decisions would have to be made unanimously, while others would be by a simple majority. No explanation of the distinction between the two was given.[38] Whatever the king's motivation in creating the council, its promulgation seemed intended to help Saud rule, while giving his half-brother Faisal, who was council president, power as well.

The Council of Ministers first convened in 1954, but despite Abdulaziz's desire to see it used, Saud seldom consulted it. Instead, he preferred to rule alone—like his father—or in conjunction with his sons and his coterie of followers. Among the latter was the infamous Eed bin Salim, who served not only as the new king's chauffeur and mechanic, but also as his procurer. In recognition of his good work, Saud also made him his chief financial advisor.[39] Saud's choices worried his brothers. Within months of his ascension, he was imperiling his family's fortune, and it became clearer why Abdulaziz had attempted to change the traditional governing mechanism of the Saudi state.

The Years of Saud

Saud's reign is today remembered for bringing the House of Saud's fortunes to their lowest point since the unification of the country. Corruption, political ineptitude, and prolifigate spending all created strains within the ruling family that resulted in a power struggle between Saud and his more competent half-brother Faisal. This conflict lasted for more than six years (1958–1964), during which important political reforms were discussed, but never implemented. Saud might have weathered these storms were it not for the hurricane sweeping the Middle East—Egyptian President Gamal Abdul Nasser's Arab Nationalism. The prophet of pan-Arabism, Nasser electrified the Arab world in 1952 when he and a handful of officers overthrew the venal Egyptian monarchy and proclaimed a new political ideology. Their message was short: there is only one Arab world, which had been divided and manipulated by the West. Nasser demanded the unification of the Arab people, the nationalization of all Western holdings, and political reform.

Revolutionary Egypt and theocratic Saudi Arabia made unlikely allies, but at first Saud funded many of Nasser's plans, and supported his nationalization of the Suez Canal. The king also allowed his new ally to send military advisors, bureaucrats, and teachers to foster Saudi development. The results were mixed: a few months after the arrival of the two hundred–man Egyptian military training unit, a plot was discovered among Saud's own troops in Taif to assassinate members of the royal family and overthrow the monarchy.[40]

Other developments were just as troubling. In 1953, thousands of Arabian-American Oil Company (ARAMCO) workers went on strike to protest their living conditions and the special privileges accorded their American colleagues. The strike was eventually broken by force and by Saud's promises of reform. Three years later, strikes again erupted, but this time the strikers were pursuing more political objectives, including calls for the creation of a Saudi Republic. These strikes were bloodily suppressed by units of the Saudi army, and a royal decree was issued forbidding future work stoppages.

That control was slipping out of Saud's and his family's hands was underlined the next year when Nasser visited the country and was afforded a hero's welcome. Nasser's dynamism contrasted with the corruption and ineptitude of Saud and his clique, and encouraged many of the king's younger brothers, especially the group centered around Prince Talal bin Abdulaziz, to form Nasserite cells. Grouped together in a dissident organization called Young Nejd, Talal and his followers sought to overturn the existing order and put in its place a constitutional monarchy.

In 1958, Saud's amateur efforts to assassinate Nasser and wreck the proposed Syrian-Egyptian union came to light. Less than three weeks later, Saud's brothers presented him with an ultimatum demanding his semiretirement. Saud acquiesced, and Faisal took over the day-to-day administration of the government. Among the supporters of Faisal's "coup" were Talal and the Young Nejd organization. Whatever promises Faisal made to Talal and his clique are not known; however, it seems likely that Faisal had at least hinted that he would support some democratic reforms in return for their support. It was only a few weeks before Talal realized that his hopes for real constitutional change under Faisal were unrealistic.

Undaunted, Talal and his supporters refused to concede defeat. After Faisal abolished press censorship, Talal's clique actively pressed for greater political freedom and courted Saudi public opinion by calculated acts of philanthropy. Constitutional reform suddenly became the key word. In May 1960, while making a visit to Cairo, Talal's full brother, Prince Nawwaf bin Abdulaziz, casually announced that there was a growing movement in his country to appoint an assembly that would draft the country's first constitution.[41] This growing reform movement was eagerly courted by Saud, who was anxious to regain full powers. Saud made his move in December 1960 when he refused to sanction Faisal's budget for the coming year. Faisal subsequently resigned, and Saud, with the support of the liberal princes, resumed full control of the government. In Saud's new cabinet, Talal and his supporters held key positions. Talal was so heartened by the turn of events that he confidently predicted that the new government would implement his reform package known as the Organic Law.

Talal's Reforms

Steeping his program in Islamic terminology in the usual al-Saud style, Talal craftily characterized his reform package as "connecting what has been disconnected between us and our Islamic heritage of consultation and justice."[42] The first article of Talal's model constitution stated that "the Saudi state is Islamic," and this was broadened in subsequent articles to read that "Islam is the religion of the State and its Sharia is the basic source of regulations."[43] Talal's constitution guaranteed private ownership and equal opportunity, and promised freedom of expression and freedom of association. The constitution severely restricted the powers of the king, who was prohibited from introducing measures unless they had first been approved by the Council of Ministers. All decrees had to be signed by the president of the council, whom the king had the right to appoint and dismiss. This was a drastic trimming of the monarchy's prerogative.

The constitution also created a National Council of 120 delegates. Of these, 40 were to be appointed by a joint commission of princes and ministers, while the remainder were to be elected. The National

Council was imbued with broad powers. Members were empowered to introduce bills, and to question the prime minister and his cabinet upon request. The council was also empowered to vote the government out of office. The king was given the authority to dissolve the National Council but with the proviso that fresh elections had to be held within three months of its dissolution.

Not surprisingly, Saud's support for such a drastic reduction in his own powers evaporated once he was firmly back in power. The Organic Law died ignominiously: On December 24, 1961, Radio Mecca duly reported that it had been submitted to Saud and his new Council of Ministers for deliberations. Three days later, the station denied ever making the statement. Saud made no mention of constitutional reform at his first cabinet meeting, and Talal and his brothers suddenly realized that they had been betrayed.[44]

Still, the prince refused to quit. In February, Talal, now the minister of finance, again broached the idea of a constitution. Saud directed his half-brother to the ulema, who curtly informed him that Sharia was the country's constitution, and his Organic Law could never be adopted. The ulema's decision was not surprising; they undoubtedly feared that their powers would be further reduced if Talal's bill were enacted. Talal still refused to concede, and he continued to press his half-brother to fulfill his promises until Saud issued a decree ordering prison for any minister attempting to change the country's existing political order. Talal resigned from the government and went into voluntary exile.

The return of Faisal to the government in the fall of 1961 failed to improve ties between the different wings of the al-Saud. Faisal was particularly bitter at Talal's support of Saud in 1960, which had facilitated his own fall. Talal, on the other hand, continued his criticism of the autocratic Saudi state. Tension mounted and culminated in August 1962 when Talal's passport was revoked by the Saudi government, obviously on Faisal's order. Talal countered by giving a scathing press conference in Beruit in which he attacked his brothers and the state, which they had created. "In our country there is no law that upholds the freedom and rights of the citizen," Talal charged. Besides reiterating his democratic aspirations for his country, Talal also admitted that contrary to the family's assertions, slavery still existed in Saudi Arabia —and that he, himself, owned thirty-two concubines and fifty slaves. He promptly freed them.[45]

Faisal's Ten-Point Program

The break between Talal and Faisal was complete. The former subsequently sought asylum in Cairo, where he was later joined by several brothers and cousins, the so-called Free Princes. The al-Saud's public bickering could not have occurred at a worse time. In the fall of 1962, the Yemeni royal regime was overthrown by Nasserite rebels. Within days, thousands of Egyptian troops were arriving in Yemen to help the rebels, and it seemed likely that the fighting would spread to Saudi Arabia. Saudi resolve was shaken when three aircrews promptly defected to Egypt. It was against this backdrop that Faisal issued his own political reform package, the so-called Ten-Point Program. The timing was convenient, especially as the crown prince had just returned from a trip to Washington and a meeting with President John F. Kennedy. In return for increased American military and political support for his embattled regime, it seems likely that Faisal gave vague promises concerning democratic reform, including the promulgation of a constitution.

Faisal's Ten-Point Program, announced one month later, fell far short of Talal's Organic Law but still contained several reforms, including the creation of a "Basic Law" or constitution. But whereas Talal had offered a gradual approach to democracy, Faisal's reforms were molded more along the traditional tribal model in which the government bought off the people with money in return for quiescence in politics. Leery of offending the ulema, Faisal defended his program's more radical tenets, noting in a special radio broadcast on November 6, 1962:

> From time to time, the form of government in Saudi Arabia has in fact undergone certain developments, which reflected the development of our community and tried, at the same time, to help the community to reach a higher level. His Majesty's Government believes that the time has now come for the promulgation of a Basic Law for the Government of the country, drawn from the Koran and the Traditions of His Prophet and the acts of the Orthodox Caliphs, that will set forth explicitly the fundamental principles of government and the relationship between the governor and the governed, organize the various powers of the State, and the relationship among these powers, and provide for the basic rights of the citizen, including the right to freely express opinion within the limits of Islamic belief and public policy.[46]

Besides a constitution, Faisal's Ten-Point Program called for the creation of a Consultative Assembly, an independent judiciary, the introduction of "innocent recreations," and the establishment of health, education, and social welfare systems. The Tenth Point also abolished slavery, and more than thirty thousand slaves were manumitted by the state, with a majority opting to continue working for their former owners. Other points of Faisal's program fared less well. Although a Justice Ministry was finally created in 1970, it remained firmly in the hands of the ulema, with limited independence. Faisal's most radical proposals—the Basic Law and Consultative Assembly—were sent to committees, where they disappeared from public view.[47]

Saud made a new bid for power shortly after the announcement of Faisal's Ten-Point Program. The resulting maneuvering and threat of armed conflict shook the Saudi state to its roots, and mobilized support against the king. In the spring of 1964, senior members of the al-Saud pressured the ulema to join them in demanding that all authority be transferred to Faisal. The ulema, who had previously been aloof to the growing struggle, complied and on March 29, 1964, issued a *fatwa*, or judgment, that recognized Saud as monarch but transferred all real power to Faisal. The *fatwa* was subsequently endorsed by a meeting of senior princes and clerics—the *Ahl al-Hal wa al-Aqd* ("those who bind and loosen," or what some analysts call the Royal Council). Saud's demotion was subsequently presented to the country as the result of an initiative from the scholars. Nothing, of course, was farther from the truth. The ulema had steadfastly remained neutral in the ongoing power struggle, leery of taking any decisions that might affect their movement or own positions.[48] That their role was enlarged for public consumption proved Robert Lacey's contention that "in 1964, the House of Saud still felt its safest, in an emergency, to acknowledge the primacy of the ulema."[49]

The final act in the al-Saud's public tragedy occurred several months later when Saud asked the ulema to reconsider their decision. Saud's refusal to accept his demotion set in motion the events leading to his final abdication, which occurred only after the ulema issued yet another *fatwa* at the request of senior princes. In November 1964, Saud flew off into exile, ending the dilemma that had vexed his country for more than six years. The lessons of Saud's reign were not lost on the family. Public bickering had nearly cost the al-Saud their country. Never again would the family show such open dissent among their ranks, for they realized that public displays of solidarity are essential to the survival of the family and the regime. That policy has become the cornerstone of the al-Saud's subsequent success, and although differences have occurred within the family from time to time, none has ever reached the intensity of those that occurred from 1958 through 1964.[50]

The Boom Years and Political Troubles

The political reforms promised by Faisal continued to languish after the fall of Saud. Instead of reform, the king and his government concentrated on the economic and social aspects of his Ten-Point Program. The escalation in oil revenues enabled Faisal to lay the foundations for the Saudi welfare state, as well as embarking on the country's development projects. The influx of petrodollars and the increased pace of modernization strained Faisal's relationship with the *ulema* and other fundamentalists. Although they had backed him in his succession battle with Saud, they distrusted him because of his turbulent womanizing past. Then there was Faisal's quite open support for some innovations, which the ulema found distressing. Under Faisal, Radio Mecca's power was boosted in 1965 so that its signal could be heard all over the country. An automated phone system was installed over the protests of the ulema, who argued that it would only encourage unrelated men and women to call one another. A Justice Ministry was created in 1970, and Faisal appointed as his minister the chief *qadi* of Jeddah, bypassing the more conservative al-Sheikh and their allies in the Riyadh ulema. Raising more suspicion was the proposal for a Supreme Judicial Council within the ministry, with which Faisal seemingly intended to supplant the ulema.[51] The council, which was headed by the minister of justice, was empowered to rule on the Islamic correctness of government decisions, as well as other social and cultural issues. Faisal also oversaw the curtailment of the power of the *mutawaeen,* the building of minarets besides mosques (many fundamentalists thought the minarets were un-Islamic because they were decorative), and the end of the rule that dictated that all foreigners in Riyadh wear *athwāb* or robes.[52]

However, Faisal allowed the ulema their small victories. The sale of Christmas trees was prohibited, and Faisal publicly chided young Saudis about their un-Wahhabi-like dress and behavior. Government officials were ordered to pray with their colleagues at set times, and fines and penalties were set in place to make sure they did.[53] A pattern slowly emerged: the king pursued selected innovations and reforms, while conceding petty points to keep his scholars and fundamentalists appeased.

However, some parts of Faisal's modernization program were too controversial to allow compromise. His introduction of women's schools was met by riots and protests, including one in the Unitarian stronghold of Buraidah that forced the king to call in the National Guard to safeguard the school (see Chapter 6). Television—one of the "innocent pleasures" whose introduction Faisal had announced in his Ten-Point Program—ignited another controversy. The projection of the human image was bitterly opposed by some members of the ulema and a small band of neo-Ikhwan activists that included members of the House of Saud. These radicals, just like Mohammed al-Wahhab and the early Ikhwan, were alarmed by what they saw as the Kingdom's increasing embrace of un-Islamic Western innovations. Fundamentalists showed their rejection of such "pollution" by growing long beards and wearing ankle-length athwāb just as the Ikhwan had done. They restively witnessed Faisal introduce television and were unappeased by its initial "test" broadcasts of exclusively Islamic programs. In September 1965, the neo-Ikhwan attacked the Riyadh television station. Among the vanguard was Faisal's nephew, Prince Khalid bin Musaid bin Abdulaziz, who was shot dead when the confrontation erupted into gunfire.[54] Television was introduced on a full-time basis two years later.

Faisal was not an utterly altruistic reformer. He established the machinery of a police state during his reign. His intolerance of dissent seems to have been sharpened during his long years of struggle with Saud, and the king had no compunction about locking up his enemies. Domestic opponents of the regime—Arab nationalists, Nasserites, and communists—were arrested by the hundreds in sweeps organized by Faisal's Interior Minister Fahd bin Abdulaziz, the current Saudi king. They were soon joined by others as domestic unrest continued throughout the 1960s. In 1967, a wave of bombings coordinated by Yemenis struck the Kingdom. Two years later, the secret police discovered two coup plots against Faisal. The first was centered in Jeddah, where Hejazi nationalists planned to dynamite several government buildings and proclaim a republic under the presidency of Yussuf al-Taweel. The second and far more serious plot was based in the

Royal Saudi Air Force and concerned a scheme by officers to shoot down Faisal's private plane the next time it took to the air. In the aftermath of the aborted coups, Faisal threw the conspirators into prison and promised a constitution and a Consultative Assembly.

Domestic unrest, however, dissipated after the first oil shock of 1973. Al-Saud promises about a written constitution and Consultative Assembly were forgotten in the orgy of personal self-aggrandizement that took place. Even the assassination of King Faisal in 1975 by a deranged nephew had little effect on the Saudi political system.[55] The succession proceeded smoothly; Crown Prince Khalid bin Abdulaziz became king, and Fahd was named the crown prince. After the obligatory promises were made concerning the creation of a constitution and assembly, the al-Saud continued to rule as before. On the surface there were only minor changes: Khalid ruled more by consensus than his strong-willed brother, and his crown prince was generally viewed as the real power behind the throne. Khalid and Fahd also relied less on technocrats, and recentralized the state apparatus. They further evidenced a marked preference for Nejdis, reversing Faisal's close links with Hejazis. There was also a resurgence in the power of the ulema, who successfully pressured Khalid to drop Faisal's relatively progressive justice minister and replace him with a member of the more conservative al-Sheikh. Khalid also released many of the political prisoners jailed by his half-brother.

On the other hand, Khalid's collegiate approach to rule seriously weakened the al-Saud's ability to make timely decisions and to resist aggrandizement of power by competing groups. This weakness was to have serious consequences within a few years.

The Mosque Uprising of 1979

The rapid influx of petrodollars and the accompanying flow of expatriates needed to build the Kingdom's infrastructure in the 1970s did not please every Saudi. Some decried the increased materialism, the Western goods, and increased government corruption. Although these rebels found the changes repugnant, they reserved special contempt for the al-Saud, who had fostered them. Criticism bit deep because of the well-known proclivities of some princes for un-Islamic activities such as drinking and gambling. As the moral decay continued, some Saudis decided that it was their duty to clean out corruption just as Mohammed al-Wahhab had done in the eighteenth century.

Among these zealots was Juhaiman al-Utaibi, born in 1936. Al-Utaibi, whose grandfather was one of the Ikhwan killed at the Battle of Sabillah, was a perfect example of how the Saudi Islamic educational system created fundamentalists. He joined the Saudi National Guard in 1955 at the age of nineteen and resigned in 1973 as a corporal. He then enrolled in the Islamic University of Medina's Department of Religious Studies where he came under the influence of the blind cleric Abdulaziz bin Baz, who preached a return to the pure Islam (see Chapter 1). However, whereas bin Baz stopped short of accusing the royal family of abandoning the tenets of Unitarianism, al-Utaibi did not.[56] While at Medina, he met other young men of similar outlook, and they fed each other's growing fundamentalism. Al-Utaibi and his followers maligned the changes that had occurred around them, heaping vitriol on television and on the widespread use of photography despite Islam's prohibition against showing the human image. They also adopted many of the trappings and mannerisms of the Ikhwan.

Al-Utaibi saved his choicest venom for the House of Saud and the ulema. Considering his family background and the fact that his grandfather had been killed by the al-Saud, al-Utaibi's views were not overly surprising. His vehemence, however, was. He blamed Saudi Arabia's corruption, spiritual decline, and materialism on the founder of the modern Saudi state.

Al-Utaibi further claimed that the al-Saud had perverted the cleansing pureness of the Unitarian message, and had in fact destroyed the adherents of true Islam, the Ikhwan. This betrayal features prominently in al-Utaibi's works. Al-Utaibi also criticized the ulema who, he said, had turned a blind eye to the Ikhwan's fate because they had entered the pay of the al-Saud. Al-Utaibi stridently singled out his erstwhile teacher bin Baz, for sanctioning this "perversion." Despite his attacks on the ulema, it appears that al-Utaibi and his followers were at least tacitly supported by some members of that body who were also opposed to the moral decay they saw, and the al-Saud's modernization programs.

Al-Utaibi and his followers came to the attention of the Saudi secret police in 1978, and ninety-nine of them were subsequently arrested in Riyadh. During their questioning, the police asked bin Baz to interrogate al-Utaibi and some of his followers. The blind cleric complied, and after talking to them for several hours, said he could find nothing treasonous in their beliefs.[57] The police also apparently thought that al-Utaibi's clique was relatively harmless, just one of several groups publishing antigovernment pamphlets and flyers. They were more concerned with fundamentalist cells within the armed forces.[58] So after six weeks in jail, al-Utaibi and his followers were released. It was one of the gravest mistakes ever made by Saudi Arabia's security apparatus.

Little more than a year later, at 5:30 A.M. on November 20, 1979, al-Utaibi and his followers—the exact number of rebels has never been released—took control of Mecca's Holy Mosque, interrupting the morning prayers. Debate continues today whether or not al-Utaibi then announced that one of his followers, Abdullah al-Qahtani, was the Mahdi, or the promised Islamic messiah.[59] Whatever the truth, al-Utaibi exhorted those present to join him and his group in opposing the al-Saud, and made a special plea to the ulema to reconsider their support for the ruling family.

The rebels' actions took the al-Saud completely by surprise. Not only were they well armed but they had avoided the security apparatus charged with protecting the state. More ominously, the rebels seemed to have supporters within the National Guard and the Hejaz. As the al-Saud gathered to debate their response, one of al-Utaibi's lieutenants announced the group's political objectives over the mosque's public address system. Besides calling for a thorough cleansing of the Kingdom of all foreigners and Western innovations, al-Utaibi's followers advocated the abolition of the al-Saud monarchy and the establishment of an Islamic republic. The rebels further demanded that the al-Saud give a full accounting of their personal wealth taken from the country. Al-Utaibi also called for the breaking off of diplomatic ties between the Kingdom and Western states, as well as the immediate cessation of all oil exports to the United States. In addition, the rebels advocated the scaling back of oil production to more reasonable levels in order to meet the financial needs of the country and no more.[60]

The seizure of the mosque presented the al-Saud with a quandary. A vigorous attack on the rebels would damage the mosque and invite charges of sacrilege. Khalid had no choice but to convene the ulema hours after the mosque's seizure and ask them for a judgment on the permissibility of the government sending in troops to retake Islam's Holy of Holies. The ulema complied but only after consulting one another for a day and a half.[61] After receiving religious approval, it took Saudi troops, allegedly with foreign help, two weeks to clear out the mosque and take al-Utaibi and nearly 100 of his supporters as prisoners. More than 200 people were killed in the desperate fight, with government losses put at 127 dead, and 461 injured. Among the rebels, 117 were killed. More than a dozen worshipers died in the first round of fighting.[62] Making the government even edgier was an outbreak of rioting in al-Hasa during the Shiite Ashura celebration (see Chapter 6).

Retribution was swift. Less than a month later, sixty-three rebels, including al-Utaibi, were publicly beheaded in small groups in cities around the Kingdom. The al-Saud also went on a public relations offensive, instructing the ulema and imams to preach during their Friday sermons about the religiosity of the ruling family, as well as the destructive nature of the uprising. Imams, like their predecessors during the Ikhwan revolt, were also ordered to stress that Islam was a religion of moderation, and that material well-being and the religion were not incompatible.[63] Other changes were forthcoming as well. Prince Fawwaz bin Abdulaziz, the governor of Mecca, who had been especially criticized by al-Utaibi for gambling, drinking, and corruption, was summarily replaced, as were three other governors. Two generals were retired, and the director of public security, Fayyad Mohammed al-Awfi, was replaced by a member of the al-Sheikh. The al-Saud also raised the salaries of the ulema and shuttered video stores accused of renting movies that contradicted Islam's teachings. Expatriates were also advised to abide by the Kingdom's Unitarian teachings.[64]

Further, the House of Saud trotted out the old promise of a Consultative Assembly for the Kingdom. Several weeks later, a nine-man committee under the leadership of Interior Minister Prince Naif bin Abdulaziz was created and charged with writing two charters: one for a basic system of government, and the second for the assembly. The committee, which was also charged with developing a system of local government, was comprised of one commoner, seven members of the ulema, and Naif.[65] The committee announced its two charters a year later.

Although promises of political reform were subsequently shelved, the lessons of the al-Utaibi revolt were not immediately forgotten. Police surveillance was tightened in the wake of the Mosque takeover and the unrelated rioting of Shia in the Eastern Province. The *mutawaeen* were given free rein in the cities; the rights of women were curtailed, and there was a crackdown on Western influences. Such concessions were necessary, as the al-Saud sought to improve their

Islamic credentials. Even Khalid noted that if al-Utaibi and his cohorts had targeted palaces rather than the Grand Mosque, the results of the uprising might have been very different.[66]

Fahd and Change

The ascension of Crown Prince Fahd in 1982 raised the hopes of Saudi progressives that long-promised political reforms would be enacted. After all, Fahd had long held a reputation for being one of the al-Saud's liberals, and he was chief architect of the Kingdom's modernization programs. However, those hopes were dashed shortly after Fahd's ascension as the *mutawaeen* ran unfettered, aggressively harassing immodestly dressed women and ferreting out alcohol and parties. Worse was the fact that Fahd's succession coincided with the first inklings of the bursting of the country's petrodollar bubble (see Chapter 5). Most Saudis believed that oil wealth was bestowed by God in recognition of their piety. Conversely, when the Saudi economy began its downward descent in the early 1980s, there were many who believed that Allah was expressing his displeasure over his people's drift from Islam into materialism and Westernism. Fahd's drinking, womanizing past further called into question his ability to serve as imam of the Saudi state. Reinforcing this attitude among many Saudis was Fahd's penchant for palace building and his ego-enhancing habit of naming almost all new public works after himself. As a result, the ulema and conservatives pressed Fahd to recoup powers they had lost during the reign of Faisal.

Fahd also had family problems. For the first time since the Faisal–Saud split, the divisions among the al-Saud were again visible. The locus of the rivalry was between Fahd and his full brothers (the al-Fahd), and the conservative faction supporting Crown Prince Abdullah bin Abdulaziz. Soon after his succession, Fahd issued a decree ordering all tribes to turn in their weapons. The decree, whether rightly or wrongly, was interpreted as the opening gambit against Abdullah, who drew most of his support from the tribes. Not only did the tribes refuse to obey Fahd's edict, they also purchased more arms to ward off any attack by Interior Ministry forces. The debacle allegedly sent Fahd, who was already in poor health, into a lengthy illness.[67]

Fahd's heavy-handed coddling of his sons sowed family resentment as well. Fahd's eldest son, Faisal, was placed at the head of the Presidency of Youth Welfare, despite allegations of substance abuse. Another son, Mohammed, was the beneficiary of several government contracts, one of which—the Philips-Ericsson telecommunications award —paid him $500 million in fees. The king's youngest and favorite son, Abdulaziz, was also given millions of dollars, despite the fact that he was barely ten years old. Other members of the al-Fahd were placed in strategic positions throughout the government bureaucracy, forcing out the technocrats whom Faisal had set in place. Fahd was also criticized for allowing the al-Ibrahim, the family of his favorite wife, to win several large contracts over other members of the royal family.

In such an atmosphere, hopes that Fahd could oversee liberal reforms quickly evaporated. The king made the usual promises about a Consultative Assembly and a constitution, and then quickly forgot them. Fahd's supporters claim that hopes of his proving a liberal reformer were always misplaced. "When he was crown prince, people thought he was frustrated by the religious leaders and Khalid," explained one associate in 1986. "That was not so. He felt his job was to develop the country, and he has done that. Now he's getting old and he does not like controversies."[68] Rather than energizing the country as had been hoped, Fahd instead vacillated.

Fahd did attempt one or two reformist measures. A few weeks after his ascension, the king addressed a meeting of scholars from the Organization of Islamic Conference (OIC). During his speech, Fahd called for the scholars to give up their monopoly on interpreting what is right and wrong in society, and suggested a refurbishment of the practice of consultation or *ijtihad* between scholars and believers that would reconcile Sharia with modern life. Observers disagree on whether Fahd was also calling for more openness in the Kingdom, but it was clear that the gist of his message was unpalatable to the ulema, who quickly distanced themselves. The king never mentioned the subject again, and concentrated on shoring up his Islamic credentials, especially in light of repeated Iranian attacks. In 1986, Fahd dropped the honorific "His Majesty," and other monikers (among the most common were "Light of the Kingdom" and "Object of One's Self-Sacrifice") and adopted the more humble "Custodian of the Two Holy Mosques."[69]

While fundamentalists were placing obstacles in the king's path, the economic downturn of the 1980s narrowed his room for maneuver. Progressives and modernizers called for more liberalization and broader consultation to counteract the effects of economic depression, which reduced Saudi Arabia's GDP by more than 50 percent from 1981 to 1987 (see Chapter 5). Progressives openly called on Fahd at the First, Second, and Third Saudi Businessmen's Conferences to institute the oft-promised Consultative Assembly. Progressives also called for freedom of the press, the unfettered inclusion of women in the work force, and greater openness in society. On the other hand, the depression also strengthened the hands of the ulema and more fundamentalist Saudis who argued that the downturn was the result of the Kingdom's straying from Islam. These fundamentalists argued that a slower rather than a more rapid pace of modernization was needed to correct the country's ills, and stressed that the country had to return to its Unitarian roots. Fahd, caught in the middle of an increasingly polarized society, did nothing.

The Gulf Crisis and Reform

Although the Saudi monarch made periodic promises about political reform, he probably showed his preferences when he prodded the al-Sabah of Kuwait to dissolve their own parliament in the mid-1980s. In all likelihood, Fahd would never have acted had Iraq not invaded Kuwait on August 2, 1990. Caught completely unprepared by Saddam Hussein's action, Fahd was compelled to promise his compatriots that true political reform would be introduced once the Iraqi threat had been blunted. Giving Fahd's promises some urgency was the fact that the Bush administration was openly advocating that Kuwait and the Kingdom broaden their political processes, in order to give its intervention a more democratic flavor. Just as Faisal had introduced the Ten-Point Program as a sop to Kennedy in order to secure American aid in 1962, Fahd made similar promises.

Fahd's hand was further forced by the mobilization of domestic pressure. The war focused the energies of both Saudi fundamentalists and progressives, many of whom were enraged that the government failed to inform them about Iraq's action for more than a day. Further inflaming passions was the arrival of the first Allied troops. Although many Saudis supported their coming, many did not, and the sight of rifle-toting, T-shirt-clad women GIs in Riyadh and the cities of the Eastern Province further heightened tensions.[70] One Saudi businessman, who echoed the sentiments of many, noted, "I supported the royal decision to face down Iraq, to bring in American troops but like everything else it was a decision the king and princes took alone and I suddenly realized the degree to which we have no say in our own fates."[71]

Critics openly wondered why after expenditures of over $300 billion, the Saudi military was too weak to defend the Kingdom without outside assistance. Others asked why the Saudi forces should be arrayed for the first time in decades not against Israel or Iran but against a brother Arab country. The ramifications were far-reaching, and perhaps deepened by an unprecedented flow of information and the arrival of 1,500 foreign journalists who attempted to probe the Saudi psyche.[72] The danger posed by the latter was recognized almost immediately: it was only through the intervention of the United States that reporters were allowed to stay.[73] "For the first time, people talk about the royal family as 'they' and 'we,' " explained one Saudi psychologist to an American newspaper. "A psychological gap has developed between the family and the country."[74]

Domestic dissent was furthered by the al-Saud's refusal to communicate the degree to which the Kingdom was threatened. Fahd never fully explained the urgency behind his decision to invite Allied troops to the country, nor the magnitude of the threat posed by Iraqi forces. Instead, Fahd sought to downplay the crisis so as not to alarm his subjects. This attitude permeated the government's early handling of the Iraqi action. When General H. Norman Schwartzkopf suggested that the Saudis erect sandbag barriers around the Ministry of Defense as a protective measure, his Saudi counterpart was dumbstruck. "Sandbags? We can't put sandbags in the streets! It would alarm the people," Prince Khalid bin Sultan bin Abdulaziz said. Schwartzkopf replied, "What's wrong with people getting alarmed?" The prince then explained, "Oh, no, you don't understand, my friend. We've never done anything like that, and people would be afraid."[75] Such reticence, however, was not lacking on the Iraqi side, and within hours of the Saudi decision to invite Allied troops, Saddam Hussein's propaganda machine was charging that Saudi Arabia had willingly defiled Islam's holy grounds by allowing an American invasion.

Saudi fundamentalists, however, were coming to the same conclusions as Hussein's propagandists, and in fact were parroting many of the very same words. The first public dissent occurred in early September when Dr. Safar al-Hawali, dean of the Islamic College at the Umm al-Qura University in Mecca, released an unprecedented tape in which he bluntly criticized the government, especially its initial news blackout of the invasion as well as the decision to invite non-Muslim troops to defend the country. In his tape, al-Hawali said the ills being visited upon Kuwait and Saudi Arabia were the result of the people and princes "misunderstanding" their religion. "It is not the world against Iraq," al-Hawali noted. "It is the West against Islam. . . . [I]f Iraq has occupied Kuwait, then America has occupied Saudi Arabia. The real enemy is not Iraq. It is the West."[76] Al-Hawali's charges found a receptive audience, especially since the government had repeatedly discredited the United States and the West in the past so as to blunt the possibility of having Western-style political freedoms introduced.

Questions begot other questions and soon Saudis questioned the entire structure upon which the Saudi state was founded. This questioning intensified after October 1990 when more than one thousand Kuwaiti notables and princes met in Jeddah to discuss the Emirate's post-war political system. After rancorous debate, Kuwait's government-in-exile promised free elections and the restoration of the disbanded parliament. The al-Sabah's concessions were electrifying, and widely covered by Saudi television and press, the latter publishing accounts featuring headlines that screamed "Free Kuwait to Have Democracy," and "Jaber Promises Democracy after Liberation."[77]

Not surprisingly, both Saudi fundamentalists and progressives began asking why such measures could not apply to their country as well. This questioning brought a stony silence from many of the al-Saud. At one meeting between a group of Saudi businessmen and Riyadh Governor Prince Salman bin Abdulaziz, those participating bluntly told the prince that the al-Saud's monopoly of power had to be broken, and the decision-making process broadened. As one of the participants later relayed, "But he [Prince Salman] didn't like what he heard."[78] In the growing push for change, the Kingdom's fundamentalists took the lead, suspecting that progressives wanted the Gulf conflict to lead to an acceleration of the modernization process and further curtailment of their powers. Those fundamentalist fears seemed justified in November 1990, when forty-seven Saudi women staged an impromptu drive-by in protest of the country's ban on women driving.

Like other incidents in the country—the introduction of the telephone, television, radio, and women's education—the drive-by was symbolic of the larger conflict between religious conservatives and progressives (see Chapter 6). The women, who were said to have alerted Salman's office before undertaking their protest, drove in a convoy of fourteen cars, accompanied by several cars filled with male supporters.[79] The convoy initially proceeded without incident, but as the women continued their drive through Riyadh, their numbers thinned as the police began stopping them. Finally, the police stopped the remaining cars outside a mosque, and after thirty minutes of driving, the protest was over.[80]

A mini-riot ensued as the protesters were surrounded by *mutawaeen,* who called them "whores, prostitutes and sinners." The women justified their actions, however, stating that "in time of war mobilization and national emergency we need to drive for the safety of our families."[81] The women also argued that their action was not un-Islamic, noting that during the Prophet Mohammed's time, it was quite common for women to ride donkeys and horses. Driving was a logical extension, they added. After nearly an hour of name-calling and debates, the women were taken to police headquarters for questioning. Their male relatives—husbands, brothers, or fathers—were interrogated as well. Only after their relatives signed documents agreeing that the women would never drive again or speak of the matter were the forty-seven released.

The next day, Riyadh was peppered with leaflets purporting to be copies of the police report. Besides listing the names, addresses, and phone numbers of the women—something unheard of in Saudi Arabia —the leaflets further charged that the women were driving in shorts, had denounced Fahd and the government, and had verbally assaulted the *mutawaeen.* The leaflets went on to charge the women with being prostitutes, and their male relatives as being secularists and pimps. The leaflets ended threateningly with the advice, "Do what you believe is appropriate regarding these women."[82] The reaction was immediate. Within hours, more than twenty thousand *mutawaeen* and their supporters had gathered outside the governor's palace in downtown Riyadh to vilify the women, and to accuse the government of acquiescing to their action. Salman appeared and attempted to allay their fears. Despite his presence, the crowd refused to disperse until bin Baz spoke and asked them to return to their homes.

Demonstrations notwithstanding, the government's response to the drive-by was initially mild. Fahd first appointed a committee of religious experts to study the issue. They decided a few days later that no

Saudi laws had been broken.[83] However, as protests and threats against the women escalated—many began receiving threatening letters and phone calls, while several who were employed as lecturers by King Saud University in Riyadh had their offices ransacked by fundamentalist students—the government had no choice but to reconsider its actions. The government also played into the fundamentalists' hands by ordering a news blackout of the protest, and muzzling liberals and progressives who were in favor of the women's action. By contrast, fundamentalists were given free rein to vent their feelings. After several days of fundamentalist pressure, the government's tone turned harsh. Interior Minister Naif bin Abdulaziz issued a statement calling the women's protest "a stupid act."[84] Naif also said that the drive-by was un-Islamic, and warned against additional protests. Naif further questioned the patriotism of the women in light of the fact that the issue was raised when the Kingdom was in crisis.[85] Bin Baz also railed against women driving, noting that he based his criticism on a desire to "protect the sanctity of women."[86]

Public pressure mounting, it came as no surprise when the government ordered the suspension or firing of those women who participated in the protest, and a ban on their and their male relatives' travel abroad. In addition, a journalist who photographed the entourage was jailed for one week.[87]

The Fundamentalist Counterattack

The women's drive-by protest confirmed the worst fears of the fundamentalists, and further inflamed neo-Ikhwan sentiments. The result was a concerted campaign by fundamentalists against royal concessions to progressives. Anti-American and anti-war tapes appeared in rapid succession. The use of audio tapes—reminiscent of the Ayatollah Khomeini's campaign in Iran—was particularly effective, given Saudi Arabia's high illiteracy rate, as well as the Arab oral tradition. Angered by the war and the women's protests, fundamentalists grew bolder in their attacks on the House of Saud. More troubling was the fact that many of these conservatives—judges, scholars, students, and university professors—came from the ranks of the Saudi elite, and bypassed the regular religious channels such as the ulema and government-sanctioned Islamic organizations. Instead, they began forming their own associations, and took to universities and mosques to press their message. They found a ready audience. Saudi fundamentalists also received financial and moral support from similar groups in Sudan, Jordan, Egypt, and Afghanistan, which the Saudi government ironically supported.

Epitomizing the new hard line was a tape entitled "Supergun," which appeared at the end of 1990. Opening with the words "Royal family princes are not owed allegiance except if they follow the rules of Islam," "Supergun" eerily repeated many of al-Utaibi's arguments and attacked the royal family for its corruption and misleading the country. Supergun also criticized the ulema for making too many compromises with the al-Saud, and the alliance with the United States, whom the tape's author called the "atheistic enemy of Islam." Surprisingly, the tape reserved its harshest criticism for the Saudi middle and upper middle classes, who were accused of turning away from Islam.[88] Another tape, "America as I Saw It," attacked the United States as a nation of prostitutes, homosexuals, and immorality, and asked why the Kingdom was in alliance with such a state. Other tapes called for the execution of secularists, the cessation of the practice of using state funds for the construction of palaces, and the adoption of an Islamic banking system, and demanded that Sharia courts hear all cases.[89]

Besides issuing tapes, some fundamentalists also took to the pulpit to criticize the al-Saud in politicized Friday prayers. Others took to the country's universities where they gave impromptu political talks. A favorite theme was the role of women, and specifically condemned any change in the status quo. These radicals also spoke against women's organizations such as the Saudi Women's Renaissance Association, a group dedicated to helping women improve themselves. The association, which counts several senior princesses as members, was assailed by fundamentalists who called it un-Islamic and its members "prostitutes."[90] The *mutawaeen* also intensified their campaign against un-Islamic influences in both Jeddah and Riyadh, and for the first time in their history began targeting upper-class and royal Saudis. In December 1990, the *mutawaeen* made two notable raids. In Jeddah, Fahd's translator was caught in a mixed-sex party where alcohol was being served.[91] In the trial that followed, two businessmen were given two-year prison terms, while Fahd's translator was given a ten-month sentence. A few days later in Riyadh, a party being hosted by a French citizen was raided by another band of *mutawaeen*. Forty-six guests were arrested after being held at gunpoint by the invaders, who also smashed furniture. Eventually freed, several of those arrested complained to their embassies, which in turn protested to the Saudi government. The government's response was to bring in the offending *mutawaeen* for questioning. Stronger action was not even contemplated, said one police officer, who explained, "We don't want any martyrs."[92]

Instead of confronting their fundamentalist critics, the al-Saud allowed them greater leeway in their criticisms, hoping to coopt them as in the past by giving them a few crumbs of greater autonomy. For example, Christmas cards were banned from entering the Kingdom, and the *mutawaeen* stepped up their campaign against immodestly dressed women.[93] Despite such concessions, fundamentalists refused to back down. Even the defeat of Iraq did nothing to end their attacks on the royal family and the political system. If anything, criticism intensified as religious forces jockeyed for position, showing a surprising degree of coordination, political acumen, and cunning as they completely outmaneuvered progressives and the ruling family. They called progressives *kuffā,* or non-believers, a deadly charge that was quite effective in silencing modernists. By denying progressives free access to the press or other forums so not to inflame fundamentalists further, the House of Saud effectively throttled its own supporters.[94] The growing political power of the fundamentalists was best illustrated in May 1991, when rumors swept the Nejdi town of Buraidah that the governor had ordered the arrest of two outspoken clerics to stifle their strident Friday sermons. Within hours, more than five thousand Saudis had taken to the streets to protest the action, which, as it turned out, had not occurred. However, the public manifestation of discontent was doubly troubling, not only for its size but for its speed of organization.[95]

Lest the king forget his promises regarding political reform, both Saudi progressives and fundamentalists presented petitions to the monarch in the spring of 1991. To ensure that their demands would be considered and not brushed aside, both groups took the highly unusual step of leaking the contents of their petitions to the Egyptian press, which readily published them. It was an action guaranteed to put the House of Saud on the defensive since Saudi society frowns on any public display of discord. Neither petition—the liberals presented theirs in February; the conservatives in March—advocated what could be called radical measures. Instead, both groups contented themselves with calling on Fahd and the royal family to fulfill previous commitments concerning a Consultative Assembly and a constitution. Both called for respect for human rights, but their interpretation of those rights differed dramatically. Whereas progressives called for a free press and equal rights for women, including driving and broader work opportunities, fundamentalists backed plans for a more tightly controlled press and the closure of un-Islamic newspapers, a crackdown on corruption, a "modern, strong and independent Islamic army," more equal distribution of wealth, and the end of interest-based banking.[96] The one hundred or so fundamentalists who signed the petition, and whose number included bin Baz, also called for a reevaluation of the Kingdom's foreign policy, including its increasingly close ties with non-Muslim countries.[97]

As the battle lines grew more entrenched, Fahd and his brethren waffled. They did prevail on the ulema to issue a statement attacking the more strident points of the fundamentalists' petition. Leading signatories of the fundamentalist petition found their passports revoked, and were visited by members of the security police. The Ministry of Justice's Higher Judicial Council, which Faisal had earlier created as a counterweight to the ulema, also issued a statement, ruling that no more political petitions should be addressed to the king or the royal family. The council's ruling had no discernible effect; instead fundamentalists addressed their next petition to bin Baz in June 1991, and took the precaution of having it published in the London-based *al-Quds al-Arabi* newspaper. The new petition marked a further escalation of the conflict, as fundamentalists sharpened their attacks on the al-Saud, accusing the government of harassing them after their first petition. But they went further. Attacking royal family nepotism, the writers made thinly veiled references to the questionable business and personal dealings of such princes as Faisal bin Fahd and a son of the interior minister, Prince Saud bin Naif bin Abdulaziz, who owned the Kingdom's sole courier service. The fundamentalists again questioned corruption within the al-Saud, especially the unequal distribution of oil wealth.[98] The petition further criticized various state fees such as those for driver's licenses, car registration, and the annual car safety inspection requirement. A few weeks later, the government announced revisions in the inspection test and lowered license fees. Fahd also announced several large donations to the Islamic News Agency in an attempt to curry favor.

However, not all the complaints came from inside the country. When "The Kingdom: Yesterday and Today," an exhibit detailing the country's economic progress, opened in Montreal in August 1991, it was met by demonstrations of Saudi university students demanding full political and human rights, elections, and a parliament. Demonstrators also protested against a lavish reception the Saudi embassy held for visiting Riyadh governor Prince Salman bin Abdulaziz.[99] As criticism mounted, hopes soared that Fahd would fulfill at least some of his promises, especially as the king said that work on his reform package was continuing. Optimism for speedy action was dashed in August 1991 when the king reshuffled his cabinet but made only cosmetic changes. Fahd also seemed to cave in to fundamentalist pressure by saying nothing when the *mutawaeen* stepped up their raids on private homes as well as their harassment of improperly dressed women. Fahd also authorized the execution of a Saudi citizen for the crime of receiving a Bible in the mail. Sadiq Mal-Allah of the Eastern Province had listened to a Christian radio broadcast, and sent off for an Arabic New Testament. Religious authorities took him for questioning, demanding to know if he had converted from Islam. Mal-Allah was held for over a year and then executed for "slandering God and his Prophet." Later when Fahd decided to stand somewhat firmer against the conservatives, his son was permitted to offer Mal-Allah's parents monetary compensation for their son's death.[100]

The royal family had no recourse but to respond to fundamentalists as attacks on the United States, the Middle East peace talks, royal corruption, and the Renaissance Association continued. In late December 1991, Prince Turki bin Faisal bin Abdulaziz, head of Saudi intelligence, took the highly unusual step of taking to the pulpit, where he cautioned fundamentalists to stop their attacks on the Renaissance Association and the royal family.[101] The sight of an al-Saud confronting critics at the mosque was unprecedented. Prince Turki's remarks were followed a few days later by a leaflet penned by bin Baz, who also attacked fundamentalists. He wrote that they "whisper secretly in their meetings and record their poison over cassettes distributed to people or . . . make these allegations in public lectures at universities. This behavior is against the will of God."[102] The government also offered $500,000 for information leading to the arrest of the authors of the more radical tapes.[103]

Fahd, himself, entered the fray after Islamic Awakening threatened

to hold a protest march in Jeddah. The demonstration was only canceled after the security forces went on alert and threatened to arrest all
participants. Later that week, Fahd told his cabinet that he was following the events with a close eye. "I am following these things with
wisdom and patience, trying to resolve issues in amicable ways," Fahd
said in remarks carried live by Saudi television. And then he added
ominously, "and if things cross all limits, there shall be another
way."[104] Later in January, up to fifty members of Islamic Awakening
were reported arrested.[105]

Fahd's Reform Package

If anything, the continued protests and agitation forced Fahd to accel-
erate his plans to introduce his reform package. The latter was finally
announced on February 29, 1992, when Fahd sent his package to the
Council of Ministers, one week after the tenth anniversary of his ascension to the throne. None of Fahd's reforms, embodied in three
decrees entitled the Basic Statute of Government, the Statute of the
Provinces, and the Statute of the Consultative Assembly, could be
described as revolutionary.[106] In fact, Fahd seemingly went out of his
way to allay his subjects' fear that the decrees would radically alter
their lives. As he said in his televised speech to the nation on March 1,
the initiatives were an "authentication of something which had already
been in existence." He continued to note that there has never been a
constitutional vacuum in the Kingdom, saying that "throughout its
whole history, the Kingdom has never witnessed such a phenomenon
because it has been ruled under guiding principles . . . and clear-cut
fundamentals, which have been referred to by rulers, jurists, scholars
and state's personnel."[107]

Fahd based his reforms on tradition. For example, his Basic Statute
of Government stressed the Kingdom's Islamic nature, noting, "The
Kingdom of Saudi Arabia is an Arab and Islamic sovereign state; its
religion is Islam, and its constitution the *Holy Koran* and the Prophet's
Sunna." Subsequent articles reaffirmed that Islam and the Sharia remained the backbone of the country's political system, while others
stressed the absolutism of the Saudi monarchy. Those hoping for
broader political participation had only to look as far as Article V to be
disappointed. That article referred to the al-Saud as "the kernel of
Saudi society," and emphasized that the kingdom is a monarchy, and

"its rule will be confined to the sons of the kingdom's founder, Abdulaziz bin Abdulrahman al-Faisal and grandsons." The inclusion of grandsons, however, meant that the number of princes who could theoretically be considered for king rose from 30 to more than 500. Another article made the crown prince subject to the king's dismissal, while yet another said all crown princes first had to be ratified by a college of the senior members of the al-Saud before ascending to the throne. The inclusion of such articles raised suspicions that they were intended to deprive Abdullah of the throne, thus allowing one of the al-Fahd to succeed. However, such fears were premature; within hours of the release of the Basic Law, another decree confirming Abdullah's succession was issued.

Subsequent articles in the Basic Statute of Government further emphasized the importance of Islam, underlined the country's capitalistic economic system, and described the state's role in providing services such as education, public health, and defense. The statute also provided for the creation of a "watchdog system" to oversee the collection and expenditure of state revenues, and other government activities.

Selected human rights were also given protection. One often-cited article promised, "The state shall provide security for all its citizens and residents within its territory. No one's liberty shall be restricted and no one shall be detained or imprisoned except in accordance with the provisions of the law." Subsequent articles prohibited raids from *mutawaeen.* "Dwellings shall be sacrosanct. They may not be entered without the owners' permission and may not be searched except under the circumstances laid down by law." Additional articles guaranteed the sanctity of postal, telegraphic, and telephonic communications, which were given protection from police surveillance except "under the circumstances laid down by law."[108] The Basic Law fell far short of offering traditional political freedoms such as those of the press, speech, and assembly. Also omitted was freedom of religion, an article whose inclusion had been pushed by the country's Shiites.

Fahd's second area of reform concerned local government. The Statute of the Provinces defined the duties and rights of provincial governors and affirmed the dominant role of the interior minister in the regional system of government. The statute divided the Kingdom's thirteen provinces into governorates, which were then divided into districts and precincts. Fahd's statute also created provincial councils, which were to be comprised of the governing prince, who would serve as the council president, and his deputy, who would be vice president. Other members included local representatives of government ministries, and at least ten "well-qualified and experienced citizens" who first had to be vetted by the Ministry of Interior, and appointed by the king. The latter had to be residents of the province from which they were appointed, and were to serve four-year terms. Provincial councils, the statute said, were to have four annual meetings, during which they were to restrict themselves to discussing the province's budget, as well as its developmental and planning needs. Council members were given the right to advance proposals concerning the above areas to the council presidents, but were prohibited from examining other areas. All council decisions also had to be approved by the Interior Ministry before being implemented.

It was Fahd's third proposal—concerning the creation of a Consultative Assembly—that received the bulk of attention. The assembly, comprised of sixty members and one speaker, has several functions. As per its name, the assembly is empowered to "express its views" on policies submitted to it by the king, as well as on international treaties and economic plans. It also has the power to interpret laws as well as examine annual reports referred to it by state ministries and agencies.

The Consultative Assembly is authorized to review the country's annual budget, as well as call in ministers for questioning. The assembly is also empowered to propose laws. The statute dictates that to be considered by the assembly, all proposals have to be sponsored by at least ten delegates. Proposals have to be approved by at least thirty members of the assembly before being forwarded to the king for a decision. Membership is restricted to men over the age of thirty, who have to swear allegiance to "the faith, the king, and the country." According to the statute, members are prohibited from holding any other government positions, and they can only be involved in commercial projects with the king's permission.[109] Forty members are needed for a quorum. The statute also committed the al-Saud to starting the assembly in six months.

The new body's real power fell far short of the old Hejazi Council of Delegates. Hopes that its membership would be elected were dashed one month later when Fahd ruled that elections and similar Western political traditions and values were not suitable for his country. "The democratic system prevailing in the world does not suit us in the Gulf," Fahd explained in a rare interview with a Kuwaiti newspaper. "Islam is our social and political law. It is a complete constitution of social and economic laws and a system of government and justice."[110] Fahd's remarks were not totally unexpected; after all, the Saudi monarch had earlier pressured both Bahrain and Kuwait to end their parliamentary experiments, and the king had also repeatedly expressed his displeasure over Kuwait's October 1992 parliamentary elections. As such, it was not surprising that the king kept the right to appoint and dismiss the assembly at will. And as one Saudi prince pointed out, free elections in the Kingdom would not have guaranteed greater political freedom. "If we go for elections now in Saudi Arabia, you would get a Parliament of fundamentalist clergy, and Bedouin groups," noted Prince Abdulaziz bin Salman bin Abdulaziz.[111]

Still, Fahd's three Basic Statutes offered some concessions by the ruling family. Although the Basic Statute of Government reaffirmed the Sharia, it also laid the foundation for a more secular approach to law, especially concerning the rights of Saudi citizens vis-à-vis the state. The Consultative Assembly, although falling far short of its Hejazi predecessors or a true assembly or parliament in the Western sense, marked a departure as well in modern Saudi history. It not only offered the first national public forum for discussion (outside the pulpit and *majlis*), but it also provided for limited public participation in the decision-making arena.

Continued Strife

"Riyadh Spring" saw the al-Saud making other gestures in an effort to arrest their flagging popularity. Besides decreeing a general amnesty for prisoners, Fahd announced price cuts on gasoline, water, electricity, telephone, and natural gas fees. Port fees were reversed, as were other service duties. All told, the measures were expected to cost the government at least SR 3.8 billion (U.S. $1.01 billion) per year at a time of widening budget deficits and government efforts to do away with subsidies (see Chapter 5). Fahd's measures, although couched in terms of helping lower-income Saudis, seemed made to blunt the appeal of religious conservatives among the Kingdom's lower and middle classes.[112]

Other changes were forthcoming. A few days later, Fahd quietly accepted the resignations of the governor of Qassim, who was his half-brother Prince Abdullilah bin Abdulaziz, and Abdullilah's deputy.

The move had long been expected, especially given Abdullilah's handling of fundamentalists in Qassim. He was replaced by Prince Faisal bin Bandar, one of the grandsons of Abdulaziz. The appointment of Faisal brought to five the number of governorships held by the grandsons of Abdulaziz, as compared to four held by the late king's sons. Continuing this emphasis on fresh leadership, Fahd continued to place his own sons in positions of power. The king appointed his son, Sultan, as vice president of Youth Welfare, where he was expected to help his brother Faisal. The appointment of Sultan led to renewed fears that the al-Fahd were continuing their attempts to change the succession process away from Abdullah and the conservatives.

Fahd's efforts at placating the country's fundamentalists, however, proved ineffective. In July 1992, the latter presented a forty-five-page "Memorandum of Advice" to Fahd, signed by more than fifty clerics and scholars. The memorandum's focus was the "wide gap" between the government's Islamic posturing and reality in the Kingdom. The memorandum attacked "the total chaos of the economy and society, administration, corruption, widespread bribery, favoritism and the extreme feebleness of the courts." Also singled out for attack were the Kingdom's resumption of borrowing from international lenders and government loans to such "atheistic" countries as Syria, Jordan, Egypt, Algeria, and Iraq.[113] Largely a restatement of the fundamentalists' March 1991 petition, the memorandum suggested that Fahd's political reforms were unacceptable and inadequate. Two months after its presentation, the memorandum was attacked and condemned by members of the ulema, in a riposte carried by the Saudi Press Agency (SPA), and given wide coverage in the Kingdom's papers. The ulema accused fundamentalists of "inventing and exaggerating" the country's problems, resorting to lies, and ignoring reality. "Whoever prepared this memorandum," the ulema said, "either had bad intentions or was ignorant of reality."[114] The ulema also claimed that some of the fifty signatories had been "deceived" into signing the memorandum, while still others were being controlled by "foreign groups and parties."[115] The statement further denied reports that bin Baz had signed the memorandum. Instead, bin Baz's name appeared first among the signers of the ulema's response.

The signs of a rift in the religious hierarchy were glaring. Seven members of the Kingdom's Council of Supreme Religious Scholars were either unable or unwilling to sign the condemnation, and their absences were ascribed to "medical reasons." Given their advanced years—many were in their seventies or eighties—such an explanation was plausible. However, it seems more likely that the ulema were bitterly divided on the subject, and that their support for the al-Saud was beginning to waver.

Criticism notwithstanding, Fahd continued work on the Consultative Assembly and appointed Justice Minister Mohammed bin Ibrahim bin Jubair as speaker of the assembly a few days later. Progressive hopes that the Consultative Assembly would act as a true forum for discussion and debate were effectively crushed, given bin Jubair's credentials, close government affiliation, and strong ties to the ulema. Bin Jubair's closeness to the royal family was well known as he had helped draft the statutes, and had also signed the ulema's condemnation of fundamentalists. Bin Jubair's appointment in turn opened up several vacancies within the Ministry of Justice. To replace him as minister, Fahd selected Abdullah bin Mohammed bin Ibrahim al-Sheikh, an appointment calculated to curry favor among the ulema. Bin Jubair's two other posts—chairman of the Grievance Board and chairman of the Supreme Judicial Council—were also given to members of the ulema, obviously in a bid to secure their allegiance. As the fundamentalists showed no sign of easing their attacks on Fahd and his brothers, the al-Saud adopted a policy of coopting the ulema to ensure that they did not join with radicals. However, Fahd's six-month deadline to appoint the full council passed without a word.

The troubles in the Saudi assembly contrasted sharply with the October election in Kuwait where opposition members picked up thirty-six of the Parliament's fifty seats. The Kuwaiti opposition's growing power was confirmed a few days later when six of the new government's fifteen cabinet positions were given to opposition leaders, who vowed to investigate some of the ruling family's past decisions. Despite skepticism that it would be allowed to proceed, Kuwait's new Parliament launched investigations into the royal family's fiscal mismanagement and fraud, the poor showing of the Kuwaiti armed forces during the Iraqi invasion, and all legislation enacted by the government after the 1986 dissolution of the last Kuwaiti Parliament. Of particular interest to the legislators was the financial mismanagement of the Kuwait Investment Office (KIO), which reportedly lost more than $5 billion through its Spanish subsidiary. In response, Parliament aggressively passed a law empowering itself to oversee all state investments, and raised the penalties for embezzle-ment. It also began investigating two members of the royal family with ties to the KIO scandal.

Kuwait's parliamentary investigation of the al-Sabah disturbed the al-Saud, because this hitherto unknown idea of accountability had been adopted as a key point by leading members of the Kingdom's own fundamentalist wing.[116] Given that fear, it is not surprising that Fahd and his brothers delayed in appointing their Consultative Assembly, and instead lobbied the al-Sabah to rein in their Parliament.[117]

Fundamentalists kept up their pressure while the al-Saud delayed. In November 1992, fundamentalists sent another strongly worded mes-sage to Fahd, calling for an "Islamic" (i.e., less Western) foreign pol-icy, and roundly castigating the ineffectiveness of the Saudi armed forces. Islamic Awakening undertook other actions. Despite the new Basic Law and its articles protecting the sanctity of homes from search, bands of *mutawaeen* continued their raids on private homes. Other fundamentalists took to shooting at satellite dishes, claiming that they spread AIDS and Western values.[118]

To counter the growing upsurge in activity, Fahd removed in De-cember the seven members of his ulema who had been unable or unwilling to sign the petition condemning the Memorandum of Ad-vice. In a low-key announcement, the Saudi Press Agency (SPA) said the septet had been replaced because of "poor health." Fahd appointed ten younger scholars to fill their positions.[119] A week later, Fahd coun-seled the ulema and imams to keep politics out of their sermons during an address to scholars in Medina. In remarks carried by the SPA, Fahd warned his fundamentalist critics to stop attacking the royal family and its policies:

> It was noticed recently that pulpits have been used for earthly matters or matters unrelated to public interests, when they should be used to pro-claim what has been proven about the Prophet Mohammed and what is mentioned in God's Holy Book. . . . I do not object to any person who wants to say a word that is beneficial to Islam, Muslims and his coun-try, but it has been noted that this has been exceeded in some cases . . . and I do not think that is something useful.

Fahd further claimed that "foreign currents" such as Iran and Sudan were behind the campaign to destabilize the government. "Do we accept that somebody comes to us from outside our country and directs us? No."[120]

Two months later, the al-Saud took additional steps against their fundamentalist foes. First, they began restricting private Saudi donations to foreign Islamic groups. Second, they began sharing intelligence with other Arab countries such as Egypt and Tunisia, who were battling their own fundamentalists. The government also pressured the ulema to take action against outspoken and radical imams and religious leaders. This was followed a few weeks later with new regulations requiring Ministry of Interior permission for the collection of money for Muslim philanthropic groups inside the Kingdom.[121]

The al-Saud, however, continued to delay the nomination of their own Consultative Assembly. In March 1993, more than six months after his self-imposed deadline, Fahd again promised that he would nominate the sixty other members of his council "shortly," so that the council "could lend a hand to the state by offering honest advice in the interest of our nation and nationals."[122] Fahd's reluctance stood in marked contrast to events elsewhere in the Gulf, where Bahrain and Oman opened new consultative councils. The Kingdom's reforms also paled in comparison to those in neighboring Yemen, which in April 1993 allowed free and unfettered elections, in which both men and women were allowed to vote for 301 members of Parliament. More than forty parties ran slates of candidates that included women. When the ballots were counted, two women had been elected, and the ruling party had won.[123] Yemen's president then proposed a constitutional amendment limiting presidents to two terms.

The Saudi government's case looked even weaker when fundamentalists struck again on May 3 with the formation of the Kingdom's first human rights committee, the "Commission for the Defense of Legitimate Rights." The committee, which was comprised of six scholars and lawyers, announced in an accompanying statement that

> Sharia has made it incumbent upon the Muslims to support the oppressed and to eliminate injustice. . . . [S]ince scholars and supporters of Sharia bear prime responsibility for fulfilling the requirements of religion, we hereby declare our readiness to contribute to help eliminate injustice, support the oppressed, and defend the rights laid down in the Sharia for mankind.

The committee then called on the Saudi population to "report any injustice to us or communicate authentic information that helps eliminate injustice, support the oppressed and defend legitimate rights."[124] The committee's brazenness in its aims was accompanied by actions. Not only did the committee telefax the news of its creation to foreign news agencies and to offices and embassies in the Kingdom, it also listed its committee members' names and telephone numbers.

The government seemed at a loss as to how to respond, especially as the committee wrapped itself in the shroud of the Sharia. On May 8, committee members met with Salman to restate their objectives. Four days later, the ulema issued a statement, expressing their "surprise at the behavior of those brethren who set themselves up as defenders of legitimate rights in Saudi Arabia." The ulema went on to say that "Sharia courts are widespread throughout the land. No one is prevented from raising a grievance to these courts. The writers of this statement know this well, and they know what confusing ramifications it can have."[125] The ulema then called on the government to prohibit the committee.

The next day the Kingdom's police moved to shut down the offices of the two committee members who were lawyers. The government also fired the four committee members who were university professors. However, the men were not arrested, perhaps in view of their status in Saudi society as members of the Nejdi legal and religious elites. In fact, only Mohammed al-Masari, a son of one of the founders, and group spokesman, was imprisoned. The police also confiscated the passport of al-Masari's American wife.

Although the committee's definition of human rights was a narrow one—for example, several members had called Shiites apostates—the committee's creation illustrated the growing split between the Kingdom's established religious hierarchy and fundamentalists. The use of the Sharia against the government was also a masterstroke, putting the government on the defensive, an action that was intensified with skillful press releases. The committee also took the step of meeting with members of the American legation in Riyadh, further wrapping their cause with the aura of respectability.

The threat posed by the human rights committee, however, led Fahd to renew efforts to shore up his standing among the ulema and traditional religious establishment. In a move calculated to curry favor among the Kingdom's religious, Fahd divided the former Ministry of

Pilgrimage Affairs and Religious Trusts into two new bodies: a Ministry of Pilgrimage, and a Ministry of Islamic Endowments, Call, Mosques and Guidance Affairs. More significantly, Fahd appointed bin Baz, head of the Supreme Council of Scholars, as the Kingdom's General Mufti with the rank of minister.

Despite such unprecedented concessions to the religious elite, critics were unmollified. A few weeks later, more than sixty academics and scholars presented a petition to Fahd demanding the release of al-Masari and the reactivation of the human rights committee. Ten of the petitioners were immediately called before the Ministry of Interior where they had their passports revoked. A few days later, the Saudi police arrested one of the committee's six founders.

Fahd's continuing problems with his Wahhabi constituents, however, led to a stunning rapprochement with the Kingdom's Shiite minority. In early August, the king released more than forty Shiite political prisoners from jail, and also permitted the return of several exiled dissidents. Those opening gambits were followed in mid-October by a meeting between Fahd and several Shiite leaders, including members from the London-based Reform Movement. The result of that meeting was an unofficial pact between the al-Saud and their Shiite critics: the latter agreed to suspend publication of several magazines critical of the al-Saud in return for Fahd's promises to release Shiite political prisoners, restore passports to more than 3,000 Saudi Shiites, improve living conditions among Shiite communities, and end discrimination against Shiites in both the workplace and government.[126]

The king finally moved to appoint his Consultative Assembly on August 20, 1993, nearly one year after the passing of his deadline. The sixty members were largely drawn from tribal and religious leaders, as well as a cross-section of government officials, technocrats, businessmen, and retired army and police officers. One-sixth of the members were drawn from the ulema or their allies, while roughly half were said to have studied abroad.[127] No opposition figures nor women were appointed and only one Shiite was given membership. However, Fahd gave no date for the convening of the assembly, and again underlined the fact that the assembly would not diminish the power of the monarchy, nor was it the precursor of a Western democratic system of government. The king further announced that his ministers would be limited to set terms of office and have to follow a code of ethics. He gave no indication whether term limits would apply to royal ministers who control the National Guard, Interior, and Defense ministries.

Fahd's nomination of the assembly did nothing to defuse tensions. In fact, only a few weeks later, a lone gunman entered Fahd's Jeddah palace and began shooting, seriously wounding two guards. The semi-official Saudi Press Agency (SPA) gave few details of the incident, and refused to identify the gunman. Instead, it said he "wasn't normal." Saudi dissident groups, however, said the gunman was a member of the neo-Ikhwan, and had attempted to kill the king for his support of the Israeli–Palestine Liberation Organization Accord (see Chapter 3).[128]

The Consultative Assembly finally met on December 29, 1993, when Fahd personally opened the body. Three days later, the assembly held its first working session, and members formed eight committees: Islamic affairs, foreign affairs, security, economic and financial affairs, social and health issues, education and culture, services and public amenities, and administration.[129] Members also found fresh restrictions on their actions as Fahd decreed that the assembly could only comment on issues he brought before it, and further forbade members from taking documents from the hall. Members were also prohibited from speaking more than ten minutes on any one subject. Assembly rules also stipulated that all topics must first be approved by the speaker.[130] Significantly, the assembly was not requested to comment on the Kingdom's 1994 budget.

The House of Saud's Dilemma

Throughout its ninety-year rule, the al-Saud have defused political tension by undermining or co-opting their rivals. Abdulaziz destroyed the Ikhwan; the ulema were brought into the power system where their independence and powers were slowly eroded; and the military was hamstrung. Abdulaziz's sons have elaborated on these tactics by creating a welfare state that repays the Saudi people for their passivity with wealth.

The Saudi monarchy's durability is enhanced because Abdulaziz and his sons, unlike most other Arab kings, were not creatures of a colonial power, but won the throne themselves. The al-Saud's stability was further strengthened because Abdulaziz and his sons have introduced all change in the context of tradition. This tactic persuades many

Saudis that developments are not so much foreign implantations as the natural organic evolution of the Saudi state. Increased government control, for example, over the fractious tribes and regions was never justified in terms of efficiency or power, but in terms of increasing the security of citizens as required by Islam. The military, educational, and political benefits of the radio in the vast Saudi hinterlands were obvious, but it, and television, were introduced as an extension of the *muzzein*'s call to prayer from the minarets. Even the government's foes revert to historical arguments when they confront the ruling family. Islamic scholars call for a parliament using the idea of "rule by consensus" practiced during the time of Mohammed and the four "righteous" caliphs.

The al-Saud's tie with Islam, however, provides both strengths and weaknesses. The Islamic card, once played, is a hard card to withdraw from the game, and can always be trumped by someone with better Islamic credentials than the ruling family. This risk has heretofore been acceptable to the al-Saud, who have used religion to maintain a traditional autocratic fusion of tribal and state institutions. However, the use of Islam has also meant that the al-Saud have been restricted in their creation and nurturing of institutions that could support their rule. For example, prior to the founding of the new assembly, the only "institution" connecting the country's ruling family and the masses was the *majlis,* which the al-Saud constantly promoted as "desert democracy."[131]

Now that the Consultative Assembly is established, it could change the people's perceptions in a fashion that may be fatal in an entirely different way to the monarchy. Many Saudis attribute government subsidies, medical care, education, loans, and contracts to the king and his family. Thus, all the separate fractions of Saudi society look to one main source for benefits. If the assembly comes into being and shows signs of power, centrifugal forces will begin to tear at the country, which is already beset by polarization and growing unrest.

The al-Saud continue to cling to the hope that their people will accept their offered reforms. Although the al-Saud have secured the support of senior ulema, they have been unable to blunt the criticism or challenge of fundamentalists. It may be that the royal family's confidence in the apathy of the average Saudi, their security apparatus, and support from foreign friends is misplaced, and that the frightful lessons learned by the shah of Iran in 1979 have been forgotten. This negligence may have deadly results.

Notes

1. William Quandt, *Saudi Arabia in the 1980s.*
2. Richard Nyrop et al., *Saudi Arabia: A Country Study,* p. 80.
3. Taken from Bernard Lewis's "The Political Language of Islam," found in *Maclean's,* February 11, 1991.
4. Al-Wahhab also criticized his own father for accepting payment before making judgments.
5. David Holden and Richard Johns, *House of Saud,* p. 21.
6. Al-Wahhab's endorsement was more than just an astute recognition of political realities. The preacher was an ardent follower of the teachings of the Hanbali scholar Ahmad bin Taymiya, who taught that the perfect Islamic state had two centers of authority: the emir and the religious scholars. The emir's chief duty was to see that the Sharia was enforced, while the ulema's task was to counsel the emir and offer recommendations based on Sharia.
7. Ayman al-Yassini, *Religion and State in the Kingdom of Saudi Arabia,* p. 31.
8. Joseph A. Kechichian, "Islamic Revivalism and Change in Saudi Arabia," p. 56.
9. Domes were considered an innovation and hence un-Islamic.
10. Alexander Bligh, "The Saudi Religious Elite (Ulama) as Participant in the Political System of the Kingdom," p. 45.
11. The product of this union was the late King Faisal.
12. Robert Lacey, *The Kingdom,* p. 67.
13. This agreement remains in effect today, with the ulema exercising control over Saudi society and the legal structure.
14. The Ikhwan are best profiled in John Habib's *Ibn Saud's Warriors of Islam* and Lacey's *The Kingdom,* pp. 142, 144–50.
15. Lacey, *The Kingdom,* p. 144.
16. Holden and Johns, *House of Saud,* p. 69.
17. Caliph literally means "successor to the Prophet Mohammed." The term was adopted by the Prophet's successors after his death, and assumed by the Ottoman Turks during the 1500s. The title was subsequently used by the Turkish sultan until 1924.
18. Interesting to note was Abdulaziz's decision to keep the Ikhwan from attacking Mecca. Abdulaziz was fearful of repeating the experiences of the nineteenth century when Mecca's cleansing had resulted in international intervention.
19. Soliman al-Solaim, "Constitutional and Judicial Organization in Saudi Arabia" (Ph.D. diss.), p. 9.
20. Ibid., p. 17.
21. Abdulaziz's creation of the Hejazi Council was also motivated by his desire to placate foreign worries and opposition to his conquest of the holy cities.
22. Holden and Johns, *House of Saud,* p. 18.
23. A serious confrontation was only avoided when Faisal, the viceroy of the Hejaz, threw himself between the two groups; see D. van der Meulen, *The Wells of Ibn Sa'ud,* p. 105.
24. Lacey, *The Kingdom,* p. 228.
25. Ghassan Salame, "Political Power and the Saudi State," in *Power and Stability in the Middle East,* p. 71.

26. Al-Solaim, "Constitutional and Judicial Organization," p. 17.

27. Ibid., p. 28.

28. Ibid.

29. Lacey, *The Kingdom*, pp. 173–74.

30. Al-Yassini, *Religion and State*, p. 54.

31. Ibid., p. 55.

32. Lacey, *The Kingdom*, pp. 201–13.

33. Abdulaziz's custom of daily meetings with the ulema was followed by Faisal. It was only in 1975 with the late King Khalid that the frequency was reduced to once a week.

34. Bligh, "The Saudi Religious Elite," p. 39.

35. H.C. Armstrong, *Lord of Arabia*, p. 214.

36. Holden and Johns, *House of Saud*, p. 99.

37. *Umm ul-Qura*, October 16, 1953.

38. Al-Solaim, "Constitutional and Judicial Organization," p. 45.

39. Lacey, *The Kingdom*, p. 308.

40. Ibid., p. 312.

41. Holden and Johns, *House of Saud*, p. 212.

42. Al-Solaim, "Constitutional and Judicial Organization," p. 71.

43. Ibid., p. 72.

44. Holden and Johns, *House of Saud*, p. 213.

45. Ibid.

46. Saudi Radio, November 6, 1962.

47. The same thing occurred in 1969 after a coup attempt by air force officers, and again in 1979–1980 following the Mecca uprising.

48. Bligh, "The Saudi Religious Elite," p. 47.

49. Lacey, *The Kingdom*, p. 355.

50. The most public feuding by members of the al-Saud since the Saud–Faisal contretemps has been that between Fahd and his crown prince, Abdullah.

51. The Supreme Judicial Council has seen a resurgence of its powers under Fahd who has sought to make it a counterweight to the ulema.

52. David Edens, "The Anatomy of the Saudi Revolution," pp. 60–64.

53. Holden and Johns, *House of Saud*, p. 263.

54. Lacey, *The Kingdom*, p. 370.

55. Faisal's assassin was the brother of Prince Khalid bin Musaid, who had died during the demonstration against television.

56. Holden and Johns, *House of Saud*, p. 518.

57. Ibid., p. 518.

58. Bligh, "The Saudi Religious Elite," p. 47.

59. Joseph Kechichian, "The Role of the Ulama in the Politics of an Islamic State: The Case of Saudi Arabia," p. 58.

60. Kechichian, "Islamic Revivalism," p. 12.

61. Bligh, "The Saudi Religious Elite," p. 48.

62. Lacey, *The Kingdom*, p. 486.

63. Al-Yassini, *Religion and State*, p. 128.

64. Ibid.

65. *The Economist*, April 15, 1980.

66. Lacey, *The Kingdom*, p. 512.

67. A similar conflict ensued in the late 1970s when Abdullah was appointed crown prince but refused to give up his control of the National Guard. See Chapter 4.

68. *The Economist*, February 8, 1986.

69. Following Fahd's change of titles, hundreds of books and brochures were rewritten to take into account the new name. A nephew of the king told the authors that with his uncle's change of honorifics, the national emblem of a palm tree with crossed swords was now a mop bucket with crossed brooms.

70. General H. Norman Schwartzkopf with Peter Petre, *It Doesn't Take a Hero*, p. 332.

71. *U.S. News and World Report*, January 21, 1991.

72. *New York Times*, March 26, 1991.

73. Schwartzkopf, *It Doesn't Take a Hero*, p. 344.

74. *Christian Science Monitor*, October 31, 1990.

75. Schwartzkopf, *It Doesn't Take a Hero*, p. 339.

76. *New York Times*, November 24, 1990, and *Washington Post*, October 10, 1990.

77. *Middle East Economic Survey (MEES)*, November 23, 1990.

78. *Time*, January 21, 1991.

79. Ibid., November 26, 1990.

80. "Reinventing the Wheel," *Ms.* Magazine, 1991. Anonymous.

81. Ibid.

82. Ibid.

83. *Time*, November 26, 1990.

84. *New York Times*, November 18, 1990.

85. *MEES*, November 30, 1990.

86. *New York Times*, November 18, 1990.

87. Ibid.

88. Ibid., March 9, 1991.

89. Ibid.

90. Ibid., December 31, 1991.

91. Ironically, the arresting *mutawaeen* had been transferred to Jeddah from al-Hasa so as not to provoke any incidents with American armed forces.

92. *Washington Post*, December 13, 1990.

93. Schwartzkopf, *It Doesn't Take a Hero*, p. 396.

94. The al-Saud's muzzling of the progressive press against fundamentalists is nothing new. In 1988–1989, Ridah Larry, editor of the *Saudi Gazette*, was prohibited by the Ministry of Information from writing any articles after an important piece appeared in *Al-Riyadh* criticizing fundamentalists.

95. *The Nation*, April 13, 1992.

96. *Christian Science Monitor*, June 15, 1991.

97. *MEES*, June 3, 1991.

98. *Washington Post*, March 27, 1992.

99. "Country Report: Saudi Arabia," *Economist Intelligence Unit (EIU)*, no. 4, 1991.

100. *Arabian Monitor*, December 1992.

101. *New York Times*, December 31, 1991.

102. Ibid.

103. *The Nation,* April 13, 1992.

104. *New York Times,* January 30, 1992.

105. *Christian Science Monitor,* January 21, 1992.

106. *New York Times,* March 2, 1992.

107. *MEED: Middle East Business Weekly,* March 13, 1992.

108. *MEES,* March 9, 1992.

109. *New York Times,* March 2, 1992.

110. *MEED,* April 10, 1992.

111. *Business Week,* November 11, 1990.

112. *Wall Street Journal,* March 25, 1992.

113. *MEES,* December 31, 1992.

114. Ibid.

115. *Mideast Mirror,* September 18, 1992.

116. Given the royal family's fusion of state and family expenses, the idea of accountability is abhorrent to them. The al-Saud would be forced to explain such anomalies as why fully one-third of the national airline's fleet is reserved for their use, and why Saudi Telecom allows them to make free international calls.

117. *New York Times,* February 15, 1993.

118. Ibid., December 14, 1992.

119. Ibid., December 21, 1992.

120. *MEES,* December 28, 1992.

121. *New York Times,* May 14, 1993.

122. *Mideast Mirror,* March 12, 1993.

123. *New York Times,* May 1, 1993.

124. *MEES,* May 17, 1993.

125. Ibid.

126. *Washington Post,* October 16, 1993.

127. *MEES,* August 26, 1993.

128. Associated Press, September 13, 1993.

129. *MEED,* January 14, 1994.

130. "Country Report: Saudi Arabia," *EIU,* no. 3, 1993.

131. Saudi commentators call the *majlis* "desert democracy" because subjects gain access to their rulers in this fashion. Cynics retort that the *majlis* helps build consensus, but does not result in significant power sharing with its participants.

3 FOREIGN RELATIONS

Our ties with the world's countries are ties of interest. There are no emotions. . . . If we find our requirements with a friendly country and if she gives us what we want, she does so in return for our money. Nobody provides anything for free.

—King Fahd, addressing military officers in 1988[1]

Some of our officials who opposed this policy [of checkbook diplomacy] used to joke that the Arabs of the Gulf region, when hit on the left cheek, turned their right pocket. This isn't happening any more. This era is over for good.

—Unnamed Saudi military official in 1992[2]

Saudi Arabia has three foreign policy objectives in the wake of Operation Desert Storm: national security, hegemony over the Arabian peninsula, and nominal leadership in the Arab and Islamic worlds. Some observers think it would do well to stick to a much less ambitious agenda: namely, national survival. The Saudi regime is facing the most serious threat to its existence since that posed by Gamal Abdul Nasser in the 1950s and 1960s.

Saddam Hussein's Iraq is to the north; Shiite Iran looms to the east; an unstable Yemen threatens from the south; and a radical Sudan lies to the west. The Kingdom is surrounded, and its own carefully crafted policies are breaking apart. The Gulf Cooperation Council (GCC) remains impotent and the Arab League and Organization of Islamic Conference (OIC) are of questionable value as well. The only viable option for Saudi security is its de facto security alliance with the United States, but this causes nearly as many problems as it solves. While the Americans supply military strength, commercial ties, and technology, they are a liability to Saudi Arabia's foreign and domestic politics. The relationship is an unpopular choice with most Saudis, and is poison in the general Islamic world. Much of America's unpopularity is due to its support of Israel, a fact that may be countered by the Gaza–Jericho Agreement between Israel and the Palestine Liberation Organization (PLO).

One of the ironies about this relationship is the amount of obfuscation practiced by each government about the other. The American government has downplayed its ties to the Kingdom because of Saudi human rights abuses. Washington has helped conceal the depth of Saudi economic troubles. Meanwhile, the al-Saud allowed the Kingdom's newspapers to savage the Americans in order to distance themselves from the "degenerative Western superpower." This ruse fooled only the very simple, who were then shocked to see, after the invasion of Kuwait, the Islamic Saudi government rush into the embrace of its "Great Satan."

Background and History

Modern Saudi Arabia's foreign policy began with the ascendancy of the al-Saud in 1902. Unlike many of his Gulf contemporaries, Abdulaziz bin Saud had a relatively well rounded world view, at least regarding the way in which foreign powers affected events in the peninsula. At the time of his conquest of Riyadh, there were two major powers in Arabia: the Ottoman Empire and Great Britain. The Turks were the power in decline, but still exercised nominal control over most of the Middle East, including the Hejaz and al-Hasa. The Turks also had strong ties with the Nejd, thanks to their strategic alliance with the al-Rashid clan of Hail.

Balancing the Ottomans was Great Britain. Britain held scattered bases throughout the peninsula at the turn of the century, including Kuwait, Bahrain, the Trucial States (today's United Arab Emirates [UAE]), Oman, and Aden. These outposts were not important in and of themselves: instead they were regarded as essential outposts along the all-vital Suez–India route. Sensing the British to be the power in ascendancy, Abdulaziz tried to attach his star to London's. In the same year he conquered Riyadh, bin Saud sent word to the British Gulf commissioner that he was interested in joining the Trucial State system.[3] The British response was to ignore his request. London's indifference was a careful political calculation. The British backed the Ottomans for their ability to pacify the Arabs so those in the peninsula could pose no threat to their possessions. As such, local chieftains such as Abdulaziz, whose ambitious dreams could upset the arrangement, were studiously ignored. Abdulaziz, however, knew he needed British support, if not British arms and monies, to succeed in uniting Arabia. His "foreign policy" during the first decade of his rule was geared toward attracting British notice. Abdulaziz's conquest of al-Hasa in 1913 finally succeeded, if only because his action imperiled Britain's Gulf holdings. Still, the British were reluctant to deal with the Saudi leader, and two months after his victory, London signed an accord with the Ottoman Empire, effectively carving Arabia into spheres of influence. Abdulaziz's state was treated as if it did not exist, and the Nejd was recognized as a Turkish province.[4]

The outbreak of World War I abruptly changed British perceptions. Both London and the Turks lobbied for bin Saud's support. In this atmosphere of wheeling and dealing, the Saudi-British Friendship Treaty was signed in 1915. The treaty, one of the first signed by a Saudi state, represented quite a turnaround from 1902 when the British had spurned Abdulaziz's advances. Now, the British promised to protect the Saudi state against domestic and foreign foes, while Abdulaziz gave London trading privileges, as well as supervision of his budding foreign policy. More importantly, the British agreed to supply arms, ammunition, and cash. Abdulaziz was nonetheless careful not to sever all ties with Constantinople. Throughout the war and unbeknownst to his British friends, Abdulaziz maintained correspondence with Turkish officials in which he emphasized his loyalty to them.[5]

The Saudi king was always distrustful of British intentions, and his suspicions grew as London moved to support the "Arab Revolt" of his arch enemy, the Shareef Husain of Mecca. Those feelings intensified as Britain's secret and not-so-secret agreements became known. The revelation of the Sykes-Picot Accord made a mockery of Allied support for the Arab world by carving up Turkish possessions in the Middle East between London, France, Italy, and Russia. Abdulaziz was further infuriated by the Balfour Declaration, which promised European Jews a homeland in Palestine, the presence of hundreds of thousands of Arabs notwithstanding. Still, Abdulaziz was astute enough to realize that his chances of uniting Arabia largely rested with Britain, and he was careful to play the complaisant ally—even when London began cutting back its support and arms shipments with the conclusion of World War I. British policy had again shifted, and London was now trying to keep Abdulaziz and the Shareef equally weak to prevent the emergence of a unified Arabian state, which might endanger Britain's recently acquired mandates in Palestine, Transjordan, and Iraq. Abdulaziz accepted the turn of events stoically. "What I cede of my rights under force," he explained to friends, "I will get back when I have sufficient force, *insh'allah.*"[6]

Without British aid, Abdulaziz continued to play the "Islamic card" to achieve his goals. This was an extension of his domestic use of Unitarianism to justify his conquest of people who practiced "debased" forms of Islam, be they Shiites in al-Hasa or the al-Rashid in the north. This Islamic strategy bore quick results when the Shareef proclaimed the resurrection of the caliphate in 1924 and announced that he was the new caliph (see Chapter 2). The Islamic world—to say nothing of Abdulaziz's Ikhwan—burst into rage. Not only were the Shareef's megalomania and venality well known, but there was also the matter of his administration of the Hejaz, which had quickly degenerated into the most extortionate fleecing of pilgrims in recent memory. Abdulaziz sent letters to Muslim organizations around the world, seeking their views. When the Indian hajj organization asked Abdulaziz to take action, the Saudi leader had the perfect excuse to move against the Shareef. He subsequently justified his attack by saying he was only fulfilling international Islamic calls for justice.[7] The British, despairing of the Shareef's unbalanced behavior, said nothing.

The Saudi leader's use of Islam as a foreign policy tool continued after his conquest of the Hejaz. To counter international fears that the new Saudi-Wahhabi state would prove just as intolerant as the first, Abdulaziz adopted a moderate tone, calling for international Islamic conferences to discuss the administration of the holy cities. Two conferences were in fact held in 1926 and 1927. Attended by the Indian and Indonesian hajj organizations, the conferences proposed that the cities be put under multinational control.[8] Of course, bin Saud had no intention of giving up his hard-won spoils, which constituted an important part of his own political legitimacy. However, he was eager to show his willingness to cooperate, and professed his intention to study the conference's resolutions. In the meantime, Abdulaziz gave the Hejaz a constitution and created local assemblies to allay international fears (see Chapter 2). Just as importantly, the Saudi leader made the pilgrimage a safe and relatively extortion-free experience for the world's Muslims.

Early Saudi foreign policy was conducted on a rudimentary basis.

After Jeddah was conquered in 1925, Abdulaziz gained his first foreign policy "expert," a local merchant named Abdullah Ali Riddha. Riddha acted as an unofficial emissary between the Saudi king and the half-dozen European missions in Jeddah, that looked after the annual needs of their pilgrims.[9] There were no Saudi diplomats per se, so local merchants traveling abroad were often empowered to issue visas and serve as ambassadors. A Ministry of Foreign Affairs was only created in 1930 with Prince Faisal bin Abdulaziz named as minister. Foreign relations were a distant priority for the Saudi monarch, unless they directly affected his rule.

So, it seems ironic that within months of his conquest of the Hejaz, Abdulaziz found himself embroiled in an international crisis caused by his Ikhwan and their refusal to stop the jihad. The "enemy" was Britain, whose mandates and protectorates ringed bin Saud's territory. London decided to put the sons of Shareef Husain on the newly created thrones of Iraq and Transjordan, which added dynastic hatreds to the already explosive mixture of border disputes and religious warfare. Abdulaziz had reason to fear revanchist plans of the Shareef's sons and had trouble restraining his Ikhwan warriors from raiding non-Wahhabi Iraq and Transjordan. Still, the last thing Abdulaziz wanted to do was risk a confrontation with the British, whose airplanes and armored cars had already proved their superiority against the Ikhwan. Abdulaziz had no choice but to rein in his warriors of God and attempt to explain the realities of international relations to them. Their refusal or inability to understand led to their destruction, but not before plunging Saudi Arabia into several years of political instability.

Saudi diplomacy coalesced in the 1930s with the consolidation of Abdulaziz's power. In 1934, the Kingdom went to war with Yemen over the Asir and Najran Oasis. The issue was expansion; surrounded by British-administered territories, the only direction in which the Kingdom could grow was southwest toward Yemen. Again, the Saudi state was contained by the Great Powers. When Abdulaziz's army threatened to seize the entire Yemeni coast, the British and Italians grew alarmed and sent a flotilla of warships to maintain the balance of power and blunt a possible Saudi thrust to Aden.[10] The threat of foreign intervention was sufficient. The Saudi advance was halted, and the Treaty of Taif was signed a few weeks later. Under its provisions, the Saudis were awarded the Asir and Najran, but other gains were returned to the Yemenis. The latter also received special work and residency privileges in the Kingdom.[11]

The Yemeni episode, however, showed a less savory side of the Saudi state, a tendency to bully its smaller neighbors. As early as 1919, the Saudis were embroiled in a dispute with Kuwait, which would have reduced the emirate to protectorate status. Saudi machinations were only foiled by British protests. Qatar was threatened with annexation, and the ruler of Bahrain secretly paid Abdulaziz protection money to avoid trouble. There were also sporadic border clashes with the Trucial States.

Abdulaziz also used the interwar period to break his dependency on London by intensifying his contacts with other European powers such as France and the Netherlands, and seeking ties and arms deals with both Fascist Italy and Nazi Germany; further afield, he signed a treaty of friendship with Japan.[12] To avoid jeopardizing his new friendships, bin Saud refused to give material support to nationalists from French North Africa and the Dutch East Indies.[13] The sole exception was Palestine. While professing friendship with London, Abdulaziz sent arms and munitions to Palestinian nationalists who were fighting British rule and the steady inflow of Jewish settlers. Securely in power, Abdulaziz was beginning to flex his diplomatic muscles, but his most important interwar international relationship was made not through treaties or an exchange of ambassadors but in the signing of a mineral concession with an American oil company. From this purely commercial enterprise would spring the vaunted "special relationship" between Saudi Arabia and the United States.

The Beginning of the Special Relationship

The Saudi-American "special relationship" is still misunderstood by both sides, despite the fact that it has been in existence for sixty years. One of the reasons for this is that it evolved with little thought or planning on the part of either nation. Abdulaziz awarded an oil exploration concession to the Standard Oil Company of California (SOCAL, the predecessor of the Arabian-American Oil Company, ARAMCO) in 1933. Oil was struck five years later. It was a propitious development, but the American government seemed utterly unconcerned. The Middle East was generally conceded to be within the British sphere of influence in 1938, and Washington had little interest in the area. It was only after the Japanese, Italians, and Germans requested oil concessions from Abdulaziz that the State Department sent diplomatic representation to Jeddah. The realization slowly dawned that SOCAL's oil fields were a vital American interest; that a belief grew as World War II progressed and Washington's oil reserves diminished. As concern about future oil shortages increased, American policymakers had an abrupt change of heart. Saudi Arabia's importance suddenly warranted greater attention and care, and a Lend-Lease Agreement was duly signed in 1943.

Closer cooperation followed. President Franklin D. Roosevelt and Abdulaziz met at the Great Bitter Lake in the Suez Canal in early 1945. A personal rapport between the two leaders took root, and the American side was diligent in trying not to offend the aging king's Unitarian sensibilities.[14] Roosevelt tried to garner Abdulaziz's support for the creation of a Jewish homeland in Palestine but the Saudi leader would hear nothing of it. Instead, Abdulaziz was so persuasive in his arguments against a Jewish-Palestinian entity that he succeeded in securing Roosevelt's commitment that the United States government "would do nothing to assist the Jews against the Arabs and would make no move hostile to the Arab people."[15] These promises were reiterated several weeks later on April 5 when Roosevelt wrote in a letter to the Saudi king that American promises had been issued in the president's "capacity as Chief of the Executive Branch of this government."[16]

Roosevelt's death voided those promises, as his successor, Harry S. Truman, was more inclined to favor Zionist aspirations. The "special relationship" had hit its first turbulence, and the trouble was just beginning. Still, relations between the two remained close. Washington was given access to the Dhahran Air Base in 1946 in return for military equipment and training. One year later, the United Nations decided to partition Palestine into Jewish and Arab sections. As the prospects of war mounted, American policymakers wondered what the Saudi reaction would be. They were thus surprised when they received a secret cable from Abdulaziz in December 1947, asking the Truman administration for guarantees of support in the face of rising Arab radicalism. Bin Saud's action seemed based on his distrust of the Hashemite rulers of Transjordan and Iraq who were pressuring the Kingdom to join an Arab coalition to fight the emerging Jewish state. Less stressed was Abdulaziz's fear that the two Hashemite states were plotting to take over the Hejaz and holy cities as well.

According to the cable sent to Truman, Abdulaziz wanted assurances that the United States "would supply the Saudi Arabian government and army with the necessary materials" to defend itself "since the threat was not only involving Saudi Arabia but also vital American interests."[17] In response, the State Department repeated promises that had been made to Crown Prince Saud bin Abdulaziz during a visit to Washington earlier that spring: "One of the basic policies of [the] United States in [the] Near East is unqualifiedly to support [the] territorial integrity and political independence of Saudi Arabia," the king was assured. "If Saudi Arabia should therefore be attacked by another power or be under threat of attack, the U.S. through the medium of [the] U.N. would take energetic measures to ward off such aggression."[18]

Abdulaziz's worries underlined the weakness of the pan-Arabist element of Saudi foreign policy, which had slowly been taking root during the 1930s. Although the Kingdom had been, with British prompting, one of the founders of the Arab League in 1945, the king had never felt comfortable with his fellow members, which included Egypt, Syria, Lebanon, Iraq, Transjordan, and Yemen.[19] He distrusted their leaders, and when war broke out in 1948 between the Arab states and Israel, Abdulaziz consciously sacrificed Arab unity, despite the fervent lobbying of his sons and advisors.[20] Abdulaziz not only refused to turn off ARAMCO's oil pipeline during the conflict, but he sent only a small token Saudi force to Palestine where it played no discernible role in the fighting. Instead, the king focused his efforts on gaining the al-Buraiymi Oasis, at the convergence of today's Saudi, Omani, and Abu Dhabian borders. Encouraged by ARAMCO, which convinced the king that the oasis was sitting on valuable deposits of oil, the Saudi monarch moved to create an outpost.[21] Saudi expansionism again precipitated an international incident as Britain moved to support its protectorates' claims. Before the issue was turned over to international arbitrators, several skirmishes had been fought.

The Advent of *Riyal Politik*

By the time of Abdulaziz's death in 1953, the three pillars of Saudi foreign policy—pan-Arabism, pan-Islamism, and the close relationship with the United States—had been set in place. It was left to Abdulaziz's successor, King Saud bin Abdulaziz, to supply the final element of Saudi foreign policy: that of *riyal politik,* the judicious use of oil money (i.e., Saudi riyals) to influence the Kingdom's friends and foes. Convinced that oil wealth would readily translate into political power, Saud played *riyal politik* with a vengeance, but was as inept at foreign politics as he was at the domestic variety and quickly found himself in serious trouble.

Saud's greatest foreign policy error was to underestimate the appeal of Egypt's Gamal Abdul Nasser. Despite the philosophical contradictions between the two men and the states they represented, Saud soon became one of Nasser's greatest backers, willingly bankrolling many of the Egyptian's schemes. Together, Nasser and Saud refused to join the British-inspired Baghdad Pact and connived to keep Jordan out of the organization.[22] Saud supported Egyptian claims on the Suez Canal, while Nasser reciprocated by backing Saudi pretensions to al-Buraiymi. The Saudi leader also gave backing to Nasser's Soviet arms deal, the Imam Yahya's claim to the British protectorate of Aden, and a revolt in Oman's hinterlands. In his lurch to accommodate Nasser, Saud willingly sacrificed the Kingdom's close American ties. Not surprisingly, Washington was nonplussed. Saudi Arabia under Saud was viewed with alarm—as shown by a State Department intelligence report issued on February 8, 1956, entitled "Saudi Arabia: A Disruptive Force in Western-Arab Relations."[23]

Saud's foreign policy, however, met with little success. British-led troops expelled the small Saudi garrison in al-Buraiymi in 1955 after Saud blatantly attempted to suborn the members of an international tribunal hearing the dispute. In Oman, loyalist troops easily put down the Saudi-backed rebels. Ties with Egypt also proved a mixed blessing. Although Saud and Nasser were nominal allies, Cairo Radio broadcast a constant stream of propaganda into the Kingdom, gleefully pointing out corruption and scandals in the royal family. Undeterred, Saud opened his country to thousands of Egyptians who arrived to man the educational, health, and government bureaucracies. Included in their numbers was a high-level military training mission. A few months later, Saudi intelligence discovered the first of several Egyptian–encouraged/sponsored plots to overthrow the monarchy and create a secular republic. Still, the Saudi king continued to work with Nasser, even giving financial support to one of Nasser's pet projects: the union of the two countries with Syria. However, Saud was increasingly being relegated to a support position, useful only for the money he provided. This was aptly underlined during the Suez crisis of 1956, when Nasser nationalized the canal without even consulting Saud.[24] The results were disastrous: Saudi oil shipments were cut in half, imports were reduced, and traffic through the canal ceased. Nasser's unilateral action meant that Saudi Arabia's oil revenues fell by more than one-third at a time of growing financial indebtedness. Saud was also forced to beg Nasser not to shut down the Saudi pipeline that went through Syria, a turn of events that wounded the king's pride. Nonetheless, Saud played the loyal ally, ordering ARAMCO to cease oil shipments to France and Great Britain, a lesson that was lost on American policy-makers in 1973.

Jealousy and pride eventually estranged Saud from Nasser. Relations came to the breaking point in 1957–1958 when Saud rushed troops to Jordan to help King Hussein put down a Nasserite uprising. Saud also rushed to repair ties with the United States, agreeing to participate in the Eisenhower Doctrine, an American plan aimed at containing Nasser's Arab Socialism. Saud signed a five-year extension on Dhahran Air Base with the United States in return for increased military aid.[25] Such a betrayal of Nasser risked retaliation, and it was not long in coming. In May 1957, the Saudis uncovered yet another plot to blow up Saud's palace in Riyadh. Implicated in the scheme was the Egyptian military attaché, whose action the Nasser government quickly disavowed.

Saud was not convinced, and without consulting his brothers, he began making his own plans to subvert the proposed union between Egypt and Syria. Saud's machinations exploded in his face on March 5, 1958, when the head of Syria's secret service announced to a stunned world that the Saudi monarch had bribed him to stage a coup and kill Nasser. Even more damaging was the Syrian's production of several checks and letters from Saud's aides. Within days, the Saudi monarch had turned over the running of the Saudi government to his half-brother Faisal, the first round in a six-year struggle to see who would control the Saudi government. Faisal's initial foreign policy was motivated by the need to secure some time to stabilize the Kingdom and its worsening financial state. Appeasement of Nasser became paramount. Faisal removed Saudi troops from Jordan, and refrained from commenting on the bloody coup that toppled the Hashemite king of Iraq. Faisal also edged away from the Eisenhower Doctrine to avoid further conflict with Nasser. This appeasement continued when Saud regained power in late 1960. Saud tried to ingratiate himself with Nasser by pledging that the Kingdom would base its foreign policy on "Arabism." Nasser was in no mood for compromise, for his much-touted United Arab Republic of Syria and Egypt had recently collapsed. Needing a quick victory, Nasser refocused his attention on "reactionary" Arab regimes. Renewed Egyptian verbal attacks on the Kingdom caused Saud to reverse himself again. In 1961, Saud condemned as "erroneous" the foreign ideologies of Egypt, and proclaimed Islam to be the Kingdom's only policy. Relations between Cairo and Riyadh again worsened, but there were other Saudi concerns. In 1961, Iraq threatened to invade the newly independent Kuwait. Britain rushed troops to the emirate to protect it, and an Arab League contingent of Saudi, Egyptian, Sudanese, and Jordanian peacekeeping troops followed two months later. Saudi-Iraqi relations quickly soured as Baghdad recalled its ambassador.[26] The Arab League force stayed in Kuwait until 1963, when a change in Iraqi governments brought an easing of tensions. The Kuwaiti incident was, however, followed by other inter-Arab disputes.

Saud, like the rest of the Arab world, was shocked to learn on September 26, 1962, that the North Yemeni regime of Mohammed al-Badr had been overthrown by Egyptian-trained officers. Al-Badr miraculously survived a tank attack on his palace to lead a royalist resistance, but Egypt soon flew paratroopers to help the revolutionary junta, the first of nearly 100,000 troops Nasser was to commit to the fray.[27]

The Kingdom was in dire straits. Not only were thousands of Egyptian troops on its southern borders threatening to invade and regain the Asir and Najran for the new Yemeni Republic, but the Saudi military was unproven and politically unreliable. Several Saudi pilots assigned to ferry supplies to the royalists had already defected, and the Saudi government was riven with discord as the Saud–Faisal conflict deepened. Against this backdrop, Faisal met President John F. Kennedy and petitioned for aid.

This calling on the United States as the savior of last resort was not without precedence. Abdulaziz had done the same in 1947 when he had felt threatened by the Hashemites. A pattern was quickly developing: although the Saudis embraced various doctrines to render their foreign policy acceptable to their Arab and Islamic partners, those policies were readily jettisoned when the al-Saud felt in danger. The Yemeni crisis was no different. Kennedy agreed to provide aid in return for Faisal's vague promises about introducing democratic reforms in his country—a pledge that Fahd was to repeat nearly thirty years later when Iraqi troops were stationed on the Saudi border. Kennedy did more than just promise; when Egyptian planes began bombing Saudi cities and installations in the south, Kennedy sent a squadron of American jets to the Kingdom. Although the latter was billed as a joint training mission, the pilots had been instructed—albeit quietly—to use force if provoked.[28] The message was not lost on Nasser, who forthwith stopped further direct military provocations against the Kingdom. Despite a massive Egyptian buildup, Nasser-supported forces were unable to defeat the Saudi-backed Yemeni royalists. A war of attrition continued, ending only in 1967 after Nasser's humiliating defeat at the hands of Israel in the Six-Day War.

Faisal's Foreign Policy

Faisal's reign marked the zenith of Saudi foreign policy. Faisal forged a cohesive foreign policy, refining the Kingdom's strategic triad and using ample doses of *riyal politik*. This is best illustrated by the Kingdom's oil policy at the time, which was retailored to meet America's growing consumption. By the end of the 1960s, the Kingdom was pumping close to 8 million bpd (barrels per day), far beyond its financial needs, but more than enough to meet American demand. Relations between Riyadh and Washington continued to improve under Faisal, especially in light of Nasser's continued threat to shared interests, and the desire to meet Soviet expansionism in the region. Faisal also tried to shore up the Kingdom's pan-Arabist policy, shredded somewhat by Saud's machinations, as well as the pan-Islamist pillar that he offered as an alternative to Nasser's radicalism.

Faisal's pan-Islamic policy was a masterstroke that served two purposes. Besides bolstering the al-Saud's political legitimacy at home, it also strengthened the Kingdom's standing in the Islamic world. Faisal approached the subject aggressively. Although the king was a devout Muslim (at least later in his life), he was also a political realist, and realized that to counteract Nasser's secular message, he would need something just as powerful. Unlike many who thought Islam's, and indeed religion's, influence was waning, Faisal took a different tack, arguing that greater not less reliance on religion was needed. Faisal renewed his efforts at strengthening pan-Islamism when he succeeded to the throne in 1964. During the next two years, the Saudi monarch made a series of state visits to Islamic states throughout the world, stressing the pan-Islamic message. The response was mixed: countries led by conservative monarchs welcomed Faisal's message; other countries professed support, no doubt influenced by the possibility of gaining Saudi financial aid. The movement was inadvertently helped in 1967 by the defeat inflicted on the Arab states by Israel. Not only was Nasser, the apostle of socialism and secularism, humbled, but it also created a new religious impetus given the fact that the holy city of Jerusalem was controlled by the Zionists.

Israel's victory served as a catalyst. Within a few short weeks, Nasser announced the withdrawal of Egyptian troops from Yemen, and Faisal promised financial aid at the Khartoum Conference to help Egypt and the other frontline states to rebuild.[29] Faisal's push for pan-Islamism and pan-Arabism was bolstered later when a crazed Australian set fire to the al-Aqsa Mosque in Jerusalem, Islam's third holiest site. International Islamic opinion was inflamed, and Faisal quickly persuaded almost all of the Muslim world to attend the first Islamic summit meeting at Rabat, Morocco. The heads of state from more than twenty Islamic countries gathered, foreshadowing the establishment of the Organization of Islamic Conference (OIC) in Jeddah.

Making Faisal's task of consensus building far easier was the massive inflow of petrodollars, which flooded Saudi coffers in the aftermath of the Yom Kippur War. The Kingdom's ability to buy friends increased dramatically. Faisal used petrodollars liberally, especially to influence events in the Arab and Islamic worlds.[30] Saudi financial aid was used to wean Egypt from the Soviet embrace, to end the first round of the Lebanese Civil War, and to ease tensions between Syria and Jordan. Saudi foreign aid eventually totaled $93 billion for the 1973–1990 period, or roughly 6 percent of the country's GNP.[31]

Israel's victory in the Six-Day War had other ramifications for Faisal and his brothers. The war left in its wake the Israeli occupation of the West Bank, Gaza, and Golan Heights. The inability to recapture—either diplomatically or militarily—what had been lost rankled Faisal deeply. He was also troubled by the changing attitude of the United States. Whereas Washington had forced Israel to return its gains after the 1956 war, Washington in 1967 was exhibiting no such concern. Faisal felt a certain responsibility to secure Jerusalem's return, given his guardianship of Mecca and Medina. The king also realized that the longer it took to reach a suitable peace, the more powerful radicals would grow within the Arab world. The latter fact especially worried Faisal, given the Kingdom's close ties with the United States, which was also the protector of Israel. Although Nasser and other Arab radicals had often labeled the al-Saud as American stooges, such charges never held much weight until Israel's 1967 victory. For Faisal and his brothers, the American link was becoming more dangerous. This point was amply underlined in March 1973 when Palestinian commandos stormed the Saudi embassy in Khartoum, killing three diplomats. A few weeks later, the Saudi embassy in Paris was assaulted.

Unfortunately, few Washington policymakers understood the Saudi dilemma. Instead, most thought the Saudis could bend their policies given close ties between the two countries, and American interests in the oil industry. Washington continued to view the Saudis as Arab moderates who could influence large sections of the Arab world through oil largess. By adopting such a stance, Washington misread Saudi (and Arab) public opinion, and more importantly, the ability of the al-Saud to disregard the strong currents flowing around them. The Saudis committed the same mistake vis-à-vis Washington. Most Americans supported Israel, and would not let it be defeated or destroyed by its Arab enemies; this attitude, in turn, entered into American policy considerations. The oil embargo of 1973 was, in retrospect, almost a foregone conclusion. The Saudis attempted to warn the United States several times that they were being pressured by Arab radicals, and even laid their position out during a 1972 speech by then Petroleum and Mineral Resources Minister Ahmad Zaki Yamani. Yamani, on a spring visit to the United States, stressed that Saudi-American cooperation was a two-way street. In return for a friendly Saudi oil policy, Yamani said the Kingdom expected a more even-handed policy in the Middle East. Henry Kissinger and the Nixon administration chose to ignore the warning.

Saudi admonitions continued into 1973. In May, Faisal met the American directors of ARAMCO and warned that American intransigence on the Israeli issue was isolating the Kingdom in the face of growing Arab radicalism.[32] Thoroughly alarmed, the directors conveyed the warning to American officials but without success. Preoccupied with its own problems, the Nixon administration was as surprised as the rest of the world when Egyptian forces swarmed across the Suez Canal on October 6, 1973, and overran Israeli positions. As Egyptian troops raced through the Sinai, and Syrian troops assaulted Israeli positions in the Golan Heights, the Saudis marshaled support among Arab oil producers for their secret plan, which promised a general reduction in oil production during the conflict. A 10 percent production cut was set into effect, with additional 5 percent production cuts promised for every month that the conflict continued. Embargoes were also threatened against states that continued to aid Israel. When the Nixon administration submitted an emergency (and inflated) $2.2 billion military aid request for Israel to Congress on October 18, the Saudis had no choice but to act. Saudi Arabia cut all oil shipments to Washington the next day.

Oil prices soared from $3.12 per barrel prior to the conflict, to more than $17 per barrel just two months later on the spot market.[33] As American gasoline lines grew, Saudi Arabia basked in its new diplomatic aura, which was especially great in the Arab and Islamic worlds. Faisal's pet project, the OIC, grew stronger as countries rushed to join it. The embargo, however, had only mixed results as regards its initial objectives. Although the Saudis did succeed in forcing Washington to treat them more on par with the Israelis in the area of arms purchases, American Middle East policy remained basically pro-Israeli. Faisal ended the embargo in March 1974.

Relations between Washington and Riyadh slowly returned to normal. There was grudging realization that whatever their differences on Israel, the two countries needed each other. The Kingdom desired American protection and arms; Washington needed a stable and moderate voice within OPEC as well as secure oil supplies. By the late 1970s, the Kingdom was selling the United States extra oil to help Washington build up its Strategic Reserve (and thus avoid the threat of another boycott). Saudi Arabia also had no qualms about bankrolling American projects in the region, such as the 1977 airlift of French troops to Zaire, or coaxing Somalia out of the Soviet orbit. The Soviet invasion of Afghanistan also underlined the need for closer cooperation.

The Post-Faisal Era

Saudi foreign policy, its conduct and objectives, changed with the death of Faisal in 1975. The Kingdom's foreign policy, like its domestic policy, became much more collegial in its formulation as the singular approach of Faisal was replaced by greater emphasis on consensus. Whereas Faisal served as his own foreign minister since 1930, his successors opted for a wider embrace of experience. Senior princes have become involved in different security concerns; for example, the current Crown Prince Abdullah bin Abdulaziz's area of expertise is

Syria and Iraq while Prince Sultan bin Abdulaziz is the Yemeni expert. This collegiate approach grew more marked in the 1980s with the rise of Saudi ambassador to the United States Prince Bandar bin Sultan bin Abdulaziz.[34] Son of the current defense minister, Prince Bandar was given an increasingly large role, at the expense of the nominal foreign minister, Prince Saud bin Faisal bin Abdulaziz. The result was a deadlock: Bandar was increasingly seen as the foreign minister of the al-Fahd clique, while Saud was the champion of the conservative block. The infighting between the two was also pronounced; in the late 1980s, Saud informed all Saudi overseas missions that they were to report to him and not his cousin.[35] Such a directive seemed to have no effect, and during the Iraqi-Kuwaiti crisis, it was Bandar and not Saud who played the larger role. Not surprisingly, Bandar is closely identified with the American alliance. Demands for his recall are a constant refrain among the Kingdom's fundamentalists.

Reflecting the change in leadership styles is a change in priorities. The focus of post-Faisal Saudi foreign policy has shifted from the West to the East, from the Israeli-Arab dispute to the Persian or Arabian Gulf. The reason is a simple one: although the Israeli-Arab conflict affected the Kingdom indirectly, Iran's growing power poses a more immediate threat, especially with the overthrow of the shah in 1979. This is not to say that the Kingdom has abandoned its other interests. In fact, Faisal and his successors fashioned a very successful Cairo–Riyadh axis after 1973, which lasted up to the late Anwar Sadat's visit to Jerusalem and the signing of the Camp David accords. The Saudis also attempted to foster their own Arab-Israeli solutions, such as the Fahd Plan, as well as advancing Saudi solutions for the Lebanese Civil War.

However, it was the Gulf that dominated Saudi attention. The Kingdom's concern began in 1971 when Britain announced the withdrawal of the rest of its forces from the Persian Gulf. The British presence had pacified the Gulf and countered both Iraqi claims on Kuwait and Iranian pretensions to Bahrain. The British presence had also served as a convenient block to Soviet expansion in the region. London's withdrawal changed the Gulf's power equation, and there was no small rush of claimants, the Kingdom included, to fill the vacuum. Iran was the hands-down winner in the resulting contest for supremacy. The shah lost no time in staking his claim for a bigger role for his country, and a few weeks after the British action, he seized three small strategic islands in the Gulf—Abu Musa and the Greater and Lesser Tumbs. The shah was motivated by greater power pretensions and the islands' commanding presence near the Straits of Hormuz. Although the shah eventually returned parts of Abu Musa to Sharjah (which was to become the UAE), his action nonetheless put the rest of the Gulf states on notice. The Saudis attempted to accommodate the shah of Iran, and hence his American protector. When the shah proposed that Iran and the Gulf states form a regional security organization, the Saudis paid polite attention, and then let the matter quietly drop.[36]

Ties between Iran and the Kingdom were always based on mutual suspicion. First and foremost, there were the religious differences between Shiite Iran and Wahhabi Saudi Arabia. The Kingdom viewed Iran as a potentially destabilizing influence on its own sizable Shiite community. Saudi Arabia also was leery of Iran on other grounds: it had a much larger and better-educated population; it was a non-Arab country; it was closely aligned with Israel; and its oil policy was always at odds with the Kingdom's policy of cautious price restraint.

Gulf tensions escalated dramatically after the 1979 success of the Islamic Revolution in Iran. For the al-Saud, the rise of radical Shiism was viewed as a threat to the tractability of the Kingdom's Shiite minority. The Carter administration's vacillation between the shah and his detractors sowed doubts as to the reliability of the Americans. The victory of the Ayatollah Khomeini and the seizure of the American embassy ended American indecision. However, the steps taken by the Carter administration to end the crisis and shore up resolve among America's Gulf friends did little to build confidence. For example, the United States sent a squadron of F–15s to the region but announced before their arrival that they were unarmed, leading Gulf Arabs to wonder why they had been sent. Lack of American resolve was also noted in the failure of Washington to secure the hostages' release, ending in the tragedy of June 1980 when a rescue mission went awry.

The Saudis also badly miscalculated by endorsing the shah's rule and pledging their support a few days before the ultimate triumph of the clerics. Such a miscue was bound to have serious repercussions. Within weeks of his victory, the Ayatollah Khomeini announced that revolutionary Iran's foreign policy was predicated on erasing the existing order in the Gulf and leading an Islamic revolution through the area. As the Ayatollah noted,

The Iranian Revolution is not exclusively that of Iran because Islam does not belong to any particular people. We will export our revolution throughout the world because it is an Islamic revolution. The struggle will continue until the call 'there is no god but God and Mohammed is the messenger of God' is echoed all over the world.[37]

Like the Bolsheviks before them, Tehran's Islamic government considered itself the vanguard of a movement, and actively sought to encourage uprisings throughout the area.

Iran's primary focus was Iraq with its Shiite majority. Besides encouraging the Shiites to revolt, the Iranians also funded Kurdish separatists and attempted to assassinate several Iraqi politicians. Baghdad retaliated by instituting a systematic campaign of repression against its Shiite majority. Leading clerics were killed, thousands of Shiites were expelled, and Iranian pilgrims were denied access to Shiite shrines. However, Iraq was not Tehran's only target. The Ayatollah Khomeini also tried to foment disturbances in the Gulf states, particularly Kuwait, Bahrain, and Saudi Arabia. Inflamed by the Ayatollah's calls to arms, and with Iranian financial backing, the Kingdom's Shiites quickly sought to assert their rights, provoking widespread rioting in November 1979 and again in February 1980. Demonstrators were brutally suppressed by units of the Saudi National Guard (SANG). Iran stepped up a propaganda assault that questioned the compatibility of hereditary monarchy and Islam. "Kings despoil a country when they enter it and make the noblest of its people its meanest," started one Iranian message in early 1980.[38]

Tehran contested Saudi claims of sole guardianship of Mecca and Medina, claiming that the Kingdom's moral position had been undermined by its close links with the United States. Saudi-Iranian ties were further worsened by differing stances on oil policy, differences that were to grow when the inevitable downturn in prices occurred. Not surprisingly, the Saudis were supportive, at first with words and later with money, when Saddam Hussein's forces invaded Iran in September 1980. Although the al-Saud distrusted Saddam Hussein and his designs, the Iranian threat was deemed the more serious. In the eight years of warfare that followed, the Kingdom supported Saddam's war effort to the tune of approximately $26 billion, including $5.84 billion in grants and aid, $9.25 billion in commercial loans, $0.95 billion in direct loans, $6.75 billion in oil aid, and $3.74 billion in military aid.[39] Riyadh's money and ancillary support (the al-Saud regularly serviced

Iraqi warplanes during the first phase of the conflict as well as passing on intelligence gleaned from their AWACs), however, did not preclude the taking of some opportunistic steps. The Saudis used the preoccupation of its two larger neighbors to form the Gulf Cooperation Council (GCC), a security organization designed to foster greater social, economic, and political cooperation. The GCC grouped the Kingdom together with Oman, the UAE, Qatar, Bahrain, and Kuwait. Saudi motivations in creating the GCC were several. The Saudis viewed the GCC not only as a vehicle toward their own hegemony over the Gulf, but also as a possible springboard to creating a third regional "superpower" to counter Iraq and Iran, both of whom were unable to prevent its formation.

As the Iran–Iraq War dragged on, Tehran's actions against the GCC members grew more strident. Iranian-backed revolutionaries nearly seized control of Bahrain in 1982, and Shiites came close to assassinating the Kuwaiti emir several years later. The Iranians also sharpened their criticisms of the al-Saud and Unitarianism. The latter, noted the Ayatollah Khomeini, was "a distortion, a tissue of lies woven out of true elements, taken out of context."[40] His deputy, Ayatollah Montazeri, went even further, calling the Wahhabi doctrine, "nothing more than a tribal aberration, a set of pre-Islamic rites."[41] The Iranians renewed and intensified their personal attacks on the al-Saud, in particular Fahd, whom they accused of pride, arrogance, and corruption. The attacks grew so strident that Fahd quickly dropped all of his honorifics and adopted the more humble "Custodian of the Two Holy Mosques."[42] Iranian criticism also focused on Saudi Arabia's unilateral running of the hajj, and the Saudi insistence that the procession be free of politics. Despite warnings, Iranian pilgrims held demonstrations in 1986 against the United States, Iraq, and Israel.

The Gulf war and its continuation also tested the Saudi-American relationship. Although the Carter administration sent four AWACS to the Kingdom as a sign of solidarity within days of the Iraqi invasion of Iran, the Saudis were angered by Washington's constant refusal to sell them the most advanced weaponry with which to protect themselves. Washington's reticence, the result of the strong Israeli lobby, did not affect other Western powers as the British, French, and Brazilians all stepped in to pick up the slack. The Saudis also questioned Washington's strategy of playing both sides off against one another by providing Iraq with intelligence and limited credits, while selling Tehran spare parts in an attempt to free the hostages in Lebanon. Riyadh was also piqued by constant pressure from Washington to open Saudi military facilities for American use. American participation in the conflict grew in the fall of 1987 when Washington offered to escort reflagged Kuwaiti tankers following Iranian gunboat attacks. The tanker war, although showing American resolve, did little to soothe Saudi jitters, and Riyadh failed to support openly an American gesture that was in the Kingdom's best interests. Relations actually soured when Fahd asked for the recall of American ambassador Hume Horan following American protests about the Saudi purchase of Chinese ballistic missiles.[43] Relations were also strained when Washington sent a general to Riyadh to command a joint operation of American and Saudi planes without the Saudis' knowledge. Angered, the Saudis promptly deported him.[44]

Saudi relations with Iraq and Iran remained tense throughout the war. Even though the Saudis were paying for the Iraqi war effort, Riyadh tried in 1985–1986 to normalize relations with Tehran, and restricted Iraqi oil exports through the East–West Petroline, blaming pumping problems. Baghdad's response was immediate: Iraqi agents detonated a bomb in Riyadh, killing two Filipinos and wounding several others. The Saudis got the message. Saudi links with Iran were also just as cool, with the focal point being the hajj, and Iranian attempts to politicize it. Tensions escalated in 1986 when Saudi police caught Iranian agents attempting to smuggle in explosives and later trying to incite demonstrations. Forewarned, the Saudis determined that the 1987 hajj would be demonstration-free. The result was the 1987 Mecca Riot in which 412 Iranian pilgrims died in bitter fighting. Despite conflicting reports, it appears that Iranian demonstrators attacked Saudi security personnel who then opened fire. The Saudis initially denied firing at all and refused to return some of the bodies. A few weeks later, Iranian mobs stormed the Kuwaiti and Saudi embassies in Tehran, destroying them and severely injuring a Saudi diplomat who later died of his wounds.

The Saudis were dismayed that their GCC allies proved refractory in presenting a common front against Iran. The UAE and Oman refused to break ties with Tehran, leaving Riyadh to sever ties unilaterally in 1988 when Iran disputed quotas placed on pilgrims from the various Muslim nations. After the rupture of relations and the Iranian decision not to send any pilgrims, four Saudi Shia set off bombs in a petrochemical plant in Jubail. The perpetrators were later caught and executed, and pro-Iranian groups vowed to kill an equal number of Saudi diplomats. The Saudis stuck to their position, and called in favors to secure pan-Islamic condemnation of Iran for the riots and support for the establishment of pilgrim quotas. Despite increased vigilance, two bombs marred the 1989 pilgrimage, killing one person and wounding sixteen. Sixteen Kuwaiti Shia were later arrested and executed for their role in the matter, provoking official Kuwaiti protests and promises from Iran for revenge.

Problems with the hajj persisted. One year later, the Saudi position claiming exclusive guardianship of Mecca and Medina was weakened when 1,426 pilgrims were killed in a stampede in the tunnel connecting Mecca and Mina. There were differing versions as to what happened. One story said the stampede was started when seven people tumbled off an overhead bridge, while another account blamed the tragedy on a breakdown in air-conditioning within the tunnel. "No one can blame this country for this accident because its authorities and people provided all facilities to the pilgrims," Fahd said in a laconic statement. "This was an accident and not intentional and I believe that any Muslim would share with this country its sorrow . . . had they not died there, they would have died elsewhere and at the same predestined moment."[45] Given the fact that most of the dead were non-Saudis and non-Arabs, Fahd's remark was interpreted as another example of Saudi callousness, especially toward Asians. "The Saudi government cannot run from the responsibility for the tunnel disaster by simply saying it was act of God," thundered Chalid Mawarid, head of Indonesia's largest Muslim organization.[46] Indonesia, which lost 680 pilgrims, and Turkey both uncharacteristically criticized the Kingdom's handling of the matter, and more ominously called for an international investigation. Such calls were subsequently rejected by the Kingdom, which also refused to appoint a committee of inquiry into the matter. The accident only stoked Iranian charges that the Kingdom was unsuited to run the hajj and that Mecca and Medina should be placed under international supervision.

If there was one result expected at the end of the Iraq–Iran War, it ought to have been Iraq's grateful friendship, but this was not the case. The Saudis aided Iraq with loans and grants, assistance in paying for part of the project connecting an Iraqi pipeline to the Kingdom's own transpeninsular network, and helped in ensuring that Iraq was able to sell oil on the world market. Once the war ended, relations between the two countries cooled.

Iraq's leaders sensed that the Saudis had taken advantage of Baghdad's preoccupation with Iran to forge the GCC against it. Saudi oil policy also clashed with that of Iraq. Saudi apprehensions were heightened in February 1989 when Iraq founded the Arab Cooperation Council (ACC), which grouped Baghdad together with Egypt, Jordan, and North Yemen. Although the ACC's primary aims were to block Iranian expansion as well as promote the Palestinian cause, the Saudis interpreted its formation as a threat to their interests and those of the GCC as well. The latter conclusion was not difficult to draw: North Yemen and Iraq were close allies, and the latter was often able to generate border incidents along the Yemeni border to put pressure on Riyadh. Saudi worries over the ACC were underscored one month later when Fahd made one of his rare visits abroad to Baghdad where he signed a nonaggression pact. Fahd also pushed the Iraqis to sign a similar treaty with Kuwait; ominously, the Iraqis refused. The reason for Saddam Hussein's reluctance was less than eighteen months away.

Saudi Diplomacy during the Kuwait Crisis

When Saddam Hussein issued repeated warnings to Kuwait and the UAE in early 1990 to stop overproducing and abide by their OPEC quotas, few Saudis thought the matter would escalate into armed conflict. Their miscalculation was matched only by Saddam Hussein's, because he assumed the world would tamely submit to the destruction of Kuwait. Saddam's rhetoric through the spring of 1990 repeated old arguments that the Iraqi leader had used since the conclusion of hostilities with Iran. More than $80 billion in debt, and facing a major reconstruction effort, Saddam Hussein had repeatedly pressed his Arab Gulf brethren to respect their quotas as a way of firming up oil prices. He had also urged the Gulf states to forgive their loans to him, arguing, not altogether unreasonably, that Kuwait and Saudi Arabia had supplied money out of self-interest because the Iranians would have invaded them if Iraq had fallen.[47]

Kuwait and the UAE failed to heed Hussein's call. Exasperated by what he saw as ingratitude, and perhaps fulfilling a well-laid plan, Saddam on July 16 drafted a protest to the Arab League, accusing Kuwait and the UAE of waging economic war against Baghdad. Iraq's position was made clearer the next day, July 17, when Hussein himself addressed the issue, charging in a speech to the nation that Kuwait and the UAE were working with "world imperialism and

Zionism" to hurt Baghdad by their overproduction. He further said that Iraq could not abide by such actions forever, and warned that unless the two Gulf powers ceased, "we will have no choice but to resort to effective action to put things right and ensure the restitution of our rights."[48] Iraqi troops began moving toward the Kuwaiti border.

Kuwait and the UAE immediately sounded alarms. Kuwait readied its armed forces, while the UAE asked the United States for a pair of tanker planes to avoid a surprise Iraqi air attack. Both countries also alerted the GCC, which met in emergency session and requested that the Arab League help defuse the crisis. The league asked Egyptian president Hosni Mubarak to effect a compromise. Mubarak traveled to Baghdad the following week. During the first days of the unfolding crisis, Saudi Arabia kept a low profile. There were several reasons for this: first, few in the ruling elite thought Saddam Hussein would attack a brother Arab country, especially one that had supported him during the recently concluded Iraq–Iran War, and second, there was the matter of personal animosity between the al-Saud and Kuwait's ruling family. Ties had never been close, and the Saudis may have concluded that the al-Sabah needed a lesson in humility. Relations between the two families were just recovering from the latest brouhaha, this time over the mascot of the Gulf Cup games. As a symbol of the games, the Kuwaitis had chosen two stallions, which had played an important part in blunting a Saudi attack in 1919. The Saudis, considering the mascots a slap at them, abruptly pulled out of the games.[49] Not surprisingly, the al-Saud allowed dynastic squabbles to overshadow more important national concerns. They showed little concern over Saddam's actions, and urged the Kuwaitis to demobilize to mollify the Iraqis. A few days prior to the Kuwaiti-Iraqi conference scheduled for July 31 in Jeddah, Fahd sent a message to the Kuwaitis emphasizing the need for a settlement and seemingly putting the onus of concessions on the Kuwaitis:

> [Y]our wisdom and foresight will, God willing, achieve our aims, our brother Arabs: to reduce all difficulties and to ensure the love and understanding between the two sisterly states.[50]

As the Jeddah conference neared, Iraqi actions—a continual arms buildup about which Washington warned Kuwait, Saudi Arabia, and Egypt on July 27—were ignored by Riyadh and the Kuwaiti emirate. Mubarak and Fahd in fact cautioned Washington to adopt a low profile so as not to endanger a successful outcome of the Jeddah summit, stressing an Arab solution to the problem. American offers of help to the Kuwaitis were also turned down, as the emir did not want to give additional credence to Iraqi claims that he was an American stooge. The Jeddah conference, which had disturbing parallels to the Munich conference in 1938 when the "prey country" was urged to demobilize and avoid confrontation only to find fresh demands, ended in failure on July 31. However, the meeting finished with some ambiguous statements suggesting that the next round of talks would be held in Baghdad on August 4. The United States, after conversations with Fahd on August 1, issued a statement expressing its hope that the next summit would be more fruitful. Hours later, Iraq invaded Kuwait.

Saudi Arabia's response in the first hours of the Iraqi attack was less than exemplary. Although the Kingdom was committed to going to Kuwait's defense as per the dictates of the GCC charter, the Kingdom did and said nothing. Perhaps it was due to shock, as Saddam had personally assured Fahd that he would pursue peaceful means to settle the crisis. There might have been some doubt whether Iraqi troops and tanks were intent on carving out just part of the emirate, or seizing the entire state. The invasion also coincided with the summer vacations of many members of the al-Saud, who were overseas and thus unable to contribute to the decision-making process. Finally, there was the unspoken fear that Hussein's troops might make a spectacular grab for the Eastern Province.

The Saudis' response was initially restricted to opening the border to thousands of Kuwaitis and other expatriates fleeing the Iraqi tanks. They also slapped a news blackout on the invasion for twenty-four hours to avoid alarming their subjects. President George Bush called Fahd hours after the invasion offering to send two squadrons of F–15s and bolstering AWACS flights, but the Saudis did not respond. In fact, their first move was to limit the internationalization of the conflict. That proved difficult: on August 2 the United Nations Security Council passed Resolution No. 660, which fully condemned Iraq's invasion and called on it to return to its internationally recognized boundaries of August 1. The resolution further called for "intensive negotiations for the resolution of their differences," looking to the Arab League to provide the forum for a solution. This prompted the Saudis to pursue an "Arab solution." Mubarak and Jordan's King Hussein met the day of the invasion and issued a joint call for a mini-summit in Jeddah on August 5. They both also conferred with Bush, asking for a muted

American reaction to allow time for an Arab solution. As Iraqi units took up positions near the Saudi border, Bush again offered the Kingdom American forces, convinced that Hussein was planning an invasion.

Events moved quickly. The GCC foreign ministers met in Cairo on August 3 where they issued a demand for the "unconditional and immediate" withdrawal of Iraqi troops from the emirate, and called upon the Arab League to intervene in the matter. At the same time, the United States pressured Saudi Arabia to accept American offers of aid before it was too late. Bandar was briefed on August 3, and "terms" of a possible American intervention discussed. Saudi apprehension over Iraq's intentions were further noted the same day when the visiting Iraqi vice president told the Saudi elite that an Iraqi withdrawal from Kuwait was nonnegotiable.

Tension rose even higher the next day, August 4. The Saudi government mobilized the National Guard (SANG), and the Arab League finally met in emergency session. The league subsequently condemned the invasion, but significantly, Jordan, Yemen, Sudan, the PLO, Djibouti, and Mauritania backed Baghdad. The rifts within the Arab League were mirrored by a similar vote taken by the Kingdom's pan-Islamic creation, the OIC. The lack of unity in the Arab League and the OIC was matched by the Kingdom's own vacillation. Although Riyadh had condemned the invasion in bilateral declarations, it had only issued conciliatory messages in its unilateral declarations. This was about to change, for the Saudis became convinced that Saddam Hussein was about to invade.

Whether or not Saddam Hussein's troops intended to invade Saudi Arabia is open to question. Saudi scouts saw no evidence of an imminent invasion during several probes in the first days of the operations. American spy satellites, however, reported seeing Iraqi troops pull up to the border, and in some cases step over it.[51] Other satellite photos have been produced that contradict this.[52] Further evidence is lacking: no plans for a Saudi invasion were ever found in the Iraqi Ministry of Defense after the war, but General H. Norman Schwartzkopf claims in his memoirs that an Iraqi defector surfaced in Cairo a few days after Iraq's move into Kuwait carrying blueprints for an invasion into the Kingdom's Eastern Province. What seems likely is that by August 3, the Bush administration had decided to thwart the Iraqi invasion. The first obstacle to that was the Kingdom, without which military intervention would have been nearly impossible.

Critics claim the U.S. government either exaggerated, or perhaps fabricated, evidence to induce the Saudis to join an anti-Iraq coalition. Such charges remain unprovable, although it seems likely that the Americans did not understate the threat facing the Kingdom. And by August 3, the Saudis already possessed ample justification for taking strong action. Saddam Hussein's declarations of nonaggression were greatly devalued by the events of the past two days. Not only had the Iraqi lied to them about his promise not to invade Kuwait, but there was the noticeable presence of Iraqi troops near the border. Still, some senior princes urged caution, arguing that a wait-and-see attitude was preferable to rushing into the American embrace. These princes said that unlike Iraq's historically rocky relationship with Kuwait, the Kingdom had enjoyed correct if not close ties with Iraq since the mid-1970s, and the two countries had no outstanding territorial differences. Second, there was the 1989 Non-Aggression Pact, which these princes said Saddam would honor. Third, they pointed out that the United States had already warned Iraq not to invade the Kingdom, a threat that Saddam would not take lightly.

Saddam also thought the Saudis would back down, counting on the al-Saud to retain their traditional caution. To this end, he made a bad miscalculation by keeping Iraqi units near the Saudi border as if to send a message. The spoken Iraqi message was conciliatory: "Some news agencies have reported fabricated news about what they called the approach of Iraqi forces toward the Saudi border," noted the official Iraqi News Agency on August 4. "Iraq categorically denies these fabricated reports. Causing confusion between the kingdom of Saudi Arabia, which is a fraternal country with which we have normal cordial relations, and Kuwait's case is tendentious."[53] The Saudis were not convinced, and continued to delay taking any action.

Saudi reticence to ask Washington for help was pronounced. Not only were the al-Saud aware of what such an invitation would entail, as regards both their international and domestic foes, but they were also leery of American intentions. Saudi distrust of Washington had grown throughout the 1970s and 1980s, especially regarding America's growing proprietary stance vis-à-vis the Kingdom's oilfields. Saudi policy had further been shaken with the Carter administration's policy toward the shah. Creating more jitters was the lack of American resolve during the 1983 Lebanese intervention, as well as American flip-flops during the Iran–Contra Affair, when Washington was playing both sides of the war. There was also the commonly held fear that guest soldiers would never leave, a common enough feature of Middle Eastern history. This in fact was one of the complaints voiced by opposition figures.

The issue of a possible U.S. intervention split the al-Saud. Although the younger princes, and especially the clique gathered around Bandar, favored an American intervention, many senior princes, including Crown Prince Abdullah, Defense and Aviation Minister Prince Sultan, and Foreign Minister Saud, did not. The opposition of the first two was surprising: not only do they disagree on most subjects, but they, as commanders of the Saudi armed forces, were obviously worried about undertaking any action that might undermine their power, or hurt their charges. Instead, they counseled a go-slow approach, and possible buying off of the Iraqis. Fahd, true to his nature, was said to be in the middle, vacillating. This was where the issue stood on August 4 when Bush again called Fahd, offering American protection. Instead of agreeing, the king asked for a briefing.

The American briefing team arrived on August 6, and immediately presented their findings. Using aerial photos taken from American spy satellites, General Schwartzkopf briefed the king and a few senior princes, including Bandar, Saud, Abdullah, and Prince Abdulrahman bin Abdulaziz, the deputy defense minister. In his memoirs, Schwartzkopf says he showed the king pictures of Iraqi troops and tanks at the border—and in some cases over the border—and said that it was unclear whether or not they would invade the Kingdom. Schwartzkopf then outlined the steps the American military would take to protect the Kingdom. Schwartzkopf's assessment was followed by a personal message from Bush, which then secretary of defense Dick Cheney gave the king: "We are prepared to deploy these forces to defend the kingdom of Saudi Arabia. If you ask us, we will come. We will seek no permanent bases. And when you ask us to go home, we will leave."[54] A brief debate ensued, during which Abdullah reportedly asked for a delay, at least until the Iraqis issued a stronger warning. Fahd's response was immediate: "The Kuwaitis did not rush into a decision, and today they are all guests in our hotels!" Fahd then turned to Cheney and Schwartzkopf and simply said, "OK." Fahd's decision, whatever its basis, changed Saudi foreign policy. By allying themselves with the Americans, the al-Saud abandoned their cautious policies aimed at consensus and instead took a much more confrontational and activist stance. With the invitation of American troops to the Kingdom, Saudi foreign policy was locked on a course that could only end in conflict with Iraq. The Saudi decision, interestingly enough, also came without the cloak of a United Nations resolution, or support from the Arab League or the OIC. Again, the Kingdom's rulers had demonstrated their willingness to jettison their country's philosophical and religious ideologies when faced with a serious threat.

Secure in American backing and the arrival of American troops and aircraft, the Saudis suddenly adopted a harder tack. The GCC finally issued a condemnation of the Iraqi invasion on August 7.[55] Bush announced his policy to the American people the next day, and was followed two hours later by Hussien announcing the annexation of Kuwait. The following day, Fahd addressed his country for the first time since the invasion. In announcing the invitation and arrival of Allied troops, Fahd clearly stated that the decision had been taken because Iraq had "massed large numbers of troops on the border of the Kingdom. . . . [F]aced with this bitter reality . . . the Kingdom expressed a desire to Arab and friendly forces to participate" in its protection. Fahd underlined that the influx of Allied troops was purely for defensive reasons, and aimed at no one. Instead, Fahd said the incoming "troops, to take part in joint exercises with Saudi armed forces, are temporarily deployed on the Kingdom's territory and will depart immediately when the Kingdom requests it." The king also stated the Kingdom's position and aims, noting, "Saudi Arabia completely rejects all measures after the aggression . . . and demands the restoration of the situation to what was before the Iraqi invasion and the return of Kuwait's ruling family."[56] Fahd's decision was confirmed by a *fatwa* from the ulema the next day.

Saudi Arabia's patience with Arab solutions to the problem was also wearing thin. One day after the king's speech, the Arab League opened its emergency summit over the Iraqi invasion. In a meeting marked by brevity, twelve of the twenty participants (Tunisia's delegate never arrived) voted to condemn the Iraqi invasion and approved the sending of troops to the Kingdom. Eight countries refused to endorse it: Iraq and Libya voted against the resolution and the PLO, Yemen, and Algeria abstained; and Sudan, Jordan, and Mauritania expressed reservations. Undeterred, Saudi Arabia hastened to put together a multinational force. As early as August 5, Morocco had offered to send troops. Other Arab countries, outside the GCC, were more reticent. Egypt only committed troops on August 11, and Syria on August 13–14.

Despite the growing chances of confrontation, Fahd and his brothers continued to make conciliatory statements to Iraq, and stressed that the forces gathering in the Kingdom would not be used for offensive purposes. However, as the Iraqi occupation continued and efforts at finding a peaceful solution to the crisis faded, the Saudis adopted a hard-line position, especially vis-à-vis Iraq's supporters in the Arab world.

On September 19, and two days after the resumption of diplomatic relations with the Soviet Union, Saudi Arabia abruptly cut all oil supplies to Jordan, citing nonpayment of bills. The same day the Kingdom expelled Jordanian, Palestinian, Yemeni, and Iraqi diplomats from the country, charging them with activities "incompatible with their status which had endangered security."[57] The Kingdom also announced new visa regulations for the Kingdom's 1.5 million Yemeni workers. At the end of September, the Saudi ambassador to Washington, Prince Bandar, issued a stinging public rebuke to King Hussein. Saudi Arabia also turned up the economic pressure by cutting off all imports of Jordanian produce.

Still, the Saudi royal family seems to have had second thoughts through the end of the year. In late September, Fahd issued a conciliatory speech in which he again called for a peaceful solution to the conflict. A few days later, Saudi Defense Minister Prince Sultan was quoted in an interview as saying that the Kingdom would not be used as a staging ground for an offensive campaign against the Iraqis in Kuwait. Sultan went on to say that his country "sees no harm in any Arab country giving its Arab sister land, a site or a position on the sea."[58] Sultan's speech was clarified the next day by the Saudi Press Agency, which said it marked no change in the Kingdom's policies vis-à-vis the United States or Kuwait.

However, those were the momentary lapses. For the most part, the new Saudi foreign policy was hard-line, and Saudi war objectives escalated markedly as the conflict continued. By late October, it seems clear that the Saudis had convinced themselves of the need to evict the Iraqis by force if necessary from Kuwait. In early November, the Saudis agreed to a doubling of the Allied forces and had accepted a new command structure, which left offensive planning in the American hands. Fahd readily agreed to the doubling of Allied troops in his country as the emphasis of the campaign shifted to its inevitable offensive phase. Again, according to Schwartzkopf's memoirs, Fahd barely hesitated before giving his approval to the doubling and possible launching of an offensive from his territory. "While we all still want peace, if we must go to war, Saudi Arabia's armed forces will fight side by side with yours," Fahd told then Secretary of State James Baker.[59] The king further stated that the Kingdom would fight alongside the United States, even if Israel were to enter the fray as the result of an Iraqi attack. The government-controlled press also unleashed a verbal attack on Saddam and his Arab allies unprecedented in Saudi history. The Kingdom's new hard-line foreign policy continued throughout the rest of the year. The Saudis consistently rejected peace efforts by Jordan's King Hussein, Morocco's King Hassan, and later Algeria's President Chadli Benjedid. The Saudis also reacted strongly to Bush's "extra mile" offer in having Secretary of State Baker and Iraqi Foreign Minister Tariq Aziz meet, with Bandar warning the Americans, "To you sending Baker is goodwill," he said. "To Saddam it suggests you're chicken."[60]

Saudi intransigence hardened markedly when Iraqi SCUDs began raining down on Riyadh and the Eastern Province. Saudi Arabia rejected Iraq's February 15 acceptance of UN Resolution No. 660 and the subsequent Soviet effort at finding an acceptable compromise that would have avoided a land war. Not only did Saudi Arabia dismiss any peaceful outlet for the Iraqis, but Riyadh also lashed out at Baghdad's allies in vitriolic terms. "The crocodile tears shed by the lackeys of the Iraqi tyrant are in fact tears of panic," noted Riyadh Radio.

> After they stood by the defeated tyrant and tied their destiny to his successes . . . they realized too late that they stood in the wrong place. [And yet], instead of returning to the right path, declaring their repentance and asking God's forgiveness and the forgiveness of those who they have wronged, these minute and negligible people stagger in the sea of their mistakes, and continue to swim against the current.[61]

The overwhelming victory achieved by the Allied forces in the land war segment (February 24–28) also failed to lower the Saudis' ire. Although Bush agreed to a cease-fire after large segments of the Iraqi forces had been destroyed or decimated, the Saudis were reportedly not pleased that the fighting was ending, instead wanting to destroy more of Saddam's forces, making a repeat invasion impossible.[62]

However, Iraq's defeat led to other issues: namely, what type of peace the Allied powers wanted. Although there was near general desire to bring Saddam Hussein to justice, the means of achieving that goal were unclear. American policymakers had no desire to see the emergence of a Shiite Iraq, fearing a repeat of the Iranian debacle of 1979–1980. This viewpoint was encouraged by the Saudis and other Gulf Arab states. The preferred solution was the disposal of Saddam Hussein, and his replacement by a less ambitious Sunni. However, Allied resolve was tested in early March as Iraq erupted into civil war, with the Shiites revolting in the south and the Kurds in the north. Again, Saudi pressure was brought to bear on the Allies not to support the rebels. The United States went along, and watched as Saddam Hussein's Republican Guard crushed the rebels. In their time of crisis, when confronted with the specter of Iraq with Saddam Hussein, or a possible Shiite Iraq, Saudi Arabia chose the former, and continues to live with the consequences of its decision.

Post–Desert Storm Strategies

Even before the defeat of Iraq in Operation Desert Storm, the Saudis began formulating their post-war foreign policy. They did so admitting the failure of their previous security arrangements. Only four months after the invasion, the Saudis and their GCC allies met in Doha, where they issued a communiqué, noting, "Iraqi aggression against Kuwait has exposed the inadequacy of the existing security arrangements within the framework of the GCC."[63] That realization notwithstanding, there was widespread disagreement as to how to remedy the situation. Some, such as Oman's Sultan Qaboos, favored enlarging the GCC security forces, and perhaps linking the organization with Iran as a counterweight to Iraq. Others, such as Fahd, preferred an Arab option, presumably including those Arab states that had joined the coalition. Fahd noted, "The Arab system has failed in confronting the catastrophe brought upon us. . . . [T]he lesson we have learned from what has happened is that cooperation between brothers must be through Arab institutions, which operate on a sound scientific basis."[64]

Saudi Arabia is still searching for a coherent foreign policy in the wake of the Gulf conflict and the failure of its pre-war strategies. The Kingdom's aims seem simple, yet difficult: national security, hegemony over the Arabian peninsula, and leadership in the Arab and Islamic worlds. Ironically, the Kingdom's least ambiguous foreign policy venture, the Gulf War, has produced the most unsettled and ambiguous foreign policy dilemma that has faced the Kingdom since its inception.

National Security

The quest for national security in the post–Desert Storm world is threatened, in Riyadh's eyes, by two powers: Iraq and Iran. The problem for the Saudis is that they still have not formulated a policy to deal with them.

Iran is considered the greater threat of the pair. Recent Saudi weapons purchases confirm this, as the Kingdom has sought to bolster its air rather than land defenses. During the Gulf conflict, Riyadh and Tehran found themselves uncomfortable allies of sorts. Iran viewed the Iraqi invasion of Kuwait uneasily. Although sympathizing with Iraq's desire to impose some discipline on OPEC and thus raise the price of oil, Tehran was also fearful that the Iraqi occupation of Kuwait was only the first step in its neighbor's expansionist policy. Indeed, Iran immediately called for an Iraqi withdrawal on August 2, noting that "Iran rejects any form of resorting to force as a solution to regional problems."[65] Tehran further reacted mutely to the deployment of American troops in the Kingdom. Although the Iranians used the crisis to mend fences with Saddam, they continued to oppose the Iraqi occupation of Kuwait, and backed UN sanctions against Baghdad. Relations between Iran and Saudi Arabia warmed considerably during the conflict, and official ties were restored in March 1991, following Omani mediation. The abrupt volte-face led to some embarrassing retractions, with the Saudi leadership explaining in one communiqué that their support for Iraq during the Iraqi-Iranian conflict was "without malice for Iran."[66]

The resumption of political ties was quickly followed by a flurry of visits. At the end of April, Iranian Foreign Minister Ali Akbar Velayati visited Riyadh, where he had an audience with Fahd. Velayati's mission seemed geared toward two objectives: writing Iran into the regional security balance, and renewing Iranian participation in the hajj. Regional security issues were difficult to resolve. Velayati quickly expressed Tehran's dislike of the proposed presence of Egyptian and Syrian troops in the Gulf. Instead, he called for an Iranian-GCC alliance to safeguard Gulf security. Alluding to the Iraqi invasion of Kuwait and the impotency of the GCC to stop it, Velayati blamed the organization's weakness on the absence of Iran.[67] The Saudis remained unconvinced.

The hajj issue was easier to settle, and the Saudis made several concessions. For the 1991 pilgrimage, the Kingdom allowed Iran to send 115,000 pilgrims, a far cry from the 1988 quota of 45,000, which had led to Iran's abrupt boycott. The Saudis also okayed an Iranian request to allow 5,000 relatives and friends of the 412 "martyrs" killed in 1987 to attend the hajj, the closest Riyadh has ever come to admitting culpability. The Iranians also showed remarkable tact, and even President Ali Akbar Hashemi-Rafsanjani took the unusual step of appealing to his country's pilgrims to follow Saudi rules and regulations, and to "restrain" themselves. In this new atmosphere of sensitivity, the Saudi forces allowed the Iranian pilgrims to hold a demonstration in front of their hajj headquarters, berating the United States and "its clients from the Iraqi Baathist regime."[68]

This new friendliness continued throughout the rest of 1991 and the first few months of 1992. The GCC continued its efforts to reach some sort of agreement that would include Iran in regional security issues. There were also rumors of an exchange of visits between Fahd and Hashemi-Rafsanjani, especially after Riyadh agreed to reduce its oil output during the spring 1992 OPEC meeting.[69] Yet despite those promising signs, relations quickly deteriorated. The fly in the ointment was Tehran's increasingly aggressive behavior in the Gulf, and especially on the island of Abu Musa. On April 16, 1992, Iranian forces on the island deported hundreds of UAE nationals, and closed the school, police station, and desalination plant. They also announced that the deportees would be allowed to return once they had acquired Iranian visas and residence permits.[70] Iran's action ended more than twenty years of joint administration of the island. Abu Musa had been seized by Iran in 1971, but later returned to Sharjah the same year, after Iran received permission to maintain a small military outpost. In the so-called tanker war during the Iraq–Iran conflict, Tehran had used the island, which dominates the southern Gulf by virtue of its position near the Straits of Hormuz, as a staging area for its attacks on tankers.

Iran's naked seizure of Abu Musa aroused the GCC from its usual somnolence. Following the failure of talks between the UAE and Iran in September 1992, the GCC supported UAE efforts to turn the matter over to the UN Security Council, and later issued a communiqué calling on Iran to return the island to the UAE. This was endorsed by Egypt and Syria the next day. The Iranian response was quick in coming. A few days after the GCC statement, Hashemi-Rafsanjani warned the GCC and its Western supporters not to attempt to regain the contested island, saying they would have to "cross a sea of blood," if they tried.[71]

Saudi fears of greater Iranian meddling in the Gulf also increased after Iran laid claims to some Qatari offshore natural gas fields, and then offered to help Doha protect itself when a border dispute broke out between Qatar and the Kingdom in the fall of 1992. Further fanning Saudi fears was Iran's purchase of Russian submarines.

But there were other flashpoints as well. Not only did Tehran continue to contest Saudi leadership of OPEC, but the two Islamic powers also began waging a none-too-subtle competition for the hearts and minds of the newly freed Muslim republics of the Soviet Union. Both Tehran and Riyadh began supporting competing groups.[72] This contest also extended to Sudan, where Iran established increasingly close political and military ties with the regime of General Omar Hassan al-Bashir. Although Shiite Iran and Sunni Sudan are strange partners, the two countries share a similar world view, and readily support fundamentalist groups throughout the region. Saudi relations with Sudan were already strained due to Khartoum's support of Iraq, as well as its financial support of Saudi fundamentalists opposed to the al-Saud. Included in the latter was the housing and training of Saudi armed militants dedicated to establishing a Saudi Islamic republic.[73]

Tense relations grew even worse when the Sudanese government of General Omar Hassan al-Bashir began accepting Iranian military advisors and aid. Al-Bashir accused the Saudi government of covertly supporting the Christian-animist forces of the Sudanese People's Liberation Army (SPLA). The Kingdom subsequently lashed back, threatening to expel the hundreds of thousands of Sudanese workers in the Kingdom, as well as launching personal attacks in the Saudi press against al-Bashir and other members of the Sudanese junta. The Kingdom also released figures detailing Saudi aid to Sudan in 1988–1992, which it said amounted to $2.7 billion. The point—a ploy used earlier by the Kingdom to counter Iraqi accusations—was clear. Riyadh seemed to be asking, "why would we support the SPLA when we're giving you financial aid?"[74]

Given the outstanding issues between them, Saudi Arabia and Iran continued to bump heads, as their current frosty relations showed no sign of thawing. In fact, relations grew even colder in 1993 when the Kingdom announced that it would tolerate no demonstrations during the hajj. The ban on demonstrations brought a quick rebuke from Iran's Ayatollah Ali Khamenei who lambasted the Saudi decision:

It is not acceptable to me that a government which has undertaken to serve the Hajj pilgrims should prevent the holding of a ceremony ... which demonstrates hatred toward the arrogant powers and enemies of the Islamic world. The U.S. and Zionists are the ones who benefit from discontinuation of such important obligations.[75]

Iran later claimed that such demonstrations had been held, a charge that Saudi Arabia vigorously refuted.

The Saudi dilemma regarding Iran is mirrored by its policy toward Iraq. Having won the war, the Kingdom is uncertain how to fashion a peace with Baghdad, especially with Saddam Hussein still firmly in power. The latter conundrum is partially one of the Kingdom's own making, as it was Saudi pressure that prevented Allied aid to both the Kurdish and Shiite uprisings. If the uprisings had succeeded, one of the casualties would have been Saddam Hussein. Riyadh's action was motivated by several factors. Not only were the Saudis leery that the fall of Saddam Hussein would lead to a fractionalized Iraq that could easily be dominated by Iran, but the Saudis also wanted to prevent the emergence of an Iraqi Shiite state on its northeastern border. The Saudi hard line vis-à-vis Iraq continues. However, it is tempered by Saudi Arabia's desire not to weaken Iraq too much, lest Iran fill the power void. As a result, Saudi policy is aimed at keeping Iraq united at all costs. To that end, it continues to support Saddam Hussein's control of the country, if only as the lesser of two evils.

Part of the Kingdom's dilemma is the absence of a credible political alternative, preferably Sunni, to Saddam Hussein. The Kingdom has established links with Iraqi dissidents, and has in turn bankrolled them. Saudi ties with the dissidents, however, have been bedeviled by the fact that most of them are Shiite. Still, in February 1992, the Saudis hosted a delegation of fifteen Iraqi opposition groups in Riyadh, a summit which was attended by the Shiite opposition leader Ayatollah Mohammed Baqr al-Hakim.[76] The summit did much to allay Riyadh fears that a post-Hussein Iraq could become a threat, as they declared that they intended to keep Iraq Arab and unified. Al-Hakim has since visited the Kingdom several times. However, Saudi policymakers remain leery of his success.

Saudi Arabia has also supported United Nations efforts to ensure that Baghdad fulfills its cease-fire obligations. Saudi Arabia has allowed American, British, and French airplanes to use its airbases to enforce the UN "no fly zones" in the south, as well as for launching retaliatory strikes against Baghdad and Iraqi military bases during several flare-ups. However, the enthusiasm for unlimited access seems to be waning, especially given the absence of clearly defined objectives. Following the UN airstrikes on Iraq in mid-January 1993, the Kingdom also called for similar international actions against the Bosnian Serbs to maintain the pretense of having an even-handed policy toward Baghdad as well as deflecting Iranian criticism. Significantly, the United States used Tomahawk missiles from warships based in the Gulf rather than jets from Saudi bases when it bombed Baghdad a few months later in retaliation for the alleged Iraqi plot to assassinate Bush. Washington's continued military actions against Hussein fan Saudi fears that such measures serve no purpose except to increase the Iraqi's stature in the Arab world.

That position notwithstanding, the Saudis have maintained a hardline posture vis-à-vis Saddam Hussein. Saudi Arabia has consistently refused to allow the sale of several hundred thousand barrels of Iraqi crude stored at Yanbu and presumably marked for humanitarian aid, saying Iraq must first pay transit fees.[77] The Kingdom has also taken a hard line as regards the lifting of sanctions against Baghdad, fearful that the return of Iraqi crude to the world market would make prices fall precipitously.

Some shadowy lines from Riyadh to Baghdad have been extended, if only through Saudi Arabia's fellow GCC members. Both Oman and Qatar now have diplomatic relations with Baghdad—in fact Oman never closed its embassy during the war—and the Bahraini prime minister publicly proposed in June 1992 that all GCC members should normalize relations with Iraq. Such suggestions have met with stony silence from the Saudis, who still feel no need for an Iraqi counterweight against Iran. Nor have Iraqi proposals met a warmer reception. Baghdad's Summer 1992 suggestion that it join the GCC, and that the organization expand to include Jordan, Syria, and Yemen, brought no official Saudi response.[78]

The ambiguous threats posed by Iran and Iraq only fuel Saudi uncertainty about the value of their new, public American alliance. Not surprisingly, the Saudis continue to waffle. Immediately after the cessation of hostilities on February 28, the Saudis temporarily reverted to their cautious foreign policy, and sought to distance themselves from American objectives and interests. Much to American consternation, they refused to take a leading role in the setting up of the subsequent Middle East peace talks between Israel and the Arabs, and the Kingdom also balked at formal and more intensive defense ties, including the prepositioning of enough military supplies to equip a division, and the free use of Saudi military facilities. The Kingdom also refused to sign a "status of forces" agreement that would have set the terms for American access to Saudi facilities.[79]

The al-Saud have always downplayed their foreign policy link with the United States for two reasons. First, too open a tie risks condemnation from Iran and Arab radicals. As protector of Islam's two holiest sites, Riyadh can not be too closely identified with the "Great Satan," a link that Tehran has drawn with surprising success. Close ties with Washington are also opposed by many Saudi fundamentalists who claim that the United States is the real enemy of the Kingdom. Fundamentalists charge that Saudi oil policy has been made subservient to American interests, and that the al-Saud are in fact American lackeys.[80]

To counter this, domestic propaganda during Operation Desert Storm tended to treat the Americans as a sort of armed expatriate worker serving the regime. Elaborate controls were placed on American religious behavior and entertainment, emphasizing the Kingdom's sovereignty. This public posturing continued after the defeat of Iraq. On the first anniversary of the Gulf War, the Saudi embassy in Washington drew criticism in the United States because its official account of Operation Desert Storm barely mentioned the United States!

Such public distancing, however, should not mask the closeness of the Saudi-American relationship. Since the Iraqi invasion of Kuwait, Saudi Arabia has committed itself to purchasing more than $30 billion worth of American weapons. Saudi acquisitions have occurred despite George Bush's arms control proposal of May 1991, and in fact have set off a massive arms-buying binge within the region (see Chapter 4). Saudi purchases have been facilitated by American domestic policy considerations and the desire to keep certain arms lines running at a time of falling Pentagon purchases. Saudi orders have also taken place despite Riyadh's increasing debt (see Chapter 5). Not surprisingly, Washington has allowed the Kingdom easy purchase, knowing full well that the Saudis can turn elsewhere for their arms, as they have in the past.[81]

Military cooperation remains close, despite differences over the prepositioning of American supplies in the country. Although the United

States has signed bilateral defense accords with Kuwait, Bahrain, and Qatar, the Saudis have opted to continue their informal understanding with Washington rather than risk condemnation from Iran and Arab radicals. However, some American military strategists are uncomfortable with the arrangement, which seems to stress quick American responses to threats to Saudi sovereignty without having preset plans in place. Saudi Arabia underlined its position in 1991 when it denied American requests for bases. However, the Saudis continue to purchase huge caches of arms, which their own armed forces are unable to use, and which effectively creates prepositioning. The United States and Saudi Arabia continue to share military intelligence gleaned from the AWACS planes currently stationed in Riyadh. Although an official treaty remains missing, it seems probable that the al-Saud and Washington are linked together in an unofficial mutual defense agreement, which some say includes assurances that Washington will come to the family's support against all external and internal threats.[82]

Commercial links between the two countries are also strong as the United States has again become the Kingdom's largest supplier of goods. Washington provides a convenient security umbrella for the Kingdom, and Saudi Arabia has reciprocated by following a sympathetic oil policy, geared toward price restraint.[83] In addition, Washington and Riyadh share common strategic concerns in seeking to contain Iran and Iraq.

Some differences remain. The question of Israel and the Palestinians continues to bedevil the relationship, even though the Jericho–Gaza Plan between Israel and the PLO, and their mutual recognition of each other, have seemingly lifted potentially hazardous obstacles. The Kingdom has stressed that the absence of a comprehensive Arab-Israeli peace only strengthens the hands of Arab radicals, who in the final analysis are inimical to the Kingdom as well. As such, the Kingdom signed on to the American peace initiative in July 1991.

Saudi Arabia's Israeli policy has consistently been respectful if unfriendly. Although the Kingdom has been a major financial contributor to the front-line states, it has also avoided direct involvement in any of the wars between Israel and its neighbors. The Kingdom and Israel share no borders, and Israel's return of several Saudi islands at the Straits of Tiran after its Sinai withdrawal ended the one direct conflict between the two powers. In fact, the Kingdom and Israel have few common interests save their relationship with Washington. As such, the Saudi regime sees a great deal of domestic risk, and little potential gain, in aggressively pursuing peace with Israel. Saudi fundamentalists quickly picked up on the fact that the Gulf conflict linked Israel and the Kingdom together, if only indirectly, and they remain opposed to any recognition of Israel. The September 1993 attack on Fahd's Jeddah palace by a lone gunman may have been the result of Saudi inching toward recognition.[84]

Riyadh, however, has made several gestures in support of peace moves. First and foremost, the Kingdom has openly backed American efforts in the current round of Middle East peace talks. Saudi financial influence has been brought to bear several times on the peace partici- pants, and surely enabled the Palestinian faction to attend peace talks. Saudi Arabia's new role was amply illustrated when Bandar attended the opening session of the peace talks in Madrid. The Kingdom also pressured Syria and Lebanon to enter the talks, and it funded the Mos- cow Middle East conference when it became apparent that the Russian government did not have the money to host the talks.[85] The Kingdom also participated in regional talks concerning water and security in the broader framework of the Arab-Israeli talks.

Fahd has also made several conciliatory statements regarding Israel, including one highly quoted plea in June 1993 when he urged his Arab neighbors to make peace with Israel. Riyadh has also made several other gestures. First and foremost, the Kingdom has begun issuing visas to people of Jewish extraction, breaking a long-standing boycott. In an unprecedented move, the Kingdom invited the leaders of the American Jewish Congress on a four-day visit during which they were assured that the Kingdom has recognized Israel's right of existence since 1982 and the abortive Fahd Plan.[86] Riyadh also ended its boycott of firms doing business with Israel.

One danger to the thawing of Saudi-Israeli relations is that the Clin- ton administration may seek to pressure the Saudis to recognize Israel before all the parts of a comprehensive Arab-Israeli peace plan are in place. Saudi recognition will hinge on Israeli withdrawal from the Golan Heights and Lebanon, as well as significant progress on the autonomy of Palestinians in the Occupied Territories.

Hegemony over the Arabian Peninsula

While Saudi Arabia's policy with the world at large is generally paci- fistic, its policy vis-à-vis its neighbors on the Arabian peninsula is, quite simply, hegemonistic. The Kingdom's motivation is simple: by dominating the peninsula, Saudi Arabia hopes to form a block that can counter Iraq and Iran. Unfortunately, from the Saudi point of view, its neighbors—Yemen, Oman, the UAE, Qatar, Bahrain, and Kuwait— have proven unwilling participants in Saudi ambitions, and have largely nullified Riyadh's attempts.

The Saudi vehicle for control over the peninsula has been the GCC, which it founded in May 1981. The GCC was not Riyadh's first attempt at forging some sort of alliance among its neighbors; in 1969 the Saudis unsuccessfully attempted to forge a similar regional alliance among themselves, Qatar, Bahrain, and the six Trucial states, which would later become the UAE.[87] Saudi Arabia's second attempt proved more successful. The timing of its creation was not by chance; the GCC coalesced when Tehran and Baghdad were occupied with one another, and thus unable to object to its creation. The GCC also came together without the Yemens, both of which objected to their exclusion.[88]

The GCC could be described as a fusion of the North Atlantic Treaty Organization (NATO) and European Economic Community (EEC), promoting economic, military, and political cooperation. Theoretically, those goals should be easily met: not only do the GCC's members share similar political systems but they also have similar rentier-based economies and share common strategic concerns. However, GCC unity has been difficult to attain. Not only is the GCC riven with personal conflicts among the different ruling families, but its smaller members also remain leery of Saudi domination. As William Quandt noted, the smaller members of the GCC are "generally viewed by the Saudis as lesser tribal leaders who for one reason or another— usually British protection—managed to remain outside the Saudi embrace."[89] The ruling families of the six member states are not personally close, and they continue to allow personal considerations to overrule their political aims—just as Abdulaziz did with the Hashemites in the late 1940s. Although the members of the GCC have a vested interest in seeing that their regimes survive, they nonetheless have contributed to their own troubles. Saudi-Omani relations have been particularly strained since Sultan Qaboos offended Fahd by ordering the latter's youngest and favorite son, Abdulaziz, out of the room during a meeting of GCC heads of state. The GCC member nations also run subsidized and competing newspapers, mostly based in London, which feature unflattering stories about each other.

Other issues temper comity. Saudi-Omani relations remain cool; many Saudis look down on the sultanate's Ibadi sect. The Omanis have also had to face Saudi intransigence on the al-Buraiymi issue, as well as Riyadh's backing of Omani rebels in the 1950s and 1960s. Border disputes abound. The UAE and Oman have several unresolved border issues, and fighting broke out between the two in November 1992.[90] Bahrain and Qatar have also exchanged blows over control of a small coral reef between them, and the recent Saudi-Qatari border clash has undermined unity even further. Even the Kingdom's relationship with Kuwait was cool prior to the invasion. Not surprisingly, the GCC did little in the first few hours and days of the Iraqi invasion of Kuwait even though the GCC charter binds its members to each other in case one is attacked by an outside power.

GCC cohesion experienced a brief surge following the cessation of hostilities. During this time, the organization explored greater military integration, following a proposal from Sultan Qaboos that the GCC should create a 100,000-man joint GCC force, which would be based at Hafr al-Batin. But as the Iraqi threat ebbed, the member states returned to their old ways. In fact, the cessation of hostilities soon resulted in a higher than normal pitch of border disputes between the GCC members. The most serious involved Saudi Arabia and Qatar. The dispute was all the more puzzling because Qatar, of all the GCC members, is the state most similar to Saudi Arabia because of their shared Unitarian religion. The Saudis claimed that the incident began when Qataris moved a border marker into their territory. When Mohammed bin Shrain, a sheikh of the Murrah tribe, investigated, he was subsequently shot by the Qataris. "The tribesmen avenged him by wiping the post out with bazookas."[91] The Qataris countered that the border post was subjected to an unprovoked attack by Saudi Defense and Aviation Minister Prince Sultan bin Abdulaziz. According to Doha, one Qatari soldier and an Egyptian on secondment died during the Saudi attack. Efforts to bring the issue to a peaceful resolution also proved unsuccessful. The issue was only settled in December 1992 when the Qatari and Saudi foreign ministers signed an agreement, following Egyptian mediation—and after Qatar had restored relations with Iraq and announced plans not to attend the GCC's annual summit meeting.

What seems likely is that Saudi Arabia, secure in its American alliance, has reverted to a more aggressive policy vis-à-vis its smaller neighbors—a return to Saudi hegemony that was started with Abdulaziz. Since the Gulf conflict, it has had new disputes with all its fellow members: it has revived border disputes with Oman and the UAE; it angered Bahrain by seeming to favor Qatar in the coral island dispute; it publicly quarreled with Kuwait over the role of Saudi forces during the Gulf conflict; and it had the falling out with Qatar. The spate of mini-crises may be the result of the Saudi leadership's manufacturing winnable fights with its smaller neighbors in order to divert attention from its ongoing domestic political situation.

Given Saudi clumsiness, GCC cooperation has suffered. Closer military integration was effectively nixed at the December 1991 summit meeting when Fahd publicly vetoed the Omani 100,000-troop plan. Fahd was driven by his fear of committing Saudi resources to a costly new undertaking when the country was grappling with its own financial problems, as well as being reluctant to commit Saudi forces to a multinational unit, in which Saudi forces would not have been predominant. Riyadh's response, instead, has been to embark on a massive arms binge, which in turn has prompted its GCC allies and Iran to do the same.

Greater economic and political integration have also proven elusive. Although the December 1992 summit meeting resulted in the election of a new chairman, Fakim bin Sultan bin Salman al-Qasimi, a member of Ras al-Khaimah's ruling family, other agreements were noticeable in their absence. More than a decade after its creation, the GCC has only been able to pass one or two commercial accords, and coordinate the six countries' electrical networks. A few joint industrial projects have been built, and Bahrain has been connected to the mainland via the Saudi-Bahraini Causeway. The paltry results have led more than one commentator to note that the GCC remains an organization looking for a raison d'être.

Saudi Arabia's relations with Yemen are no less complicated, and are predicated upon the 1934 Asir War and the civil war of the 1960s. Since its taking of the Asir and Najran Oasis, Saudi Arabia has feared Yemeni irredentism. Of all the powers on the Arabian peninsula, only Yemen offers a credible challenge to Saudi supremacy —a fact that Riyadh recognizes. Not only does Yemen have the human resources—its population is at least 1.5 times greater than that of the Kingdom—but it also has growing financial independence given increased oil production.

Prior to 1990, Saudi Arabia's Yemeni policy was based on stymieing unification attempts between the two Yemens. Riyadh gave generous amounts of foreign aid to North Yemen, including free hospitals, subsidized food, and large credits. The Kingdom also regularly paid bribes and subsidies to Yemen's different tribes to subvert the union, which nonetheless took place in 1990 and has managed to survive Saudi pressure ever since.

Iraq's invasion of Kuwait and Sanaa's subsequent support radically altered Saudi-Yemeni relations. Yemen's attitude seemed largely the result of its traditional friendship with Iraq (each has found in the other a convenient counterweight against Saudi Arabia). Yemen also remained bitter toward Kuwait and the GCC, which had excluded it from membership in the early 1980s. Prior to the invasion, Yemenis were the only nationality group who needed an entry visa to work in the Kingdom as per the dictates of the Treaty of Taif. That changed within weeks of the invasion, as the Saudi government revoked their status and required them to find sponsors. Hundreds of thousands could not, and were subsequently forced to leave; others were arrested by the Saudi security forces and tortured (see Chapter 6). Today, estimates of the Yemeni population in Saudi Arabia range as low as 60,000. Saudi Arabia has also undertaken a number of other retaliatory measures against the Yemeni government, including the cessation of Riyadh's paying of pilgrims' fees for Yemenis.

Relations between the two countries remain cool in the aftermath of Operation Desert Storm. The defeat of Iraq allowed the Saudis to step up their pressure on Yemen. Border incidents had already occurred after the discovery of oil in the late 1980s. Yemen's oil production is slowly increasing, bringing in needed hard currency, and also lessening its financial dependence on the Kingdom. This has not gone unnoticed by Riyadh. A few short weeks after the end of Operation Desert Storm, Saudi Arabia began warning oil companies that their operations in the northern part of Yemen should be avoided, as the area was contested. To underline its position, Royal Saudi Air Force jets flew warning sorties over the contested area.

Further contributing to tension between the two countries is the status of the Treaty of Taif, which is supposed to be renewed every twenty Hejira years, and which expired in 1992. The treaty reportedly only ceded the Asir and Najran to the Kingdom until 1992. Negotiations only began in September 1992 after Yemen appealed to the United States, France, and Great Britain.[92] Finding an agreement has been elusive: not only do the Yemenis want the Asir returned, but the Kingdom wants to use the treaty's stipulations to serve as a basis for delineating the eastern borders between the two countries. There are also conflicting claims to offshore islands, which have further inflamed territorial issues.

The Yemeni government has also charged that the Saudis are paying saboteurs to blow up government installations and kill various Yemeni politicians, in order to provoke a civil war. Complaints about foreign meddling have been made by Yemeni president Ali Abdullah Saleh, who blamed "unnamed" foreign partners for bankrolling bombs and assassinations. Pro-government newspapers said a few days later that the "unnamed" country was Saudi Arabia.[93] Making matters worse from the Saudi perspective has been Yemen's political progress, which has won kudos from Washington. Despite its "backwardness," Yemen held parliamentary elections in 1993, in which forty parties participated, and in which two women won seats.

The Saudis have taken a number of steps to guard against the Yemeni threat. In an apparent abandonment of its earlier *riyal politik*, Riyadh has begun to solidify control in the area. Besides making plans for another military city in the Asir to guard against a Yemeni strike, the Kingdom also announced plans to erect a $3 billion electronic fence along the length of its border with Yemen to control border incidents. The fence also seems intended to cut down on the amount of smuggling between the two countries, a perennial problem.[94]

To counter Yemeni claims, Saudi Arabia has also begun investing heavily in the area, especially the port of Jizan. The Jizan Agricultural Development Company was formed in May 1992, and Riyadh has upped its infrastructural investment. Saudi Arabia has also tried to isolate its neighbor diplomatically. When Oman and Yemen signed a treaty delineating their border, the Kingdom immediately protested, and tried to force Oman to scrap it. Not surprisingly, the Saudis then renewed their own border conflict with Oman to pressure Muscat in the right direction. The Saudis have also attempted to dissuade UAE and Omani efforts aimed at normalizing relations between Riyadh and Sanaa. Relations with Yemen have grown even more difficult in 1994 as Sanaa has drifted closer to civil war.

Leadership in the Arab and Islamic Worlds

Saudi Arabia has always walked a delicate line in its quest for leadership in the Arab and Islamic worlds. Petrodollars ensured a certain degree of political power for the Kingdom, and by its guardianship of Mecca and Medina, it had claims to the titular leadership of the world's one billion Muslims. However, both are balanced by the fact that the Kingdom is closely linked and identified with the United States, whose interests are inimical to many in the Arab and Muslim community. Juggling the two has been a Saudi preoccupation, and a task that has not been too successfully accomplished.

The Iraqi invasion was a bitter lesson for Saudi Arabia and Kuwait as regards the reliability of their Arab and Islamic neighbors. The Arab League, the OIC, and even bilateral agreements with countries that had received billions in Saudi aid proved small comfort during the Kuwaiti crisis. That the American link proved in the final analysis to be the only reliable thread in Saudi foreign policy has in turn affected Riyadh's post-invasion calculations. Prior to Operation Desert Storm, the Kingdom seemed unwilling to countenance any break in the facade of Arab unity. Now, Saudi Arabia, again with American backing, has adopted a policy of almost intentional confrontation with its formerly close allies. Possibly, this is a result of great bitterness toward those nations and groups that eagerly lined up to take Saudi money but did little when the Kingdom was in danger.

To avoid complete ostracism in the Arab world, the Kingdom's post-Kuwait foreign policy has included among its aims a tighter embrace of Egypt and, to a lesser extent, Syria. The emergence of a Cairo–Damascus–Riyadh axis is not surprising; both Syria and Egypt are firm enemies of Saddam Hussein, and both participated in Operation Desert Storm. Both also received substantial monies from Riyadh for doing so.

Hopes for greater Saudi-Syrian-Egyptian coordination and cooperation were centered on the so-called Damascus Declaration. Immediately following the cessation of fighting, Syrian, Egyptian, and GCC ministers met in Damascus on March 6, 1991, to forge a framework for a common defense force that would have guarded Kuwait and the Kingdom against future Iraqi attacks. The so-called Damascus Declaration would have provided the basis for the stationing of Egyptian and Syrian troops in Kuwait and the Kingdom, thereby foregoing the need for American (i.e., non-Arab, non-Muslim) help. According to preliminary discussions, both Egypt and Syria would have stationed 3,000 troops apiece in Kuwait. There, they would have been joined by 10,000 Saudi troops and an equal number from the remaining five GCC states. In return, the GCC would pay Syria and Egypt for their manpower.[95]

However, negotiations bogged down as the Iraqi threat diminished. Although Egyptian president Hosni Mubarak pushed for the creation of a Rapid Deployment Force (RDF), the GCC was less enthusiastic. GCC sources eventually claimed that the delay in inking a 6 + 2 Pact (the six members of the GCC with Egypt and Syria) was delayed on "protocols," which was initially interpreted as meaning that although the GCC was willing to set up a multi-billion-dollar development fund for its two Arab neighbors, they were resisting more binding multilateral pacts involving cultural, political, and economic matters.[96]

The GCC states later balked about making direct payments to Cairo and Damascus, and instead insisted that their monies be deposited in a development fund that would have been made available to private entrepreneurs in each country. However, the main point seems to be that the GCC, and especially Saudi Arabia, were reluctant to allow large contingents of Egyptian and Syrian soldiers to mingle with their armed forces.

Nonetheless, GCC reticence was taken graciously by Cairo and Damascus. Hosni Mubarak recognized the futility of the endeavor as early as May 1991 when he ordered the last Egyptian troops to return to Cairo. The debacle of "hiring" Egyptian troops aside, Egyptian-Saudi ties are especially close. Not only does Egypt provide a counterweight to both Iraq and Iran, but it is also the most populous Arab country, and the intellectual center of the Arab world. The two countries share strategic concerns, first among them the rise of the fundamentalist regime in Sudan. The two countries have also linked efforts to fight fundamentalism in their own countries, and have taken a leading role in the subsequent round of Arab-Israeli peace talks. There are close economic links as well: the hundreds of thousands of Yemenis expelled from the Kingdom were largely replaced by Egyptians. Egypt also provides manpower of another sort: Egyptian security forces were "imported" during the 1988 hajj, and have allegedly stayed ever since.

Saudi relations with Syria have always been more circumspect, and tinged in part by fear. Syria's support of Arab radicalism has always alarmed the al-Saud, and the secularist tendencies of the ruling Baath party are diametrically opposed by many Saudis. Nonetheless, Syria has been a major recipient of Saudi aid, even before the Gulf conflict. The al-Saud have also courted Damascus's favor over the past two decades, especially as regards the settlement over the Lebanese issue. In such talks, Crown Prince Abdullah is usually sent as the Saudi emissary, given the fact that his relatives are Syrian. Syrian participation in Operation Desert Storm was considered essential by Riyadh, so as to give the operation a pan-Arab flavor, as well as to preempt radical suggestions that the Saudis were American stooges, isolated in the Arab world. The Saudis and Kuwaitis allegedly paid more than $1.6 billion worth of loans and credits for Syria's participation.

Saudi relations with the rest of the Arab world have been largely determined by their actions during the invasion. The Kingdom's relations with Jordan and the PLO, for example, are frosty, and promise to remain so for the foreseeable future. The Kingdom had long subsidized and supported Jordan as a convenient buffer between itself and Syria and Israel. As such, King Hussein's position during the Kuwaiti debacle was regarded as abject betrayal. Worse, many in the Kingdom believed the Jordanian monarch had made plans to reclaim part of the Hejaz for the Hashemites if Iraq's Kuwaiti gambit had succeeded.

Upon the outbreak of hostilities, Jordan's ambassador was asked to leave the country, and the Kingdom also implemented a ban on all Jordanians attempting to enter the country (this ban was also applied to Yemenis, Sudanese, and Palestinians). The Jordanian ambassador was only allowed to return in December when the ban was lifted on other nationalities.

Saudi-Jordanian relations remain cool. Saudi Arabia has reduced its Palestinian and Jordanian work force, and has ceased all financial and oil assistance. Saudi pique has been registered in a number of other ways. Shipments of frozen sheep from the annual hajj to Jordan's poor have been halted.[97] The Kingdom has also taken several diplomatic initiatives against Jordan. One of the more unusual was the Saudi proposal that a Palestinian state be created from the West Bank and Jordan, replacing the Hashemite dynasty.[98] The Saudis have also contested King Hussein's proposed restoration of the al-Aqsa Mosque, and have instead made a far more generous offer of money.[99] The Jordanians also claim that Saudi Arabia has funneled funds to fundamentalists opposed to the monarchy, although such a charge seems unlikely given Saudi apprehension at the wave of growing fundamentalism in the area, including the growth of Hamas in the Occupied Territories. Nonetheless, the Kingdom released data detailing more than $6.2 billion in aid and grants to the Jordanian state since 1988. Mirroring the Saudi detailing of aid to Iraq and Sudan, the revelation showed the depth of Saudi ire. King Hussein has been left to make unreciprocated gestures such as turning over to the Saudis a number of dissidents, and breaking away from Saddam Hussein.

Saudi relations with the PLO have fared no better. After PLO Chairman Yasir Arafat publicly endorsed the Iraqi invasion of Kuwait, the Saudis announced that their financial support of the organization would cease. Arafat's betrayal, after years of financial support (in fact, Riyadh was the most constant supporter) rankled the Saudis deeply. "From now on, we support causes, not people," said one Saudi official. "We are making the point that Yasir Arafat is finished here, but that other Palestinian leaders who appreciate all the financial help we have extended to the Palestinian movement over the years and who have not turned against us will be welcome."[100] The Kingdom's ire took Arafat by surprise, and he hastened to offer an explanation. However, Fahd uncharacteristically refused to see him. Instead, Fahd received Hani al-Hassan, a senior PLO official sympathetic to the Gulf monarchies.

Rhetoric notwithstanding, relations between the Saudis and the PLO have eased somewhat. In the fall of 1991, the Kingdom announced that it would no longer prohibit its citizens from making contributions to the Palestinian cause.[101] Although official donations to the PLO have ceased, the Saudis also offered to provide upward of $100 million for a reconstruction and development fund for Jericho and Gaza following the announcement of the Israeli-PLO accord. However, Saudi officials quickly added that the fund would not be administered by the PLO.

The thaw continued in early 1994 when Arafat was finally given permission to visit the Kingdom. Although his three-day stay was billed as a private visit so the PLO leader could perform *umrah,* or minor pilgrimage, Arafat nonetheless met Fahd and other senior Saudi officials.[102] Whether or not Arafat will eventually be forgiven for his support of Iraq has yet to be seen. Saudi relations with the PLO seem predicated on the realization that the PLO remains the best alternative to check more dangerous Palestinian organizations such as Hamas.

The Kingdom's pan-Islamic policies are also undergoing reevaluation. Although the OIC issued a statement condemning the Iraqi action on August 4, many members were opposed. Saudi requests to the OIC's members for troops also produced varying results. Among Asian nations, only Pakistan and Bangladesh sent troops, partially in the hope of increased Saudi financial aid. Other countries such as Indonesia and Malaysia were conspicuous in their refusal. Pro-Iraqi demonstrations also occurred in Pakistan, Bangladesh, India, and Malaysia. The demonstrations in Pakistan were so divisive that the government nearly withdrew its troops from the Kingdom. As it was, Pakistan's 11,000-man contingent saw no action because of the strength of anti-American feeling found in Islamabad. Even Pakistani Prime Minister Benazir Bhutto refused to support UN sanctions when they were first announced.[103] Saudi support among the rest of the Islamic world was mixed, and largely conditioned upon what aid members thought they could squeeze from the Saudis.

Not surprisingly, the Kingdom's reliance on its Islamic brethren has decreased, especially with the rise of fundamentalism. This apprehension with fundamentalism exposes the critical ideological-religious problems facing the al-Saud. Historically, the Kingdom has funded Islamic radicals in every country, seeing this support as an affirmation of Islamic leadership. Prior to Operation Desert Storm, Saudi petrodollars helped construct mosques all over the world, funded Islamic terrorists in the Philippines, and underwrote anti–Salman Rushdie marches in Europe and Asia.

The great irony of Saudi-funded Islamic fundamentalism has been that many recipients of Saudi aid have turned against Saudi Arabia, and have in fact funded and supported the Kingdom's own hard-liners arrayed against the al-Saud. This disloyalty has led the Saudis to terminate support for many Islamic groups, even though that means abandoning them to the ministrations of Iran. The Kingdom has acted in several ways. Financial aid has been severely reduced. The change in the Kingdom's aid policy was announced by the Saudi ambassador to Algeria, Hassan Fekhi, who said that the Kingdom was also facing a problem with fundamentalist groups, many of whom had also embraced extremist causes.[104] In addition, the Kingdom has implemented new restrictions aimed at limiting private contributions to what it considers Islamic groups. New policy was enacted in 1993 when the government announced that only organizations sanctioned by the Ministry of Interior could receive donations.[105]

The threat, however, is that Saudi reconsiderations may lead to increased Iranian influence in the Islamic world. Such a development could be unsettling, given Iranian suggestions that Mecca and Medina be administered by a pan-Islamic body, which would effectively break Saudi control of the holy cities—one of the planks of al-Saud legitimacy. There is a catch as well. By claiming to be the most Islamic country in the world as it is wont to do, Saudi Arabia runs the risk of being undermined by some more Islamic power at all times.

Interestingly, the Saudis may also be sounding a new note in their pan-Islamic policy. A trial balloon was floated in *Asharq al-Awsat*, the pan-Arab London-based newspaper partially owned by Riyadh's Governor Prince Salman bin Abdulaziz. An article published on the Kingdom's 60th National Day questioned whether radical, fundamentalist Islam is really necessary: "But is the Islamic world really facing a bloody battle with the Christian world? Are the Crusades really continuing? Although there has been much stoking of the fire of that idea, it no longer finds the widespread acceptance it had a year ago," the unnamed writer said, adding that the Kingdom can play a role in healing relations between Muslims and Christians. "This is where the Saudi role appears qualified to find fertile ground."[106]

Notes

1. *Saudi Gazette*, July 27, 1988.
2. *New York Times*, March 1, 1992.
3. Robert Lacey, *The Kingdom*, p. 76.
4. Ibid., p. 110.
5. Nadav Safran, *Saudi Arabia: The Ceaseless Quest for Security*, pp. 75–77.
6. Lacey, *The Kingdom*, p. 137.
7. Ibid., p. 187.
8. D. van der Meulen, *The Wells of Ibn Sa'ud*, pp. 106–7.
9. Ibid., p. 17.
10. Ibid., pp. 169–70.
11. Those privileges ended in September 1990 following Yemen's support for Iraq in the Gulf conflict.
12. Lacey, *The Kingdom*, pp. 240–41.
13. van der Meulen, *The Wells*, p. 108.
14. Lacey, *The Kingdom*, p. 273.
15. *Washington Post*, February 9, 1992.
16. Lacey, *The Kingdom*, p. 274.
17. *Washington Post*, February 9, 1992.
18. Ibid.
19. van der Meulen, *The Wells*, pp. 170–73.

20. Ibid., p. 173.

21. Saudi aspirations in al-Buraiymi were also stoked by the fact that the oasis had one of the last surviving slave markets in the region.

22. Safran, *Saudi Arabia: The Ceaseless Quest,* pp. 78–80.

23. Lacey, *The Kingdom,* p. 312.

24. Ibid., p. 314.

25. Safran, *Saudi Arabia: The Ceaseless Quest,* p. 81.

26. Ibid., p. 82.

27. Ibid., p. 93.

28. *Washington Post,* February 9, 1992.

29. Lacey, *The Kingdom,* p. 384.

30. For an overview of oil money being used as a political lubricant, see Steve Longrigg, "The Economics on Oil in the Middle East."

31. *Washington Post,* April 3, 1991.

32. Lacey, *The Kingdom,* ch. 5.

33. Ibid.

34. Bandar is one of the more controversial members of the al-Saud. Flamboyant and personable, he has become a social fixture in Washington where some of his actions—buying a $2 million mansion adjoining his own, and then razing it so he could get a better view of the Potomac—have attracted wide attention. The prince has also been linked to several scandals, including arms peddling (see Chapter 4).

35. Several Saudi diplomats provided this information.

36. Iran was not the only power to propose a regional alliance. The United Kingdom, Saudi Arabia, and Iraq all proposed their own variants.

37. Lawrence Freedman and Efraim Karsh, *The Gulf Conflict, 1990–1991: Diplomacy and War in the New World Order,* p. 7.

38. William Quandt, *Saudi Arabia in the 1980s,* p. 39.

39. *New York Times,* March 1, 1992.

40. Amir Taheri, *Holy Terror: Inside the World of Islamic Terrorism,* p. 167.

41. Ibid.

42. Fahd explained his decision as follows: "I have wanted to replace the words His Majesty by something I adore and am honored to carry and that is Custodian of the Two Holy Harams." Saudi Press Agency, October 27, 1986.

43. Various theories abound as to why Hume Horan was recalled; staffers at the American embassy in Riyadh told the authors that it was likely tied to Horan's meeting with the king concerning the Saudi purchase of Chinese missiles. When Horan protested, Fahd reportedly told him that every country had a right to defend itself. Later in the conversation, Fahd asked for American assurances that Israel would not attack its rockets. Horan infuriated the king by then repeating Fahd's own words that every country including Israel had a right to defend itself.

44. General H. Norman Schwartzkopf with Peter Petre, *It Doesn't Take a Hero,* p. 275.

45. *New York Times,* July 4, 1991.

46. Ibid., July 19, 1991.

47. For more background, see Freedman and Karsh, *The Gulf Conflict,* part 1.

48. Ibid., pp. 48–49.

49. "Country Report: Saudi Arabia," *Economist Intelligence Unit (EIU),* no. 1, 1990.

50. Freedman and Karsh, *The Gulf Conflict,* p. 56.

51. Schwartzkopf, *It Doesn't Take a Hero,* p. 304.

52. *Utne Reader,* May–June 1992.

53. Freedman and Karsh, *The Gulf Conflict,* p. 90.

54. Schwartzkopf, *It Doesn't Take a Hero,* pp. 302–6.

55. Saudi Press Agency, August 7, 1990.

56. *Middle East Economic Survey (MEES),* August 13, 1990.

57. Ibid., September 24, 1990.

58. *MEED: Middle East Business Weekly,* November 22, 1990.

59. Schwartzkopf, *It Doesn't Take a Hero,* p. 372.

60. Freedman and Karsh, *The Gulf Conflict,* p. 241.

61. Ibid., p. 379–80.

62. Ibid., p. 405.

63. *MEES,* July 7, 1991.

64. Ibid., January 7, 1991.

65. Freedman and Karsh, *The Gulf Conflict,* p. 108.

66. "Country Report: Saudi Arabia," *EIU,* no. 3, 1991.

67. *MEES,* May 8, 1991.

68. *The Middle East,* August 1991.

69. Ibid., May 1991, and August 1991; and "Country Report: Saudi Arabia," *EIU,* no. 3, 1991.

70. *MEES,* April 20, 1992.

71. Associated Press, December 26, 1992.

72. Eqbal Ahmad, "A Tug of War for Muslims' Allegiance," pp. 24–25.

73. *New York Times,* August 23, 1993.

74. "Country Report: Saudi Arabia," *EIU,* no. 3, 1992; and *Wall Street Journal,* March 16, 1992.

75. *MEES,* May 29, 1993.

76. Ibid., July 6. 1992.

77. *MEED,* July 9, 1993.

78. *MEES,* July 13, 1992.

79. *Middle East Report,* July–August 1992.

80. *Mideast Mirror,* September 18, 1992.

81. *New York Times,* August 23, 1993.

82. Scott Armstrong, "Eye of the Storm."

83. *New York Times,* August 23, 1993.

84. Saudi Press Agency, September 13, 1993.

85. *New York Times,* January 28, 1992.

86. *Washington Post,* January 23, 1992.

87. Louis Turner and James Bedore, "Saudi Arabia: The Power of the Purse-Strings," pp. 405–20.

88. The Yemens were denied membership in the GCC for a number of reasons; not only were their political systems different but the Saudis were also leery about possible Yemeni domination of the GCC, especially given their large populations.

89. William Quandt, *Saudi Arabia,* p. 24.

90. As late as 1989, Oman had no diplomatic representation in the UAE. *The Economist,* January 21, 1989.
91. Reuters, October 3, 1992.
92. *MEES,* May 11, 1992.
93. *Al-Quds al-Arabi,* August 6, 1992.
94. *BusinessWeek,* February 18, 1991.
95. *MEES,* July 22, 1992.
96. *The Middle East,* June 1991.
97. *MEED,* July 3, 1992.
98. *Time,* March 18, 1991.
99. *MEED,* July 3, 1992.
100. *New York Times,* August 25, 1990.
101. *MEES,* March 29, 1992.
102. *Middle East International,* February 4, 1994.
103. Freedman and Karsh, *The Gulf Conflict,* pp. 345–46.
104. *MEED,* June 19, 1992.
105. *New York Times,* May 1, 1993.
106. *Asharq al-Awsat,* September 23, 1993.

4 MILITARY AND SECURITY FORCES

> The Saudi citizens were expecting that the Kingdom's force of men and sophisticated weapons would place it at the peak of the best military levels in the Middle East region, and that [the Saudi] armed forces could confront the region's armies, especially because [the Kingdom's citizens] have allocated hundreds of billions from [their] annual income to spend on the army. They were astonished, however, when [the Kingdom] announced to the world that [it] could not defend [its] borders by [itself], something which exacerbated the impact of the crisis on the sons of [the Saudi] people, caused them pain, and triggered their denunciation.
>
> —Amman's Radio al-Liwa, February 12, 1991

Saudi Arabia's armed forces have always faced a dilemma. Charged with defending the country from outside attack, the military and security apparatus must also protect the al-Saud from internal enemies. The two goals are not mutually compatible because one of the principal suspects of internal subversion is the military itself. Thus, the fear of military coups makes the development of an efficient armed service a low priority for the royal family. To render the military coup-resistant, the al-Saud have compartmentalized the armed forces in a manner that impedes its fighting ability. This is achieved by a complicated series of checks and counter-checks that weakens the command structure and promotes interservice rivalry.

Not surprisingly, the Saudi armed forces performed poorly during the Gulf conflict. Within days of the Iraqi blitzkrieg, the government was constrained to seek protection from the West. Such an ignominious showing would perhaps have been forgiven except that the Saudi military and security forces are among the most pampered in the world, and have absorbed more than $100 billion in arms since 1965. Overall military and security expenditures for the same period have exceeded $300 billion. This outlay has not gone unnoticed by Saudi critics, who now ask how the al-Saud could spend so much money and get so little military strength in return.

Background

The Kingdom's environment is an important military asset in many respects. The harsh climate and terrain always dictated military tactics and strategy as the desert offered invaders no nourishment and, more importantly, no water. Conflicts in Arabia were usually waged between static forces grouped around water resources, and mobile armies, which staged hit-and-run strikes before retiring to the trackless sands. Desert warfare traditionally rewarded the Bedouin, who had superior mobility, and penalized townspeople, who were slow to react.

Fighting was largely limited to raids on other tribes or small oasis settlements. The raids, called *ghazzu*, generally consisted of a few brave young men attempting to steal camels from their neighbors without being caught. The raids followed certain rules of etiquette: camels rather than material possessions were the aim; sheep and goats were left unmolested; no raiding occurred between midnight and dawn; and women were respected.[1] The *ghazzu* was the sole training for many Bedouin for the infrequent wars that erupted in the peninsula.

Sustained military campaigns were unknown. The logistical problems of maintaining large field armies in the desert were nearly insurmountable, particularly when balanced with the rather paltry benefits in the event of booty. The harsh desert environment and subsistence-level economy also mitigated against long, drawn-out maneuvers. Warfare instead developed into prolonged feints and thrusts by small groups of men—poorly equipped and poorly trained, unwilling to risk their lives, camels, or horses—who would avoid conflict until an advantage materialized.[2]

Such an approach to fighting suited the Bedu, who were notoriously fickle warriors and unstable allies. Their involvement in military actions often lasted only as long as the bribes did: the history of Arabia is littered with sudden betrayals, abrupt switches of alliances, and what others might call a complete lack of scruples. Still, the Bedouin could occasionally surprise outsiders. The Roman prefect Aelius Gallus learned this in 24 B.C. when he invaded Arabia on his way to Yemen at the head of an army of 10,000 men. Gallus attacked to secure the frankincense trade routes but was forced to retreat due to heavy losses from guerilla raids from Bedu, as well as the heat and lack of water.[3]

The first leader to harness the Bedouin's fighting potential was the Prophet Mohammed, who welded the disparate tribes together by promising them eternal rewards if they fell fighting for the spread of Islam, and earthly riches if they succeeded in their military campaigns. Motivated by religious zeal and earthly greed, the Bedu became a feared fighting force—for a time. They stayed united until Mohammed's death in A.D. 632, when they revolted, and were subsequently crushed by the Prophet's successors. The key to Mohammed's success surprisingly remained ignored by other would-be empire builders. It was only in the mid-eighteenth century that Mohammed bin Saud succeeded in uniting the peninsula by recasting the Prophet's formula and forging the alliance with Mohammed al-Wahhab (see Chapter 2). Using religious fervor and the lure of earthly booty, bin Saud was able to mold the tribes into a fighting force, which he and his sons subsequently used to conquer most of present-day Saudi Arabia. However, their success proved temporary. Alarmed by their taking of Mecca and Medina, the Ottomans eventually sent a well-equipped army against the first Saudi-Wahhabi state. Better weaponry, including howitzers, and the judicious and generous placement of bribes to rival tribes gave the Ottomans success. The first Unitarian state was utterly destroyed.

However, the lessons gleaned from its failure were not lost on Abdulaziz bin Saud when he began his bid to restore his family's political fortunes. The young bin Saud resurrected the political union between the al-Saud and al-Wahhab, and used it to his political advantage. However, Abdulaziz also had an awareness of the power of modern weaponry, gleaned from his years of exile in Kuwait, where he first encountered British field guns and naval vessels. The latter had played a part in the deterrence of an al-Rashid attack on Kuwait in 1901. That outcome impressed the young Saudi, who was to show a keenness for acquiring the latest weaponry throughout his life.

Abdulaziz inadvertently "revolutionized" military tactics on the peninsula by his reliance on foreign weaponry, at least when he had the funds to purchase it. His first such victory occurred a few months after his capture of Riyadh when his forces met the al-Rashid army outside the small Nejdi village of al-Dilam. Deploying Kuwaiti marksmen armed with the latest rifles in set positions, Abdulaziz handily defeated the al-Rashids, who Bedu-style rushed upon a supposedly unsuspecting foe in a mad, unorganized attack.[4] Although the battle totally exhausted Abdulaziz's cache of expensive munitions (and the funds with which to import them), it also convinced him of the efficacy of his strategy. Henceforth, the Saudi leader was to seek Western munitions in all his diplomatic forays.[5]

Abdulaziz's second military "innovation" occurred by chance. Learning of a new religious community outside Riyadh, the Saudi leader was able to recruit the Ikhwan, or Brotherhood, to his side (see Chapter 2). The Brotherhood proved to be a potent military force, as well as the perfect mechanism with which to settle the tribes. Adherents flocked to the king's banner for both religious reasons and the prospect of booty. In doing so, each Ikhwan recruit took vows to fight for Islam, to give up his nomadic existence, and to prepare for war against unbelievers. The Ikhwan's utter ferocity and fearlessness proved essential in routing bin Saud's enemies. The conquest of the Hejaz, however, made the Ikhwan, like the revolutionary vanguards of most movements, a liability, as well as a threat.

Not surprisingly, Abdulaziz began laying the foundations for his own army to safeguard his family and the state he had founded. Bin Saud created his new force from townsfolk, using as his nucleus the old Turkish-trained Hejazi army.[6] At the time of his conquest of Jeddah, the Hejazi Armed Forces had several thousand men under arms as well as a few rickety airplanes piloted by White Russian émigrés, some lightly armored cars, and a few pieces of light artillery. Abdulaziz's first steps were to refine his forces, paying particular attention to the development of his fledgling air force and the introduction of wireless posts. The latter two were high priorities because they robbed the Bedouin of their most important assets: the element of surprise, and the ability to fade into the trackless wastes of the desert. This was amply proved in 1922, when a 2,000-man Ikhwan unit staged an unauthorized raid into Transjordan and massacred the inhabitants of two small villages. On their return to the Kingdom, they were intercepted by British armored cars and planes thanks to information gathered from wireless posts. Only eight men returned. Abdulaziz, astonished by the ease with which his vaunted holy warriors were dispatched, became even more enamored of modern weaponry.

Abdulaziz assigned the formation of his new units a high priority because the prospect of an Ikhwan revolt grew each month. He lavishly paid for recruits, paying the then unheard-of sum of three pounds sterling for each volunteer, and six pounds sterling for each emir or leader who rallied to his cause. In addition, all were promised similar sums once the battle had been decided. The king was also helped by his British allies, who rushed the Saudi leader guns and ammunition, and provided information about the rebel forces. On March 31, 1929, religious fervor met modern technology at the Battle of Sabillah when the Ikhwan collided with Abdulaziz's new army, which featured armored cars and machine guns. The Brotherhood was utterly crushed in half an hour. The Ikhwan continued to fight for another year, but against wireless radios, machine guns, and armored cars, they never had a chance.

Abdulaziz used his new army only one more time. In 1934, the Saudi leader undertook an invasion of Yemen, capturing the Asir and Najran Oasis in the process. Following the campaign, Abdulaziz promptly demobilized the army, retaining only a small bodyguard.[7] There were several reasons for his decision. First and foremost, the Saudi monarch did not have the financial resources for a standing army (see Chapter 5). Second, the demobilization was consistent with tradition. Large standing armies, as desert sheikhs knew, only served to encourage ambitious rivals to spin their own intrigues.

Abdulaziz did attempt to secure modern weaponry for his forces when funding permitted. Although the British had always been the king's favored arms source, London grew increasingly reluctant to furnish the king arms, especially as any new Saudi expansion was likely to occur against its mandates and protectorates. Their refusal spurred Abdulaziz to seek modern weaponry elsewhere. Poland provided some modern rifles, and in the mid-1930s, Abdulaziz came to an agreement with Mussolini's Italy for the creation and training of the Royal Saudi Air Force (RSAF). Abdulaziz also had no qualms about doing business with Adolph Hitler and Nazi Germany. Relations between the two countries were established in January 1939, and scarcely six months later the Saudi king signed a contract for the immediate delivery of 4,000 German rifles, munitions, and the construction of an armaments factory near Riyadh. This occurred despite Abdulaziz's nominal alliance with Great Britain![8] The deal, however, was left unconsummated, as the king's perilous finances never allowed payment.

The fortunes of the Saudi military were changing. First, with the discovery of oil in 1938, Saudi coffers started swelling with petrodollars, making military expansion possible. Second, the United States government—in reaction to prompting from the Arabian-American Oil Company (ARAMCO)—was expressing more of an interest in its investment in Saudi oilfields.[9] In 1943, the United States signed a Lend–Lease Agreement with Saudi Arabia, and began delivering small military supplies. This new relationship culminated in the American construction of an air base at Dhahran in 1946, and an agreement that gave Washington unlimited access to it. Two years later, Washington undertook to train the RSAF.[10] And third, the Saudi military began receiving more attention in 1947–1950 when tensions began rising between the Kingdom and Hashemite Iraq and Transjordan. Alarmed, Abdulaziz sent a top-secret cable to Washington in December 1947, seeking assurances of support. Promises notwithstanding, Abdulaziz requested a military alliance with the United States three years later. The Truman regime responded by sending Assistant Secretary of State George McGhee to Riyadh to oversee the creation of a military aid program.[11] One year later, the United States Training Mission in the Kingdom was established. Washington was eager to supply training and weapons, especially as close military ties were viewed as one way to influence the al-Saud and their country's foreign policy.

The Saudis also sought to institutionalize the military. In 1944, the Ministry of Defense was created and Abdulaziz's son, Prince Mansour, appointed minister. It was an unwise choice; Mansour was ambitious and talented, and immediately began creating special military units loyal only to himself. Although never proved, it seems likely that the prince was using his position to challenge the succession of Saud, if not the power of his father as well. In 1951, Mansour suddenly took ill and died in mysterious circumstances at the age of twenty-nine.[12] His units were promptly disbanded.

Military growth continued under King Saud bin Abdulaziz, who laid the foundations for the modern Saudi armed forces, first turning to Egypt's Nasser for guidance and help. Saud's choice in allies was unwise as problems immediately arose with the arrival of a two-hundred-man Egyptian military mission in early 1955. Several months later, the first conspiracy to overthrow the government was uncovered among a cabal of army officers in Taif.[13] It was to prove the first of several such attempts undertaken with Egyptian encouragement and connivance.

Saud reacted in several ways. Not only did he create a royal guard to protect himself and his family; he also resurrected the last remnants of the Ikhwan and put them into a new fighting force aimed at protecting the al-Saud against all comers, including the Saudi Army. Called the White Army, the units took their name from the Ikhwan habit of wearing white martyr headcloths as they went into battle. The new army, constituted only as a tribal levy and not an Islamic brotherhood, served as a counterweight to the established army while providing the means to harness the country's restive tribesmen to the al-Saud's side. Later, the White Army's name was changed to *Harass al-Watani,* or the Saudi Arabian National Guard (SANG). SANG soon evolved into a completely separate arm with full ministry status.

Saud also sought to expand his other forces. In 1957, the Royal Saudi Navy (RSN) was formed. The air force was also strengthened. However, his most important move was to restore the tattered military ties between the United States and the Kingdom. During a state visit in 1957, the Saudi monarch renewed his country's military agreement with Washington, with the latter receiving use of Dhahran Air Base for an additional five years in return for American military and economic aid. The agreement notwithstanding, Saud expelled the Americans in 1961 in a fit of pique. It was left to Crown Prince Faisal bin Abdulaziz to restore close American military ties when the Yemeni Civil War erupted. Wanting to safeguard the Kingdom's territorial integrity, Faisal secured the resumption of American military aid, and the buildup of the Kingdom's armed forces continued. The latter was aided by the 1965 foundation of a joint Anglo-American Commission charged with developing the Kingdom's armed might.

As Saudi Arabia entered the seventies, it had the basic components of its armed forces in place. The army, air force, navy, National Guard, and Ministry of Interior all existed. Saudi Arabia also had a powerful military patron, the United States. The military was not perfect; the coup virus was still strong. However, the Kingdom's armed forces were starting to coalesce. To ensure loyalty, each main unit—the Ministry of Defense, the Ministry of Interior, and the National Guard—was headed by a prominent member of the al-Saud.

The Boom Buildup

The need to develop a strong military took on added significance in the early 1970s, especially following the 1971 British withdrawal from the

Table 4.1

Budgeted Saudi Defense and Security Allocations, 1980–1994

Year	Overall budget expenditures (SR billion)	Defense allocations (SR billion)	Percentage of all outlays
1980	245.0	69.9	28.5
1981	298.0	82.5	27.7
1982	313.4	89.9	28.7
1983	260.0	75.7	29.1
1984	260.0	79.9	30.7
1985	200.0	64.1	32.1
1986	—	—	—
1987	170.0	60.8	35.8
1988	141.2	50.3	35.6
1989	141.1	55.0[a]	38.9
1990	143.0	51.9	36.3
1991	—	—	—
1992	181.0	54.3	30.0
1993	196.9	61.6	31.9
1994	160.0	—[b]	—

Source: Ministry of Finance and National Economy.
Notes: No budgets released for 1986, 1991; many purchases occur off-budget.
[a] No defense figure released in 1989; estimate.
[b] No defense figure released in 1994.

Gulf. Iran quickly moved to fill the void. Confronted by a potential threat, Saudi Arabia undertook its first large-scale effort to expand its military. The 1973 Arab-Israeli War, and the subsequent oil embargo, gave the Kingdom the wherewithal to fund its purchases. Military purchases from the United States totaled only $45 million in 1970; three years later they were $1.15 billion. Security purchases from all suppliers rose from $839 million in 1972 to $6.51 billion in 1975, $13 billion in 1978, and $20.58 billion in 1980. Overall, more than $250 billion was spent during the boom on the military and defense-related projects.[14] The boom period saw the signing of billion-dollar contracts for military bases, aircraft, warships, tanks, and other weaponry. Even in 1984, when the boom was quickly fading into recession, Saudi military expenditures remained high, both at the per capita level and as a percentage of gross national product (GNP) (see Table 4.1).

For 1984, Saudi military expenditures were estimated by the International Institute for Strategic Studies at $20.70 billion, compared to

$5.2 billion for Israel, and $142.70 billion for the United States. Per capita expenditure was said to total $2,518 in Saudi Arabia, $1,333 in Israel, and $644 in the United States. As a percentage of GNP, Saudi military expenditures totaled 18 percent, compared to the United States' 6 percent and Israel's 23 percent.[15] The high rate of spending continued up to Operation Desert Storm. For the period 1986–1990, Saudi Arabia ranked sixth in the world in military expenditures as percentage of overall government spending with 32 percent (Yugoslavia with 53 percent was first, followed by Sudan with 47 percent; Israel ranked eleventh with 26 percent; the United States was fourteenth with 25 percent). The Kingdom ranked fourth in the world in 1989 for military expenditures as percentage of gross national product with 19.8 percent (Nicaragua was first with 28.3 percent; Iraq ranked second with 23.0 percent; Israel was fourteenth with 9.2 percent); it ranked second in the world as regards per capita military expenditures with $1,313 compared to first-place Israel with $1,335. The United States was third with $1,204.

Ironically, Saudi Arabia's huge military buildup was initially not centered on weapons at all. For the first few years of the boom, defense spending was concentrated on building the necessary infrastructure such as roads, housing, bases, and hospitals.[16] The defense budget for 1975 is indicative; of the billions of dollars allocated, 85 percent was spent on infrastructure.[17] Among the purchases for the year was a huge $1 billion order for furniture that the Ministry of Defense gave one North Carolina firm.[18] Defense allocations also covered a wide gamut of undertakings, including the construction of the Saudi-Bahraini Causeway, started in response to an abortive Iranian-backed coup against the Manama government. Even more expensive than the causeway was the ministry's immense marble headquarters in Riyadh, complete with underground bunkers able to withstand nuclear attack. The price tag was a reported $1 billion.

In their buildup, the Kingdom's planners opted for a simple defense strategy: to trade space for time in order to seek foreign help. To deter foreign incursions as well as guard against the concentration of too many army troops near the capital and other major population centers —the al-Saud had learned from the mistake of Libya's King Idris— major bases were constructed far from the Kingdom's main population centers and on each of the three most likely avenues of invasion. The largest undertaking was the King Khalid Military City (KKMC) at

Hafr al-Batin in the desolate northeastern corner of Saudi Arabia near Iraq and Kuwait. KKMC sits astride the route that any invading army from the north would have to take in order to reach the country's oil-rich al-Hasa.[19] The SR 18 billion (U.S. $4.8 billion) complex was built under supervision of the U.S. Army Corps of Engineers. From the air, it resembles a large octagon in an uncluttered sandbox. Designed to house three brigades and their dependents for a population of more than 50,000, KKMC is a heavily armed military base complete with water and power supplies, homes, mosques, maintenance facilities, and a hospital.

A second military city is located at the northwest corner of the country near Tabuk. Intended to guard the country against possible incursions from Israel, Jordan, or Egypt, the Tabuk military complex contains an air base, paratroopers, commandos, and half of the Kingdom's heavy armor. Any invader from the northwest would also risk entrapment between the Red Sea and mountain escarpment if he proceeded toward the important cities of Yanbu, Medina, Mecca, and Jeddah. The third major base is in the south, near the Yemeni border at Khamis Mushayt. There, invaders can only proceed along two easily defended land routes guarded by two mechanized brigades and armored units. Several air bases are also located in the Asir to provide support. Deteriorating relations with Yemen and Jordan, however, have prompted the Kingdom's military planners to consider erecting two other multi-billion-dollar military cities near Jizan and Medina. Plans appear to have been delayed, however, by the Kingdom's budgetary crunch.[20]

Besides building a basic infrastructure, the Kingdom also spent billions of dollars on foreign weaponry as part of its military policy of deterrence. Possession of the most up-to-date weaponry, noted one Western military expert, was given top priority so as to send "a message to Saudi Arabia's neighbors."[21] Still, most of the Kingdom's purchases have remained underutilized. Arms purchases were also another method of redistributing the sudden windfall in petrodollars. Bribes and "commissions" rocketed. This pattern was established from the beginning. An order for Lockheed C–130 transport aircraft set well-known arms merchant Adnan Khashoggi on the path toward wealth.[22] Khashoggi had no qualms about representing rival companies, and among his clients he counted Lockheed, Raytheon, Rolls-Royce, and Marconi. Khashoggi, who got his start as a commercial middleman, led Northrop and Lockheed executives through the maze of Saudi royal intrigue. By the end of the 1970s, Khashoggi had earned $106 million from Lockheed, and another $54 million from Northrop. Representing a French firm netted him another $45 million on armored cars.

Nor was Khashoggi the exception to the rule. During U.S. congressional investigations into the Lockheed and Northrop influence-buying scandals, the Senate was astounded to learn how Saudi generals as well as princes pressed around the "commission" trough. Among their number was Prince Sultan bin Abdulaziz, the current defense and aviation minister whose insistence on commissions gained him the unflattering sobriquet of "Prince Five Percent."[23] Overall, several billion dollars worth of the Kingdom's defense budget is said to have ended up in the hands of top princes, generals, colonels, and majors. Despite Saudi government moves to end the practice, it seems likely that it continues. In 1991, a former United Technologies (UT) employee filed a lawsuit against his employer, alleging that UT paid two Saudi princes several million dollars to secure a helicopter contract. The suit also alleged that the Saudi ambassador to Washington, Prince Bandar bin Sultan bin Abdulaziz (son of the defense minister), was the middleman.[24]

Saudi Arabia's recession put only a small dent in the country's defense and security spending. Budgeted defense expenditures declined slightly, although defense outlays as a percentage of overall expenditures stayed approximately the same. However, the Saudis had no choice but to set priorities, and insist on more competitive terms. Bidding for subsequent defense contracts became more spirited. Besides insisting that major defense purchases include offset investment programs, the Saudis also pushed for innovative financing, including oil barter deals, as the recession continued. The first such "austerity" deal occurred in 1986 when the British won a $7.5 billion award (which was later supplemented by another $15 billion order) for Tornado fighters, trainers, missiles, and auxiliary services. In return, the Saudis agreed to supply British Aerospace (BA), the chief contractor, with 400,000 barrels of crude per day. However, the deal's success was uneven: as oil prices fell, Saudi payments fell far short of BA's timetable of deliveries, and the Ministry of Finance eventually had to arrange a loan to cover the shortfall.[25]

Table 4.2

RSAF and SALF Major Aircraft, 1993

Aircraft	Present number	Ordered/ Intent on buying
McDonnel Douglas F–15	80	72
Panavia Tornado (ground attack)	48	48
Panavia Tornado (interceptor)	24	—
Northrop F–5	105	—
British Aerospace Hawk (trainer and combat versions)	30	60
Pilatus (propeller trainer)	30	30
Lockheed C–140 (heavy cargo)	2	—
Lockheed C–130 (cargo)	63	—
Lockheed C–130 (tanker)	6	—
Lockheed C–130 (hospital)	3	—
KC–3 (tanker)	8	—
Boeing EC–3A (AWACS)	5	4
Westland helicopters	—	90
Bell Scouts helicopters	—	15
Apache AH–64 attack helicopters	—	36
Cessna 172 light transports	12	—

Source: Western embassies.

Service Overview

Prior to the Iraqi invasion of Kuwait, the Saudi armed forces had less than 100,000 men under arms, excluding paramilitary and special Ministry of Interior forces. The Saudi armed forces are divided into five main units: the Royal Saudi Air Force, the Royal Saudi Navy, the Royal Saudi Army, the Saudi National Guard, and Ministry of Interior Forces.

The Royal Saudi Air Force

The Royal Saudi Air Force (RSAF) has always been the favored service in the military establishment, and it is the only service with offensive capabilities. Not only has the RSAF received the bulk of military expenditures, but its forces are also the best equipped and best trained (see Table 4.2). Its personnel is also heavily sprinkled with members of the al-Saud. The 15,000-man RSAF has traditionally had the strongest ties with its American counterpart. Saudi pilots train in the United

States, and the two forces also coordinate their strategies. This link, however, has come at a price: the RSAF has also been the most coup-prone service in the Kingdom.

The RSAF's defensive role is anchored by a sophisticated, multilayered air defense system. The system's eyes are five American-built Boeing EC–3A Airborne Warning and Control System (AWACS) jets, which were obtained in 1981 after a bruising battle in the United States Senate. The sale of the AWACS fulfilled several objectives: besides giving the Saudis an early warning defense system, it also gave the United States Air Force an important listening post in the Gulf without having to establish an official base.[26] Much of the overall $8.9 billion package, in fact, was spent on developing infrastructure and command centers.[27] The AWACS are also tied in to the Saudi air defense system through the so-called Peace Shield program, which is a Command, Communications, Control, and Intelligence (C3I) system designed to link the Saudi air defense systems together.

The AWACS's 350-mile radar sweep gives the Saudis a critical fifteen-minute warning before enemy aircraft can hit their coastal oil and water installations. This allows them to orient their air defense systems to face the threat. The outermost layer of air defense is the F–15 Eagle, which the Saudis initially obtained in 1978 despite strenuous Israeli opposition. The Kingdom eventually purchased sixty-two F–15s with the proviso that they not be based at Tabuk, near the Israeli border. Prior to Operation Desert Storm, the Saudis reportedly had more than eighty F–15s, augmented through the ample purchase of replacement machines.[28] Saudi Arabia has also ordered seventy-two F–15Ss, a slightly downgraded version of the F–15E.

In addition to the F–15s, the Saudis have twenty-four air defense/interceptor variants of the Panavia Tornado fighters, which have a longer flight endurance than the F–15s, and nearly as much speed. According to Saudi sources, the Tornado interceptor variants are not particularly well liked. These two-man craft place great demands on manpower, and their Rolls-Royce engines suffer from accelerated wear. The next line of defense consists of the Northrop F–5E fighter. These supersonic aircraft have a combat radius of 1,056 km. The RSAF now has sixty-five F–5Es, twenty-four F–5Fs, and sixteen F–5Bs. The Saudis' British-made Hawk trainers can also carry armament in a pinch, can fly at Mach .88, and have a combat radius similar to that of the F–5E.

If an intruder evades the interceptors, he confronts several lines of missile defenses. First are the Patriot missiles, which have not only anti-missile but anti-aircraft capabilities as well. Eight units of Patriots with 300 missiles are currently in place, and the Kingdom has confirmed another order for an additional thirteen batteries with 761 missiles.[29] They are followed by improved Hawk missiles that can hit aircraft at altitudes up to 16,000 meters at a range of 40 kilometers. The next line of defense uses the Shahine, which is an improved version of the French Crotale missile. This weapon was acquired in a unique deal, which permitted the Saudis to fund the development of the missile while retaining certain rights to it. The Shahines have a range of 15 kilometers, and can hit aircraft at a height of up to 6,800 meters. The mobile Shahines can be shifted to high threat areas. The final defense system consists of Swiss Oerlikon anti-aircraft guns, and French 30-millimeter twin anti-aircraft guns, with an approximate range of 3,500 meters. The Saudis also possess Stinger shoulder-fired anti-aircraft missiles for close-in defense.

Billions of dollars notwithstanding, the Saudi air defense system is not perfect, and has had several glaring failures. In 1982, a defecting Iranian F–4 Phantom jet capable of carrying 9.75 tons of bombs passed over Ras Tanura on its way to Dhahran. It landed as the Kingdom's F–5s were taking off. That same year, a defecting Iran Air Boeing 707 crossed the Gulf and Saudi Arabia, and landed at Cairo, undetected by the AWACS aircraft.[30]

Besides providing aerial defense, the air force's other job is to transport army units across the vast Saudi country. It has a fleet of C–130 transport planes, a number of which are configured as aerial tankers. Several more are configured as flying hospitals. Only two C–140s can carry heavier combat vehicles. It takes the Saudi army a week to ten days to concentrate significant forces on a front. During an outbreak of fighting between the Yemens in 1979, the Kingdom had to request U.S. Air Force C–5As to redeploy tanks to the southern border.[31]

The RSAF gained a new dimension in 1988 with the purchase of Dong Feng Oh intermediate-range ballistic missiles from the People's Republic of China. The missiles, which can carry a one-ton conventional or unconventional weapon, were purchased ostensibly to counter the growing Iranian missile capability. The fifty-plus missiles, which are based south of Riyadh near al-Sulayyil and al-Kharj, were purchased and installed without American knowledge, and allegedly through the offices of Saudi ambassador to Washington Bandar. They were discovered by chance by an American nurse wandering through the desert, who reported her find to the embassy. The missiles themselves are not considered militarily effective due to their inaccuracy, but they do give the Kingdom a retaliatory option that does not risk Saudi manpower. Given the Saudi desire to acquire nuclear technology —preliminary negotiations have been proceeding between Riyadh and Bonn over the sale of a small nuclear reactor since 1987—the missiles could also conceivably carry nuclear weapons.[32]

The RSAF's facilities are far larger than the air force's actual needs. Although all of this seems like overbuying, the Saudis are mindful that their equipment and bases can be used by allies in the event of emergencies. This is exactly what occurred during Operation Desert Storm, when American, French, British, and other Allied aircraft used Saudi bases with ease. Despite protestations to the contrary, Saudi Arabia has become the West's "aircraft carrier" in the Gulf, and has been used as a staging area for sorties against Iraq since the conclusion of the war.[33] Allied aircraft are currently based at Dhahran, Taif, Riyadh, and Khamis Mushayt.

The Royal Saudi Navy

Saudi Arabia's most pressing strategic concern is free access to the seas. On the Persian Gulf, the Kingdom is threatened by Iranian closure of the Straits of Hormuz. The problem is a significant one, as witnessed during the Iran–Iraq War, as well as the ongoing Iranian–United Arab Emirates (UAE) contretemps over control of the strategic Tumbs Islands and Abu Musa (see Chapter 3). Saudi access to the Red Sea is also conditional, with Egypt, Yemen, and Eritrea controlling the chokepoints. The Royal Saudi Navy (RSN) was founded to counter those threats.

Although the Kingdom is a massive peninsula surrounded by water, its people, excluding some pearlers and fishermen, do not have a maritime tradition. Nonetheless, billions of dollars have been invested in the RSN. Americans designed the RSN's main bases in Jeddah and Jubail. France supplied the Kingdom's largest ships, four Medina-class frigates more advanced than any in the French navy. The 2,600-ton frigates are armed with Otomat missiles, Crotale naval SAMs, and automatic 100-millimeter cannon. The $3.45 billion frigate deal also supplied two "Durance"-class oilers, twenty-four missile-armed Dauphin helicopters, and shore defense missile systems. The RSN also has three

Jaguar fast-attack patrol craft, fifty-three coastal patrol boats, six landing craft, and four small minesweepers.[34] The RSN also placed orders for six Sandowne-class minesweepers as part of the al-Yamamah deal. As of 1993, one had already been delivered and two others were being built.

The 9,500-man RSN, whose numbers include 1,500 marines, is considering the purchase of perhaps three more heavier frigates. Canada, for instance, is exploring the possibility of selling three 4,600-ton Halifax-class frigates. France has also signed a $4 billion preliminary agreement for the supply of three Sawari-class frigates of approximately 3,200-ton displacement. Two more distant arms acquisitions will be naval patrol aircraft and submarines. The candidates for patrol craft are the American Orion PC-3, and France's as yet unbuilt Atlantique II. The Saudi desire to acquire submarines seems more predicated on prestige than actual need. A submarine deal, if consummated, could cost upward of $4 billion, and include six to eight submarines, bases, and support facilities. The Saudis seemed on the verge of making such a purchase in 1987, and boats from the Netherlands, Germany, France, and the United Kingdom were said to be in the running. However, negotiations were never finalized. Renewed interest in submarines resurfaced in late 1992 when Iran announced its purchase of one Russian Kilo-type submarine and its order of two more. In addition, the Gulf's supposed inability to support submarines was disproved in October 1992 with the entrance of American and Iranian submarines.[35]

The RSN is dependent, as the other services are, on foreign maintenance, and seems to be the least effective of the Kingdom's armed forces. Of the two frigates stationed at Jubail, one almost never leaves the mouth of the base harbor, and the other usually patrols within eyesight of the coast. The same is true for the frigates based in the Red Sea. As long as it keeps its eye on the land, the RSN is unlikely to evolve into an effective force with a high esprit de corps.

The Royal Saudi Army

The modern Royal Saudi Army (SALF) is an outgrowth of the Hejazi troops Abdulaziz inherited in 1925. Comprised largely of town dwellers, the army was essentially established after the unification of the Kingdom, and played no part in its creation. Abdulaziz immediately decommissioned the army following the Yemeni conflict of 1934. Oil wealth brought a resurgence in its numbers, and by 1951 it stood at 7,500–8,000.[36] Today, the army numbers approximately 50,000 men, slightly larger than the Saudi National Guard (SANG). The SALF possesses armor units, paratroop units, artillery detachments, and air defense artillery (anti-aircraft) units. It is loosely organized along the American model.

The Saudi army is a defensive force, and currently has 550 main battle tanks, of which 250 are U.S.-built M–60 A3s and 300 are French AMX–30s. The Saudis have also ordered 465 M–1A1 and 235 M–1A2 tanks, which provide the tank commander the same thermal imaging sights possessed by the gunner.[37] Overall, the Saudis seem intent on bringing SALF's tank strength to 1,200 even though they lack the personnel to staff more than a third. SALF's mechanized infantry units employ 600 U.S.-built M–113 Armored Personnel Carriers (APCs) plus 250 French AMX–10P tracked APCs. They also have over 400 of the new Bradley Infantry Combat Vehicles, and have ordered 200 more. Defense sources told the authors that the Saudis will be unable to use all the new weapons, and will store the surplus for use by their allies should another invasion take place. This allows them to pre-position war matériel without appearing to grant the Americans bases. The Saudis are also interested in the Multiple Launch Missile System used by the U.S. Army's artillery.

Despite modern weaponry, the effectiveness of the SALF remains questionable. The quality of its volunteers remains low, and training and motivation lag. Making recruitment even more difficult is the fact that few Saudis want to serve at SALF's three main bases—Tabuk, Hafr al-Batin, and Khamis Mushayt—all far from the Kingdom's main population centers.

Saudi National Guard

The Saudi National Guard (SANG) is a combination of national army and tribal subsidy. SANG is the only Saudi military arm that has native roots; it evolved from Ikhwan remnants as well as tribal levies. It is not a reserve force in the mold of the U.S. National Guard, but a full-time force, wholly independent of the Ministry of Defense, with its own logistics, weaponry, and organization. This is because SANG's mission is not so much to deter foreign aggression as it is to provide internal security. Its troops protect sensitive domestic installations such as desalination plants, oil facilities, and power stations. The guard has also been used to quell domestic disturbances, such as the Mecca uprising and Shiite rioting in 1979, and the Mecca riots in 1987.[38]

SANG has an authorized strength of 35,000–45,000 although its combat strength may be as few as 18,000–25,000. Full-time guardsmen are said to number 10,000. SANG has several distinct units, distinguished from each other by their uniforms. The regular, full-time SANG soldiers wear dark-green fatigues, with the red-checkered "Ghutra" headdress. Some of the modernized unit soldiers wear red berets. The Liwa units, consisting of men that can be mobilized by tribal leaders for service, wear a more traditional Arabian *thobe,* or robe, with crossed bandoleers. Many Liwa are equipped by the Kingdom with old rifles, but many others have personal AK–47s. These men have no established transport system, and are mustered when needed by their tribal sheikhs. The Firqa nonmodernized units, whose members dress similarly to their Liwa counterparts, use trucks for transportation, and are light infantry, with little organic fire support and heavy weapons. Firqa units are organized along tribal lines and guard installations and embassies. They come from Bedouin tribes and are considered less vulnerable than townsmen to subversion.

SANG's modernized brigades were established under a U.S.-Saudi agreement. As early as 1971, the United States was invited to assess the role of SANG, and two years later an agreement was signed to arm and train the guard. A private firm, the Vinnell Corporation of Fairfax, Virginia, was given the supervisory contract.[39] SANG's two New Brigades are light mechanized units. Rather than using maintenance-heavy tracked machines, the New Brigades use wheeled armored cars, including the venerable Cadillac Gage V–150 and 1,100 new General Motors armored vehicles. However, the former may soon be replaced by the Swiss-Austrian Mowag amphibious wheeled carrier chosen by the U.S. Marine Corps. Most of the Gages mount .50-caliber machine guns, but others carry Vulcan anti-aircraft guns, TOW anti-tank missiles, or 90-mm high-velocity anti-tank guns. Each brigade has an anti-armor platoon. The First Brigade also uses 105-mm howitzers, while the Second uses the 155-mm howitzer.

Regardless of the weaponry, the guard has purchased new systems at a slower pace than SALF and has opted for simplicity.[40] In spite of this, or perhaps because of it, the guard's performance during Desert

Storm was rated better than that of the army. Like the other services, training remains problematic as many recruits are illiterate while others have low levels of education. The relative lack of sophistication of the guardsmen is best illustrated by the special videos officers use to acquaint soldiers and their families to housing on bases. The films describe how to use toilets, washing machines, lights, and refrigerators. The videos also discourage cooking on the floors of the houses and encourage the use of stoves.

Although SANG has proven resistant to foreign ideologies, it has nonetheless been prone to infection by Islamic fundamentalism. The group of zealots who seized the Great Mosque in Mecca in 1979 included a number of the supposedly reliable National Guard, and some guardsmen reportedly funneled arms to the rebels as well. There is also the question of SANG's close identification with Crown Prince Abdullah bin Abdulaziz. Abdullah is so possessive of SANG and the political strength it gives him that he refused to surrender it upon being named crown prince. By contrast, the current monarch, King Fahd bin Abdulaziz, gave up the Ministry of Interior portfolio when he became crown prince. Abdullah's refusal, due to the fact that he had no full brother to whom to pass SANG, created a succession crisis that was only defused with the mediation of Morocco's King Hassan II.[41] Abdullah's control of SANG also gives his family important business contracts. For example, SANG uses Austrian trucks made by Steyr, a company that Abdullah represents. The unit's officers also drive Ford Crown Victorias, because the agent for Ford happens to be Abdullah's son, former SANG Brigadier General Prince Miteb bin Abdullah bin Abdulaziz.

Ministry of Interior Forces

Although not a military force per se, the units of the Saudi Ministry of Interior form an important bulwark in the Kingdom's security system. Besides the police forces (traffic, criminal, and prison), Ministry of Interior forces also include the Royal Guard, the *mubaheth*, or secret police, the Coast Guard, and frontier forces. All report directly to Prince Naif bin Abdulaziz, Fahd's full brother. Another full brother, Prince Ahmad bin Abdulaziz, is the deputy minister.

The Royal Guard numbers approximately 2,000 and is charged with protecting the king and royal family. Formed in 1955 by Saud, following the discovery of a coup attempt, the Royal Guard is heavily armed and semi-independent. The *mubaheth* are the Kingdom's political police, charged with protecting the regime from internal enemies. The exact size of the force is unknown. Their success also seems uneven: the *mubaheth* failed to detect the Mecca uprising and have been unable to counter the growth of fundamentalists opposed to the regime. Smaller Interior Ministry units are the Saudi Coast Guard, which is armed with helicopters and eight SRN–6 hovercraft, and the frontier forces, which patrol the borders and handle customs inspections. Overall, the ministry's paramilitary forces total approximately 10,500 men.

The ministry's most important force may be the *mujahidoun*, or fighters. This shadowy adjunct of 40,000 armed men is a secret, plain-clothes reserve available at an instant. They are recruited from direct descendants of Abdulaziz's men and report once a month for their pay. They silently watch at night over sensitive locations in the Kingdom's main cities, such as banks and telephone exchanges. The organization's headquarters is a broad, three-story concrete building behind a ten-foot-high iron fence. Its sign, contrary to other government offices, is written only in Arabic. *Mujahidoun* report directly to the interior minister and are only vaguely known by the general public.

The Ministry of Interior's police state apparatus took shape during the reign of Faisal, who oversaw a general crackdown after several aborted coup attempts. The ministry exercises wide control over the lives of both Saudis and expatriates. Controls on the latter include the need for permission to travel between cities, perform the hajj, buy cars, or leave the country. When the ministry works in concert with the *mutawaeen* (which it often does), no personal habit is above investigation. Its wiretapping program is extensive. Sources at Saudi Telecom say the Philips-Ericsson telephone system was designed with ministry wiretapping in mind.

Naif has augmented government control with a large American-built computer system. The National Information Center (NIC) was built by Computer Services Corporation (CSC) of the United States at a cost of over $300 million. Three supercomputers keep files on every citizen, visitor, or alien resident in the Kingdom. The computer maintains records divided into driver's licenses, hajj pilgrims, vehicle registrations, visas, passports, and *dafatir al iqama,* or work permits. It maintains criminal records, foreign worker registrations, applications by foreigners for visas, and their passport information. The computer also maintains the *mumnuween* (forbidden) file. When a person's name is entered into this category, usually for opposition to the regime, he or she is subjected to unending bureaucratic delays and problems. The computer is part Big Brother, part needed modernization, as the manual system it replaced was exceedingly inefficient and documents were often lost or misplaced.

In addition to the NIC, the Ministry of Interior has taken delivery of French command centers linked to helicopters equipped with television cameras and audio systems. These will film riots and other disturbances and transmit the information to the command center. The first such center was built for Eastern Province Governor Prince Mohammed bin Fahd bin Abdulaziz, whose province contains the Kingdom's Shiite population. The ministry has also taken delivery of a Japanese fingerprint storage computer.

Operation Desert Storm and Its Aftermath

Saudi Arabia's armed forces never received a full chance to prove their mettle during the Kuwaiti crisis. First, they were never mustered to come to the aid of the emirate despite the defense stipulations found in the Gulf Cooperation Council (GCC) accord. They also assumed a secondary role following the arrival of hundreds of thousands of Allied troops. The inability of the Saudi armed forces to offer at least some deterrence was the result of years of interservice rivalry and a confusing system of checks and counter-checks implemented to forestall potential coups.

The weakness of the Saudi command structure was manifested within days of the Iraqi invasion. Civilian commanders, as the first Allied officers discovered, often lacked the necessary clout to make or follow through on decisions. Allied requests for water, supplies, and fuel—all things promised by Fahd when he issued his invitation to allied troops—were tied up in bureaucracy. As his top Saudi generals told their counterparts, "We want to help, but we're not authorized to spend the money."[42] Conditions only improved once a royal commander, Lieutenant General Prince Khalid bin Sultan bin Abdulaziz, was appointed to head the Saudi and Arab forces. Even Khalid had troubles with his own command structure, often making agreements to pay for different contracts, and then belatedly realizing that he himself was unable to deliver.[43]

The combat readiness of the Saudi armed forces was also uneven.

The RSAF was considered the best, but the SALF was a different matter. "You must help with my ground forces," Prince Khalid told Operation Desert Storm Commander General H. Norman Schwartzkopf within days of the latter's arrival in the Kingdom. "They are in terrible shape."[44] SALF faced several problems. First and foremost was its complete lack of logistical services, including mechanical, technical, medical, and cooking units. Instead, SALF relied on civilian contractors to meet most of its logistical needs. This dependence on civilian contractors severely restricted its mobility and kept it tied to its bases, impacting its combat effectiveness. One of the more telling anecdotes in Schwartzkopf's memoirs involves Prince Khalid, who asked within weeks of the Iraqi invasion, "Where can we buy field kitchens? We need to be able to feed our troops."[45]

Training was also lacking. One Saudi tank commander on the Kuwaiti border found twenty-four of his group of twenty-eight M–60 tanks inoperable after a few weeks of duty and bitterly complained, "The Americans have sold us defective equipment. All my tanks are broken." Closer inspection showed that the tanks had only needed a change in air filters, a job that American tank drivers do themselves. SALF tank captains, however, were unaware of the simple operation and instead took their tanks out of action, waiting for them to be "repaired" by a civilian contractor.[46]

Once actual hostilities broke out, some Saudi forces proved exemplary. An air force pilot earned fame by shooting down two Iraqi jets, and Saudi jets flew 6 percent of the thousands of sorties against Iraq.[47] The battle for al-Khafji produced the war's second Saudi hero, a SANG tribesman who used anti-tank missiles to destroy several Iraqi armored vehicles while he and his unit were under fire. These cases of individual bravery could not erase the fact that SALF was unable to retake al-Khafji after Iraqi armor first stormed the town. Their failure was so glaring that Fahd wanted to bomb al-Khafji to oblivion to prevent the Iraqis from holding any Saudi territory. When fighting took place, the more lightly armed SANG outperformed the SALF and proved far more flexible in adapting to the rigors of war. Along with Qatari units, it spearheaded the recapture of al-Khafji, although some reports claim that most of the fighting was done by Pakistanis.[48]

Schwartzkopf noted that the Saudi leadership and armed forces manifested little desire to go on the offensive. At various times, the Kingdom's political and military commands suggested the best way to liberate Kuwait was to launch an attack against Iraq via Turkey. The latter opinion was probably an indication of both the state of the Saudi armed forces, as well as the cultural difficulties experienced by many Arabs in the Allied coalition in reconciling themselves to a campaign against a fellow Arab country. However, the willingness of the Kingdom's forces to go into battle improved once Riyadh and al-Hasa were subjected to SCUD attacks.

When the offensive was launched to liberate Kuwait, the performance of Saudi armed forces was mixed. On the coast, SANG and some army units performed well and quickly secured their objectives. However, the Saudi forces on the central invasion route were slow off the mark according to U.S. advisors. Their sluggishness was such that Schwartzkopf had to threaten Khalid that if the Arab forces, which included the Saudi and Egyptian units, did not speed up their attack, he would send in the U.S. Marines to liberate Kuwait City.[49] The American assessment of both Schwartzkopf and other American officers was later disputed by the Saudi side.[50]

There were other trouble spots, as well. Some RSAF pilots refused to fly sorties during the conflict, and there were several defections as well. The first occurred three months after the Iraqi invasion, when a Saudi pilot fled with his F–15 to Sudan rather than fight against Iraq.[51] When actual hostilities began in early 1991, French radio reported the defection of five Saudis with their aircraft to Amman, while another unconfirmed report had several Saudi pilots flying to Yemen. American military sources also reported that desertion was fairly high among the SALF but not SANG. In addition, certain units showed questionable political reliability, especially in fighting against a brother Arab country. Twice, Allied servicemen were fired on by unknown Saudi assailants.[52] Other developments were just as disturbing: after the conflict, both SALF and SANG personnel began growing beards to show their solidarity with fundamentalists opposed to the al-Saud. Anti-regime tracts also appeared among some units.[53]

The Iraqi invasion of Kuwait brought immediate changes to the Saudi armed forces. Within days of the Iraqi invasion of Kuwait, the al-Saud announced plans to double the size of SALF, and the king called for volunteers, even suggesting he was considering conscription. Enlistment rules for SANG were changed as well. Previously, it had followed quotas to prevent specific tribes from dominating the organization. Those quotas were abolished, and the organization was also

Table 4.3

Selected Saudi Arms Expenditures, 1991–1993

Year	Weapon system	Cost (U.S. $ billion)
1991	Patriot missiles	3.30
1991	AWACS maintenance	0.35
1992	72 F–15s with missiles	9.00
1992	362 Hellfire missiles	0.61
1992	F–15 training and support	0.50
1992	M–1A tanks and armored carriers	3.00
1992	Strategic Reserve Program	4.00
1993	SANG technical support	0.82
1993	Hawk and Patriot missile support	0.58
1993	48 Tornados	7.00

Source: Western embassies.

opened to townspeople for the first time in its history.[54] By October, more than 170,000 Saudis had volunteered for military training, overwhelming training facilities.[55]

Besides laying the foundation for a larger force, the Saudi government also undertook a round of arms buying and arms-related expenditures. Less than six weeks after the invasion, the Kingdom announced plans to purchase up to $20 billion worth of new American weapons, including tanks, aircraft, personnel carriers, and support services (see Table 4.3). The Saudis also decided to invest more than $4 billion in the Strategic Reserve Program. The latter's contractors are Swedish firms Skanska AB and ABV, who will build hardened oil and refined product storage facilities in underground caverns. Like the al-Yamamah Tornado deal, this will be paid for by oil barter.[56] By mid-1993, the Saudis had placed orders for more than $30 billion worth of American arms, the result, as one American official noted, of Bandar's going on a "binge."[57] Many of the purchases have since been delayed or postponed given the Kingdom's financial crunch and the fact that Saudi payments to the United States have fallen into arrears. Rather than taking action, the Pentagon has continued to allow Saudi Arabia to place orders on preferential terms despite increasing doubts as to the Kingdom's financial strength (see Chapter 5). The latest such incidence occurred in January 1994, when the Clinton administration gave the go-ahead for a Saudi restructuring of nearly $10 billion worth of arms debt in order to allow Riyadh to purchase more than $6 billion worth of civilian airliners.

In the first blush of the Iraqi action, the Kingdom reiterated the need for greater inter-GCC cooperation, and even supported a plan from Oman's Sultan Qaboos to create a 100,000-man Peninsula Shield Force to be stationed at Hafr al-Batin. But with the defeat of the Iraqi forces in late February, calls for greater military cooperation within the organization lost their urgency. By December 1991, the proposal for the Peninsula Shield Force was killed, following Saudi pressure.[58]

Today, greater GCC military cooperation seems unlikely, given the overall uncertainty regarding the organization itself (see Chapter 3). Saudi Arabia and the other GCC members are unlikely to support any plan that would take money from their own military developments, especially given the number of rivalries. This latter impediment has grown with the recent round of Saudi-Qatari border skirmishes and an intensification of the Qatari-Bahraini border dispute (see Chapter 3).

On paper, a unified GCC force could be potent. The GCC has nearly 1,000 tanks and nearly 300 jet fighters. These numbers are also growing rapidly. Since the conclusion of the Iraqi debacle, the GCC countries have ordered more than $40 billion worth of arms. Included in this are more than 1,000 tanks and a similar number of armored vehicles, an armor buildup military analysts call the largest since World War II.[59] The GCC's buildup has also forced other powers in the region, especially Iran, to accelerate their own acquisitions. However, there remains no synchronization in arms purchases among the GCC members, despite calls in favor. This lack of coordination is a waste of resources, as Oman, Bahrain, Qatar, Kuwait, and the United Arab Emirates (UAE) all face critical diseconomies of scale given the relatively small size of their individual forces. While common military purchases would make a lot of sense from the standpoint of cost, spare parts, and training, few steps have been taken in this direction. So far, the closest coordination of purchases took place when Qatar bought Mirage F–1s because Kuwait had them. Several GCC countries also have U.S.-built Hawk SAMs and Patriots.

Greater GCC military cooperation with Egypt and Syria in the so-called Damascus Declaration also seems to be a dead letter. Announced at the end of hostilities, the Damascus Declaration provided a sketchy framework for the placement of Syrian and Egyptian troops in the GCC region under a combined military command. Enthusiasm for the idea quickly faded due to financial concerns as well as GCC leeriness about exposing their troops to Egyptian and particularly Syrian influences. Instead, the GCC states have shown a marked preference for signing bilateral defense pacts with the United States. As of 1993, Kuwait, Bahrain, and Qatar all had defensive treaties with the United States. The Kingdom, however, has refused to sign any such accord, or other memos outlining Saudi-American military cooperation. Instead, Riyadh seems to prefer the existing informal arrangements, especially given fundamentalist opposition to close Saudi-American ties.

Remaining Difficulties

The Saudi armed forces are facing several challenges in the aftermath of Operation Desert Storm. Recruitment of quality men remains a problem, especially given plans to raise the number of Saudi men under arms to more than 200,000. At present, service in the Saudi military is voluntary, as the royal family wants no disaffected class in the army. The government has considered conscription, and Fahd occasionally mentions the idea in public. Yet while Defense and Aviation Minister Sultan thinks it is a good idea, SANG Commander Abdullah thinks it would introduce undesirable elements in the military forces. The result is that the idea continues to languish. The need, military analysts point out, is for better-educated servicemen, rather than substantially higher numbers. Recruitment of quality people lags as military careers in the Kingdom offer little prestige. Although soldiers are relatively well paid and granted free housing, the Kingdom's military tradition is a young and checkered one.

A second challenge is to maintain the loyalty of the armed forces. The government has adopted several strategies to combat insurrections since the coup-ridden 1950s and 1960s. For example, the government draws recruits for its different branches from different pools of manpower, making it difficult for any one group to spread its tentacles through several different services at one time. Townspeople dominate the RSAF, SALF, and RSN. Asiris are most numerous in the police and internal security forces, and tribesmen comprise SANG. Army bases have been established far from population centers to guard against coups. Air bases are generally located near cities so SANG forces can be airlifted in to easily deal with uprisings. Communication between the services is kept to a minimum, to the point that they seldom share maps or other mundane information.[60] This keeps the military inherently inefficient but also makes it less able to turn upon its masters.

The Saudi armed forces also contain special bureaus or sections to ferret out potential insurgences, with the coup-prone RSAF having two.[61] In addition, the al-Saud protects itself by having hundreds of princes in the armed services where they keep an eye on the rank and file.[62] The flip side of this is that princely officers are seldom permitted to rise above a certain rank. Otherwise, their presence could antagonize the commoners in the armed forces. The Saudi commander of Operation Desert Storm, Lt. General Khalid, son of the defense minister, was promoted after the conclusion of Operation Desert Storm only to resign a few months later. Some sources said he had grown too ambitious, and wanted to be named chief of staff, a position reserved for commoners.[63]

Training remains problematic. Given the Kingdom's reliance on high-technology weapons, many of its recruits are overwhelmed. Many Saudi volunteers are illiterate or have only a primary education (see Chapter 6). Not surprisingly, technology often exceeds the skill levels of many recruits, lending some basis to the argument that the Kingdom's defense establishment might be in better straits today if less money had been spent on high-tech weapons and more on education and health.

Tangential to training is the intensive maintenance most Saudi weapons systems require to remain operational in the harsh desert conditions. For example, the RSAF suffers from constant maintenance problems. Its F–15 is a match for any other aircraft in the region, but only if the ground crew keeps it in the air. It takes eighty men to keep one F–15 flying, compared to forty for the F–5. The Kingdom's intermediate-range ballistic missiles similarly require hundreds of technicians. A second problem is the breadth of weaponry in the Saudi arsenal, due to the refusal of the United States to provide the Kingdom with all its weapon needs. For example, the RSAF flies not only American aircraft but British and Swiss planes as well, putting additional pressure on its maintenance teams. The result is that most of the Kingdom's maintenance work is done by contract labor, which entails political considerations.

Expatriates are also hired in support and combat roles. More than

20,000 Pakistani mercenaries were hired in 1980, about half of whom were used in armored combat units stationed outside Tabuk, and the other half in support roles. In 1987, they went home. Unsubstantiated stories said the Saudis insisted on their departure due to the fact that many of the soldiers were Shia Baluchis and as such constituted a security risk. The second explanation was that a Pakistani unit either refused to fight or was mauled and retreated during a Yemen border incident.[64] After their withdrawal, the Saudis examined the possibility of hiring Bangladeshis, and military visits were exchanged between the two countries but no agreement signed. Egypt, on the other hand, has supplied police and troops since 1988, when Egyptians participated in the hajj security effort. The deal, which reportedly called for $5 billion and 15,000 Egyptian soldiers, was angrily denied by Interior Minister Naif. However, the Egyptian mission in Riyadh initially confirmed the story.[65] It seems likely that several thousand Egyptian security or paramilitary forces remain in the Kingdom.

Besides troops, the Saudis have also employed foreign officers to serve in individual capacities, largely training and logistical matters. Their numbers have been said to reach a few thousand and have included nationalities as diverse as American, Pakistani, Egyptian, Bangladeshi, Syrian, and Jordanian (before the Iraqi invasion of Kuwait). Another large foreign component is comprised of the employees of foreign employers contracted to the Saudis, largely in operations and maintenance (O&M) procedures.

There is a growing debate within the Saudi command structure as to what sort of armed force the Kingdom needs. Some of the country's elite tend to favor strengthening the air defense capabilities while continuing to use the American protective shield against ground-based threats. These princes believe that Iran is again the Kingdom's main threat and favor purchasing more planes and missiles. They are opposed by princes who favor transforming the country's largely defensive ground forces into more offensive, highly mobile units, armed with the latest American technology. Support for such an undertaking has grown with a vigorous rewriting of the conduct and actions of Saudi troops during the Gulf conflict. Indicative of the new "inflation" was the diplomatic incident that occurred during the Kuwaiti visit of former U.S. President George Bush in April 1993. Following Saudi protests that the praise of America's contributions slighted the

Kingdom's soldiers, the Kuwaiti government issued a special report extolling Saudi efforts. Saudi sensitivity over the issue is revealing.[66]

Conclusion

The Saudi armed forces face several daunting challenges. Increasing the size of the Kingdom's forces as well as improving their abilities will take years, if not decades, to implement. Forging a unified fighting force is also decades away—especially considering the current absence of coordination and communication among the Saudi forces. But perhaps the most dangerous threat facing the Kingdom's military is the al-Saud's constant over-buying of weapons, a policy that has been encouraged and supported by American politicians in recent years, eager to protect the U.S. military industry while winning votes. The Clinton administration, like the Bush administration before it, has seemingly forgotten the lessons of Iran. The purchase of billions of dollars of the world's most advanced weaponry could turn out to be more dangerous to the al-Saud, the Kingdom, and regional security than to the foes they are meant to deter. More than one observer has commented that the threat to the Kingdom, always portrayed as external, will forever be internal. Against that type of enemy, long-range missiles, supersonic aircraft, and tanks will never be a great deal of help.

Notes

1. Robert Lacey, *The Kingdom*, p. 27.
2. Ibid., p. 70.
3. Philip K. Hitti, *History of the Arabs: From the Earliest Times to the Present*, p. 46.
4. David Holden and Richard Johns, *The House of Saud*, p. 69.
5. Lacey, *The Kingdom*, p. 124.
6. Nadav Safran, *Saudi Arabia: The Ceaseless Quest for Security*, p. 45.
7. Ayman al-Yassini, *Religion and State in the Kingdom of Saudi Arabia*, p. 119.
8. Lacey, *The Kingdom*, p. 257.
9. Washington policymakers only took an interest when Japan began asking the Kingdom for oil exploration concessions shortly after the ARAMCO strike.
10. Al-Yassini, *Religion and State*, p. 119.
11. *Washington Post*, February 2, 1992.
12. The most commonly heard story is that Mansour was poisoned by his brothers.
13. Lacey, *The Kingdom*, p. 312.
14. The actual amount is probably much higher; many defense and security

expenditures occur off-budget, sources say, and Saudi budgets are notoriously inaccurate.

15. A. Reza S. Islami and Rostam Mehraban Kavoussi, *The Political Economy of Saudi Arabia*, p. 61.

16. Construction of armed forces hospitals has proven to be a huge source of graft and corruption in the country. Although the Saudi Ministry of Health has more than 160 hospitals with approximately 25,000 available beds, SANG and the defense and interior ministries have insisted that they be allowed to build and staff their own facilities. As of 1990, SANG had 2 hospitals, the Ministry of Interior had 1, and the Ministry of Defense, 22. Together, they had more than 5,000 beds. Like the services, armed forces hospitals have no coordination, no common buying policies, and no interservice cooperation.

17. Islami and Kavoussi, *Political Economy*, p. 26.

18. Joseph Kraft, "Letter from Arabia."

19. The initial three brigades that planned to stay at Hafr al-Batin have been halved due to manpower shortages. Although the military city is a top-secret project, the authors found blueprints to the complex left in the desert by a Korean subcontractor.

20. *MEED: Middle East Business Weekly*, March 20, 1992.

21. *Financial Times of London*, April 13, 1988.

22. Lacey, *The Kingdom*, ch. 49.

23. Sultan is the Kingdom's exclusive agent for the Société Française d'Exportation, a major arms-exporting agency.

24. *Wall Street Journal*, October 7, 1991.

25. *Middle East Economic Survey (MEES)*, August 24, 1992.

26. *The Economist*, June 6, 1981.

27. Scott Armstrong, "Eye of the Storm."

28. The Saudis have stealthily built up their fleet of F–15s through "replacement machines." Military sources say the Saudis regularly claim to crash F–15s when they have not, so that they can order "replacements."

29. *MEED*, January 22, 1993.

30. Safran, *Saudi Arabia: The Ceaseless Quest*, p. 444.

31. Mazher A. Hameed, *Arabia Imperilled: The Security Imperatives of the Arab Gulf States*, p. 159.

32. The likelihood of such a sale remains remote, especially given the Kingdom's current fiscal crunch. However, the rockets could carry biological weapons or the so-called "Islamic bomb," especially if fundamentalists were to establish an Islamic state.

33. *Middle East Executive Report*, July 1992.

34. Hameed, *Arabia Imperilled*, p. 136.

35. It was previously believed that the Gulf was too shallow to support submarines. Associated Press, September 27, 1993.

36. Safran, *Saudi Arabia: The Ceaseless Quest*, p. 68.

37. The second stage of the tank deal of 150 units has been on hold. *New York Times*, August 23, 1993.

38. SANG's ferocity—and its habit of shooting first and asking questions later—is well known in the Kingdom. Given their Ikwan backgrounds, they are especially feared among the Shiite community.

39. Vinnell's contract with SANG has been extended through the end of 1998 in an $819 million agreement. Reuters, June 20, 1993.

40. Safran, *Saudi Arabia: The Ceaseless Quest*, p. 130. SANG's weaponry also reflects the "go-slow" philosophy of Crown Prince Abdullah.

41. Hassan often mediates differences between the al-Fahd and Abdullah. See Chapter 2.

42. General H. Norman Schwartzkopf with Peter Petre, *It Doesn't Take a Hero*, p. 329.

43. Ibid., p. 365.

44. Ibid., p. 340.

45. Ibid.

46. Ibid.

47. According to an American source, the pilot initially panicked but was talked through the attack by American controllers on an AWACS plane.

48. Lawrence Freedman and Efraim Karsh, *The Gulf Conflict, 1990–1991: Diplomacy and War in the New World Order*, p. 365.

49. Schwartzkopf, *It Doesn't Take a Hero*, p. 460.

50. *New York Times*, October 21, 1992.

51. *Washington Post*, November 15, 1990.

52. "Country Report: Saudi Arabia," *Economist Intelligence Unit (EIU)*, no. 2, 1991.

53. *The Nation*, April 13, 1992.

54. *The Economist*, September 22, 1990.

55. *MEES*, October 10, 1991.

56. *MEED*, March 13, 1992.

57. *New York Times*, August 23, 1992.

58. *MEED*, April 10, 1992; and *The Middle East*, February 1992.

59. Associated Press, February 14, 1993.

60. Western military attachés in Riyadh are the source for this information.

61. Adeed Dawisha, "Internal Values and External Threats: The Making of Saudi Foreign Policy," pp. 129–43.

62. Ghassan Salame, "Political Power and the Saudi State," in *Power and Stability in the Middle East*, p. 76.

63. Other sources said Khalid was ordered to resign after profiteering on military contracts. *Washington Post*, March 15, 1992.

64. Safran, *Saudi Arabia: The Ceaseless Quest*, p. 130.

65. Not only did the Egyptian embassy confirm the troop deal to the authors, but the transaction was further verified by several Egyptian co-workers whose army relatives had been transferred to Mecca and Medina as part of the agreement. Saudi sensitivity over the matter is due to Iranian hopes to make the hajj an event under international Muslim sponsorship.

66. *Mideast Mirror*, April 22, 1993.

5 THE SAUDI ECONOMY

If you didn't become a Saudi in the days of King Abdulaziz, you will never be a Saudi.
If you didn't become rich during the days of King Khalid, you will never be rich.
If you didn't become poor during the days of King Fahd, you will never be poor.

—A modern Saudi saying

Saudi Arabia's economy remains driven by oil and oil revenues. Sales of crude oil comprise approximately 35 percent of the Kingdom's GDP, and oil indirectly accounts for far more through oil industry contracts. The Kingdom's planners have attempted to diversify the country's rentier economy with mixed results. Although other sectors of the economy contribute hefty amounts to the Kingdom's overall GDP, their real levels are difficult to discern, especially given the government's recycling of petrodollars through industrial and agricultural subsidies. Real producing sectors of the Saudi economy are more difficult to pinpoint.

Oil has also proven a mixed blessing. Although it has given the Kingdom riches and paid for the country's push into the twentieth century, the Saudi oil industry has had relatively little direct impact on the economy's overall development. The Saudi oil industry is largely self-contained and uses skills not required by other sectors. Exploration and drilling take place in remote areas, thereby stymieing the construction of support services and industries. Technology transfer is also minimal, and the industry employs relatively few people. The oil industry enriches the Kingdom but does not support its economic and industrial development in the way toy assembly did for Singapore and Taiwan.

This is not to understate oil's importance. Oil sales constitute the bulk of the government's revenues and therefore have a tremendous impact on subsequent government expenditures. Despite attempts at building up the private sector, government expenditure remains the economy's chief engine. When government expenditures are high, the Saudi economy booms. When they are low, the economy suffers. Even the country's most ardent supporters of the private sector concede that it will be years if not decades before the economy will be able to sustain substantial growth without sizable government outlays.[1]

Background

The Saudi economy has long been a creature of its environment. When Arabia's climate changed 18,000 years ago, the impact on the region's economy was immediate. The sudden lack of rain ravaged what had been a relatively flourishing herding and gathering society. Croplands and pastures withered and died in the merciless drought, forcing many of the peninsula's inhabitants to flee to the coasts where they eked out existences in trade or fishing. Others migrated completely beyond Arabia. For those who stayed behind, the only viable options were to become nomadic herdsmen, or seek oases and survive by cultivating date palms and some grains.[2] Oases slowly became established settlements but were restricted in size due to limited water resources. For the most part, they were self-sufficient entities whose craftsmen met their few essential needs. Their sole link with the outside world and each other was the occasional caravan that crossed the desert.

The little economic development that took place in early Arabia was due to religion. Religious demand for Yemen's frankincense, perfumes, and other aromatic resins supported a relatively well developed, commerce-based economy in Yemen and the Western Highlands. One of the primary stops for the caravans was a town called Mecca. Several centuries before Christ, men and women were drawn to the city to worship at the base of a black rock, which legend said had been thrown to earth by God, and which today's scientists believe is a meteorite. Over time, other religious shrines were created, and Mecca prospered as a pilgrimage site. It continued to do so even when Christianity became the state religion of the Roman Empire and the pagan use of frankincense in funerals and other ceremonies abruptly ceased. Mecca's transcendental importance was established with the foundation of Islam in the seventh century A.D. when it became the focus of the Muslim movement and the repository for the wealth of Muslim conquests. But as the center of Islamic power shifted first to Damascus and then to Baghdad, Arabia again drifted into stagnation for the next thousand years.

Saudi Arabia's economy remained primitive at the turn of the twentieth century. The Hejaz had the peninsula's most advanced economy thanks to the annual influx of pilgrims who arrived each year to perform their trek to Mecca. Trading was well developed, but most of the merchant families were recent arrivals from the Hadhramaut of Yemen. The area had also benefited from eighty years of rather neglectful Ottoman rule, which had nonetheless seen the establishment of a simple infrastructure, including the Hejazi railroad, a commercial code, and the first rudimentary banks. To a smaller extent, a similar trading society existed in al-Hasa, where a small group of Indian, Iranian, and Bahraini merchants had settled. On both coasts, fishing provided a mainstay for some, while on the Persian or Arabian Gulf, pearling was important as well.

However, the people of the central region continued to live as they had for centuries. Economic activity was restricted to oasis farming, bazaar trading, nomadic herding, and raiding. All finished goods, and such luxuries as rice, sugar, and tea, were imported. The contrasts between the Nejdi and Hejazi economies were startling. It was said that when Abdulaziz bin Saud conquered the latter in 1925, his revenues increased severalfold—an indication of the importance of the hajj trade, but also a telling commentary on the economic imbalance between the two regions.[3]

Abdulaziz's ascension had mixed effects on the Kingdom's economic development. Far more interested in political than economic affairs, the Saudi king paid little attention to his country's economy. The exceptions occurred when they threatened his own finances, which were in a constant state of insolvency. "That's my financial system," Abdulaziz would tell visitors, pointing to gold called up from the royal treasury. "I ask for money and it appears. What more do I need to know than that?"[4] The Saudi monarch made no distinction between his personal royal fortune and state revenues, and economic development was left to chance. The ironic catalyst for change was the Great Depression. As the number of pilgrims fell from 130,000 in the late 1920s to a paltry 40,000 in 1931, Abdulaziz found himself in dire financial straits as pilgrim fees, which constituted the bulk of state revenues, plummeted. In his desperation, the Saudi monarch reversed his decision not to grant new mineral concessions to foreigners, a decree he had made out of deference to his more religious followers who were opposed to non-Muslims entering the country. When he was approached in the early 1930s by two oil companies seeking mineral exploration rights, Abdulaziz felt that he had nothing to lose and everything to gain by agreeing. After less than spirited bidding, the American company, Standard Oil of California (SOCAL), bested its British rival and signed a contract that immediately gave the king 35,000 pounds sterling, with promises of additional payments. Although the king was skeptical that anything would be found—he actually hoped that the drilling would yield water—his budget problems were at least temporarily eased.

SOCAL's initial results confirmed Abdulaziz's skepticism: the first six wells proved unsuccessful. SOCAL's luck changed with the seventh when on March 16, 1938, it struck a huge pool of oil. Within months, the SOCAL venture had paid Abdulaziz an additional 200,000 pounds sterling and had assured him that it was only a portent of things to come. The sudden inflow of money spurred economic development. The increased payment of oil royalties enabled Abdulaziz and his rapidly expanding family to increase their spending, which resulted in a trickle-down effect on the rest of the economy. The king and his sons, as well as selected courtiers, had no trouble disbursing their newfound riches on palaces, automobiles, and other luxuries. Imports from Europe and the United States mushroomed from $3.8 million in 1938 to $162.4 million in 1956.[5]

Oil's other benefit was that it provided the impetus for the development of the country's infrastructure, especially in the oil fields of al-Hasa. As SOCAL and its successor, the Arabian-American Oil Company (ARAMCO), discovered, their contract with Abdulaziz provided them access to oil but precious little else. There was no infrastructure to speak of, no armed forces to protect the wells, no educated work force or administrators, and no real government apparatus. Instead, it was left to ARAMCO to construct a basic infrastructure around their facilities. Roads, housing, modern ports, a water system, clinics, schools, and power plants were erected as the company established its own little fiefdom within the Saudi state. ARAMCO also created new business opportunities for Saudi merchants and contractors, while offering jobs to thousands of people in al-Hasa.

Despite the nearby example of ARAMCO, the first flush of oil wealth did not spur any similar rush by the government into developmental spending. It was not that Abdulaziz was unsympathetic to providing for his people's needs—it was simply beyond his understanding. The budget of 1946 was revealing. Revenues were estimated at 13.2 million pounds but expenditures were 17.5 million pounds. The deficit, 4.3 million pounds, was approximately 25 percent of the entire budget. Making matters worse were the outlays. Two million pounds were allocated for servicing existing debt, and another two million were earmarked for the royal garage. One million pounds were reserved for court hospitality and entertaining. Only 150,000 pounds were set aside for new schools and education.[6] Equally disturbing were the quantities siphoned off by some of the king's family and retinue as corruption grew. By the time of his death in 1953, Abdulaziz had overseen the expenditure of more than $400 million in oil revenues but had little to show for it in the way of basic infrastructure save the Riyadh–Dammam railroad, a new breakwater outside the Jeddah port, several roads, and water wells.[7]

Development was left to Abdulaziz's heir, Saud bin Abdulaziz. "My father's reign may be famous for all its conquests and its cohesion of the country," Saud told the country shortly after ascending the throne. "My reign will be remembered for what I do for my people in the way of their welfare, their education and their health."[8] Saud was true to his word; it was during his reign that the Kingdom's first large infrastructural projects were undertaken. The results were truly amazing. In 1954, the Kingdom's infrastructure outside al-Hasa was nonexistent, and the country only had 327 kilometers of roads.[9] Under Saud, thousands of kilometers of highways were started, as were dozens of hospitals, hundreds of schools, and two new universities. The port facilities were expanded to handle the inflow of imports, and Saud transferred the growing government apparatus from Jeddah to Riyadh, where he constructed rows of monoliths for his new ministries.

It was the first big public spending in the Kingdom's history, and it was financed by oil revenues. The latter continued to climb and by 1955 accounted for almost all of the government's foreign exchange, more than three-quarters of its revenues, and two-thirds of the gross national product (GNP).[10] Still, oil revenues were outpaced by the sheer magnitude of the projects undertaken as well as the growing corruption and Saud's personal extravagance. The country was nearly bankrupt, and Crown Prince Faisal bin Abdulaziz instituted an immediate freeze on development projects, save for roads and highways, when he took day-to-day control of the government in 1958. Several years of austerity followed, and developmental spending only recommenced in the early 1960s when the Kingdom's finances had improved. Under Faisal, the pace was slower and corruption less endemic. Some problems remained: lack of quality and poor planning often had telling consequences. Many new highways had to be replaced within two to three years due to shoddy construction.[11]

Faisal's prudent planning—as well as rising oil revenues—paid dividends. Per capita income mushroomed from SR 1,853 (U.S. $412) in 1962/1963 to SR 5,189 (U.S. $1,391) in 1971/1972.[12] Part of that income growth was the result of trickle-down economics. Just as important was the fact that almost two-thirds of all Saudi families received money from the government, through military duties, tribal grants, education stipends, or contracts, as Faisal sought to buy his people's loyalty (see Chapter 2).

Growing riches were accompanied by some economic diversification. A 1967 economic survey revealed that although nearly half of all Saudis were employed in agricultural pursuits including herding and fishing, the service, construction, and trade sectors were growing as well, employing 21.8 percent, 10.3 percent, and 9.5 percent of the work force, respectively.[13] Another study of the country's 43,616 registered business establishments was also revealing. Approximately 66 percent were said to be in service trades, while 21 percent were engaged in manufacturing. The latter figure was somewhat misleading as the government included such enterprises as tire repair shops as manufacturing concerns.[14] The survey also showed that the Hejaz was home to fully half of all registered companies, with the Nejd and al-Hasa trailing with 23 percent and 17 percent, respectively.[15] Ninety-five percent of all firms employed five people or less.[16]

Prior to 1970, the emphasis in the Kingdom's developmental spending had been on infrastructural projects. That emphasis continued in 1970 with the announcement of the Kingdom's First Five-Year Plan. Put together by Western consultants and the Kingdom's new Central Planning Organization, the plan laid the foundations for the country's future economic development and diversification. Three years later, political events made the plan entirely irrelevant.

Table 5.1

Saudi Oil Revenues, 1973–1994

Year	Total revenue (U.S. $ billion)	Year	Total revenue (U.S. $ billion)
1973	4.34	1984	31.47
1974	22.57	1985	18.32
1975	25.68	1986	13.55
1976	30.75	1987	17.49
1977	36.54	1988	16.64
1978	32.23	1989	20.24
1979	48.44	1990	31.50
1980	84.47	1991[a]	43.70
1981	101.81	1992[b]	42.30
1982	70.48	1993[c]	37.40
1983	37.35	1994[c]	30.50

Source: Saudi Arabian Monetary Agency (SAMA) Annual Reports.
[a]*Economist Intelligence Unit* estimate.
[b]*Middle East Monitor* estimate.
[c]Authors' estimates.

The Boom Years

Saudi Arabia's boom, which occurred after the 1973 Arab-Israeli War and the subsequent oil boycott, was completely unexpected. Few people, not even Faisal, were aware of the changes the Kingdom was launching when it refused to sell its oil to the United States and the Netherlands in 1973. The price of oil more than quintupled from $3 a barrel in 1972 to almost $17 by December 1973. It continued to climb for the rest of the decade, and following the fall of the shah of Iran, the spot price of crude was more than $40 per barrel. For Saudi Arabia, which had steadily increased its production, the inflow of petrodollars was nothing short of spectacular. Oil revenues topped $4.34 billion in 1973 and subsequently jumped to $22.57 billion the next year (see Table 5.1). They then mushroomed to $48.44 billion in 1979, $84.87 billion in 1980, and peaked at $101.81 billion in 1981, a 17,000-fold increase in less than 40 years.[17] This windfall in petrodollars was even more startling when examined from the country's money supplies. Reflecting the dramatic increase in oil revenues, "money supply" M1 exploded from SR 1.428 billion in 1964 to SR 4.524 billion in 1973, SR 26.775 billion

in 1978, SR 60.184 billion in 1981, and SR 86.032 billion in 1984.[18]
The Kingdom's GDP similarly rocketed, tripling from 1975 to 1980.
The Saudi economy was suddenly awash with funds.

The inflow of petrodollars brought new problems. Even before the
oil embargo of 1973, Faisal's economic planners had been having
difficulty absorbing all of the country's oil revenues. The Kingdom's
native population was approximately 3.5 million, and the economy was
still in a rudimentary stage of development despite Saud's initial programs. The country could not hope to absorb the money gained from
pumping 9 million bpd—a production level kept high to meet Western
needs. In fact, given steadily spiraling oil prices, many Saudis argued
that the Kingdom's oil was worth more in the ground where its value
was safeguarded from inflation. This dilemma initially left the al-Saud
at a loss for what to do with their windfall. They had three choices.
One option was to place their new petrodollar wealth with Western
financial institutions and watch inflation diminish its worth. The second choice was one that was followed by Kuwait: to invest petrodollars in Western economies through the purchase of equities. The
al-Saud, however, opted largely for the third alternative of undertaking
one of the largest and most expensive development plans ever seen in
the world.

Prodded by their Western consultants, the House of Saud dramatically expanded the country's Second Five-Year Plan, which was to go
into effect in 1975. Infrastructural projects were stressed, and roads,
hospitals, schools, military bases, seaports, and airports were constructed. Cement factories and oil refineries were undertaken; ground
was broken for the twin industrial cities of Jubail and Yanbu. Trans-
continental oil pipelines were laid and giant water desalination plants
set in place. Billions more were spent on weapons and the defense and
security apparatus (see Chapter 4). Having the biggest was suddenly
equated with having the best. Typical was the construction of Jeddah's
King Abdulaziz International Airport. Despite the fact that its traffic
needs were relatively small, the airport covered an area equal to the
five largest airports in the United States put together.

To ensure the population's support for the al-Saud, Faisal laid the
foundations for a generous welfare state. Education and health care
were made free, and students were given generous grants to attend
school.[19] Food prices were kept artificially low through widespread
subsidies. Bread was one example. Although the price of one loaf was

SR 1.00, the American Embassy estimated the actual cost to the government at more than SR 5.00. Prices of other staples—rice, cooking oil, sugar, meats—were similarly subsidized. Utility prices were also underpropped. Saudi consumers were charged only eight cents per cubic meter for the water coming from the country's new desalination plants even though the cost to the government was U.S. $1.20. Similar subsidies were implemented for electricity, gasoline, and cooking gas. Other government subsidies abounded. Fares on all transport, Saudi Arabian Airlines (Saudia), the train, and inter-city buses were kept artificially low. Subsidies have had unintended results. Given the low prices of many goods, many Saudis suffer no qualms about wasting previously expensive goods, given their subsidized cost. Water consumption is one example: Saudi city dwellers use more than 500 liters per day, roughly ten to twenty times the average of their rural Arab brethren.[20] By 1983–1984, direct subsidies accounted for 14.7 percent of the Saudi budget.[21]

The government also disbursed billions of riyals for agricultural, industrial, and service enterprises through its credit agencies. Middle- and low-income Saudis were given interest-free housing loans of at least SR 300,000, of which 25 percent was forgiven if payments occurred on schedule.[22] Petrodollars percolated down in other ways. To foster the development of a strong private sector, the government handed out thousands of contracts to Saudi entrepreneurs on a cost-plus basis, abolishing open bidding. Contractors were paid 20 percent of the award cost up front, and if a person were clever enough and competent, that was often more than enough to finish the project.

Another stratagem for the distribution of oil wealth was through real estate. Since the royal family theoretically owned all land, it soon became common for the king or princes to grant land to their subjects or to themselves, and then have the government repurchase it for the construction of new office buildings or highways. Real estate prices soared, and in some instances, land prices doubled every week.[23] Car imports tripled in one year, and the ports became clogged with ships waiting to offload their cargoes as imports rose from U.S. $3 billion in 1973 to U.S. $17 billion four years later.[24]

The real estate boom created scores of millionaires and fueled a massive binge in consumer spending, bolstered by the arrival of hundreds of thousands of expatriate workers "imported" to build and manage the Kingdom's new hospitals and roads, schools and ports. It was a time of get-rich schemes by the thousands. As the American envoy to

Riyadh noted, "The sky over Riyadh is black with vultures with new get richer-quicker plans under their wings."[25] It seemed as if the gusher would never end. "I still remember driving to work every morning and seeing long lines of Saudis waiting for our doors to open," recalled one banker. "They would be holding their money, large wads of notes in plastic garbage bags. I remember once we had a man come to the bank with a large Samsonite suitcase stuffed with riyals."[26] The combination of subsidies and government giveaways, plus the absence of taxes, led to massive enrichment of the Saudi people. As King Fahd bin Abdulaziz later noted, "A Saudi has to be very unlucky, very stupid and very lazy not to do well."[27]

Government spending fueled a boom in the construction industry. Overall, national expenditures on construction more than quadrupled during the 1976–1979 period to approximately $3 billion worth of new projects being assigned each month, a level which was maintained till late 1981.[28] The construction industry grew so quickly that it soon comprised more than 30 percent of the country's non-oil GDP.

Government expenditures were so great—they were to total over $776 billion over the life of the first four Five-Year Plans—that from 1975 to 1980 they actually outstripped private sector expenditures.[29] By contrast, public expenditures comprised only 28 percent of total spending in the United States, 19 percent in Turkey, and 20 percent in South Korea.[30] This reliance on public sector spending would have serious consequences in the future.

Besides infrastructural projects, the government also undertook a massive investment in resource-based industries (RBIs)—industries based on processing hydrocarbons—due to the country's huge hydrocarbon reserves. RBI investment was heavily promoted to diversify the Saudi economy, fuel economic growth, spread development to different regions, and absorb the oil windfall while not adding too much to inflation.[31] Saudi Arabia's investment, 20 percent of non-oil GDP, was substantially larger than that of other oil producers.[32] Overall, the $12 billion plan oversaw the construction of two huge export refineries, three olefin units, two methanol plants, two steel mills, and one fertilizer plant.

Other industrial investment, and especially joint ventures with the West, was eagerly courted as part of the government's economic diversification program. Besides subtly pressuring leading suppliers such as Japan, the United States, and members of the European Economic Community (EEC), Saudi Arabia instituted a package of incentives

Table 5.2

Saudi Economic Statistics, Selected Years, 1970–1992

Year	Total GDP (U.S. $ billion)	M1 Supply (SR billion)	M2 Supply (SR billion)	Cost of living index (1988 = 100)
1970	3.89	2.36	2.85	32.5
1975	39.65	10.56	12.10	50.1
1980	115.17	59.22	77.48	103.0
1981	156.80	73.49	97.90	105.6
1982	154.33	85.19	113.77	106.8
1983	121.06	83.25	113.17	107.8
1984	109.97	82.93	118.62	106.5
1985	93.60	84.02	124.56	102.9
1986	74.86	86.38	127.35	99.9
1987	70.42	92.01	133.27	99.0
1988	76.03	93.66	134.14	100.0
1989	82.88	91.75	136.41	101.1
1990	99.00	102.26	141.55	103.2
1991	105.65	—	—	—
1992	110.83	—	—	—

Source: SAMA Annual Reports.

that offered foreign investors subsidized financing through the Saudi Industrial Development Fund (SIDF) if they created joint ventures with at least 25 percent Saudi equity participation. If Saudi equity totaled 51 percent, the joint ventures were offered access to the entire Gulf Cooperation Council (GCC) market. Generous ten-year tax holidays were offered, and industrial concerns could import their machinery and raw supplies duty-free. In addition, industrial concerns were offered subsidized prices for land, water, and energy. Foreign entrepreneurs soon accounted for a quarter of all investment in the country. The government also instituted buy-Saudi policies, mandating that all foreign companies that won government contracts had to subcontract at least 30 percent of their award to local concerns, including joint ventures. By 1984, there were more than 1,200 industrial plants operating in the country.[33]

The Recession of the 1980s

Just as oil fueled the boom, it was also the culprit in the subsequent bust of the 1980s. Proving Saudi Petroleum and Mineral Resources Minister Ahmad Zaki Yamani correct, higher oil prices led to the exploitation of more expensive oil fields in Alaska and the North Sea. Higher prices also encouraged conservation, alternative energy sources, and increased fuel efficiency, all of which reduced oil demand. By early summer 1981, the price of crude oil was softening and Saudi Arabia began cutting its production as OPEC's swing producer in a vain attempt to arrest the fall. The Kingdom's production dropped from 9.9 million bpd in 1980 to between 2 and 3 million bdp in 1985, roughly one-quarter of what it had been at the peak of the boom. The Kingdom's content of OPEC's sanctioned production fell from 35 percent in 1982 to only 20 percent in 1985. Despite that, the price of crude had still plummeted, falling from a high of more than $40 per barrel in early 1980 to less than $10 in 1986. The impact on Saudi Arabia's fortunes was telling. Oil revenues fell from a high of $101.81 billion in 1981 to $37.35 billion just two years later. By 1986, Saudi oil revenues totaled only $13.55 billion. Saudi GDP showed a similar plunge, dropping 55.1 percent in the space of six years (1981–1987). Imports of both goods and services fell by one-half in the five-year period from 1983 to 1987, and the current account deficit totaled $54 billion for the same time period.[34]

The full impact of the recession, or "economic restructuring" as the Ministry of Finance and National Economy preferred to call it, was felt gradually.[35] Government spending started sliding in 1982, but its initial drop was slight as the government decided to draw down its rather substantial foreign reserves, estimated at between $115 billion and $120 billion, rather than making stiff cutbacks in programs and projects.[36] The government also instituted several cost-cutting measures. First and foremost, open bidding on all new contracts was instituted, a move that reduced potential bid corruption and project costs by 50 percent.[37] The government also halved its advance payment to contractors from 20 percent to 10 percent. The result was felt immediately: many contractors had come to rely on those payments as means to finish older, existing projects, and now experienced cash flow problems.

Contractors often completed projects, delivered them to the client ministry, and then experienced payment delays for months or even years. Sometimes delays were justified: the easy money of the boom years had led many contractors to cut corners in order to reap larger profits. However, government inspectors began finding shortcomings, real or imagined, everywhere. Horror stories were common. Carlson al-Saudia, a joint venture of Carlson Company of the United States and Prince Saud bin Fahd bin Abdulaziz, son of the present king, had no choice but to declare bankruptcy while waiting for payment, a move that stranded thousands of Filipino workmen in the desert. Another major contractor, Laing Wimpey Alireza, a Saudi-British joint venture, despaired of ever being paid after repeated delays, and finally cut its losses and spirited its employees out of the country to avoid Saudi ire. In staggered groups, executives and senior officers went to different parts of the country and then departed on vacations on exit–re-entry visas. Such stealth was necessary to avoid the taking of "commercial hostages," and it succeeded; the company retrieved all of its workers without a single one being held (see The Legal System, p. 200). The company later told the *Financial Times of London* that their losses were attributable to late payments from the government. Saudi officials vehemently denied the allegations but were powerless to act.

The issue of payment delays soon reached billion-dollar proportions and afflicted both Saudi and foreign contractors. As of 1986, the Korean embassy estimated that its contractors were owed at least $4 billion. A similar amount was owed French contractors, who received partial payment for their work on the Saudi power grid, but only after Paris had filed a high-level protest. American companies were affected as well, and when then–Vice President George Bush visited Riyadh in 1986, he was presented with a position paper that claimed the embassy was already representing at least a dozen U.S.-based companies in their disputes with the government, while another fifty to sixty were said to be battling for themselves.

The accusations about the Saudi government grew so heated that Fahd had no choice but to deny them in a public broadcast in which he complained about a "rancorous campaign . . . launched by foreign radios, television and press" on the issue. Several weeks later, the Saudi Council of Ministers issued a warning stating that "companies which falsely claim delayed government payments may be barred from working in the Kingdom."[38]

Although foreign companies were badly hit by delays, those taking the hardest blows were their Saudi counterparts, many of which were bloated through government largess, often overextended, poorly capitalized, inefficiently managed, and unable to secure additional financing as the banking crisis froze lending. It was a domino effect: contractors were pressed for funds and in turn delayed payment to subcontractors who in turn delayed payment to suppliers. Hundreds of Saudi firms went bankrupt in the ensuing morass, including such behemoths as the Shobokshi Group and Ghaith Pharaon's Redec Corporation.

Hopes that the massive investment in RBI industries would take up the slack also proved baseless. The fall in oil prices affected the new cost-effectiveness of the Saudi plants; as they began coming on line in 1985, petrochemical prices slumped to their lowest levels in years. As a result, the new plants contributed only $1 billion to non-oil GDP rather than the $4 billion originally planned. Far from boosting non-oil GDP, the new RBI industries could not even offset the fall in construction industries.[39] RBI industries, which were only economically feasible thanks to massive government feedstock subsidies, also failed to meet other objectives. These capital-intensive ventures were largely constructed from imported materials and employed relatively few people (initially only 7,500), and therefore contributed relatively little to other sectors of the economy.

By 1985, the Saudi economy was in an undeniable recession, and the government had no choice but to reduce expenditures. As the downturn worsened, the government increasingly pressured the Saudi private sector to take up the slack caused by the decrease in public expenditures. The Saudi private sector had the financial resources; most estimates placed the amount of Saudi private sector overseas assets at more than $100 billion. However, the will to shore up the economy was lacking. Many Saudi entrepreneurs were unwilling to shed their short-term investment mentality. Also hurting was the government's refusal to countenance any political concessions, especially as regards greater private sector involvement in the country's economic decision-making process.[40] Several devaluations, payment delays, and an overregulated stock market also dampened investor enthusiasm. Confidence was not helped by the government's failure to issue a budget in 1986, nor by the cancellation of two new oil refineries, a lubricant base oil refinery, and several other infrastructural projects. Indicative of the new penny-pinching was the fate of a planned desalination and power plant for the Asir, which was retendered and scaled down four times. Rather than admit funding was a problem, the government said the bids were flawed.

The recession also saw further cutbacks in government aid, including the number of loans granted by the five state lending agencies. Total outstanding loans by the five peaked at SR 166.907 billion in

1986 and fell thereafter. Commercial banks were reluctant to take up the shortfall, especially when they were confronting a burgeoning bad loan problem, an unresponsive legal system, and mounting provisions for bad debts. The banking system's new tightfistedness was best illustrated in late 1989 when one of the Kingdom's largest contractors, Mabco, went bankrupt after failing to secure fresh financing. Making the case all the more ironic was the fact that the company had just received a contract to build the new concourse building at King Fahd International Airport in al-Hasa. However, because the company had not secured any pre-payment from the government, banks refused to grant it a SR 84 million loan. The matter grew so contentious that officials from the Saudi Arabian Monetary Agency (SAMA) later sat in on the negotiations between Mabco and its bankers. Despite none-too-subtle pressure from SAMA, the banks refused to comply, and Mabco, government contract in hand, had no choice but to file for bankruptcy.[41] Mabco's story was repeated in scores of cases.

The recession caused the first reassessment of the Kingdom's generous welfare program with its costly reliance on subsidies. As the recession continued, the Kingdom's planners had no choice but to act. Fortunately, the Kingdom's retrenchment on many subsidies coincided with falling commodity prices, especially as the agricultural export war between the United States and the European Economic Community (EEC) heated up. As prices of chilled meats, barley, wheat, milk, and corn fell in the resulting competition, the Saudi government was able to erase subsidies on selected products.[42] The Kingdom was lucky; previous attempts to cut agricultural subsidies had run into stiff opposition, especially given the unwritten code between the Saudi population and al-Saud that gave the latter political power in return for providing a fairly affluent life-style (see Chapter 2).

Other attempts at erasing subsidies on gasoline, water, electricity, and bottled gas proved less successful. In each instance, concerted public outcry blunted the initiative. The first such attempt occurred in April 1984, when the government announced plans to increase the price of gasoline by 70 percent in order to cover the SR 4 billion debt the state oil concern Petromin had run up due to subsidized fuel. Immediate protests rolled back the original price increase, and although smaller hikes were later implemented, they were far less than those originally sought. Efforts to downsize subsidies on electricity and water, whose annual support cost the government at least SR 4 billion per year, also proved unsuccessful. The Industry and Electricity Ministry announced electricity rate increases in 1984, but they were rescinded the next year. Efforts to raise water rates met with similar failure. However, the government's action had an unintended side effect: both local and foreign investors became even more cautious about locating projects in the Kingdom, especially given the fear that it was only a matter of time until such subsidies were abolished. Government attempts to cut agricultural production subsidies met with limited success as well.

These setbacks forced the government to shift its tack in 1987–1988 and try to increase government revenues. Due to the regime's fear of losing political support, and unanswered questions on the Islamic correctness of taxes, direct revenue measures on Saudis were never seriously contemplated.[43] Instead, Fahd's government focused on less conspicuous revenue-generating measures, which he tried enacting by stealth.

Fahd announced the 1988 budget on December 31, 1987. Contrary to rumor, it contained no mention of new taxes or service charges. The reason became apparent a few days later when the official gazette, *Umm al-Qura*, published a detailed listing of several new revenue-raising measures the king had "neglected" to mention in his address. An airport departure tax of SR 10 for domestic flights and SR 50 for international flights headed the list. Other user fees included an SR 10 surcharge for all electricity and water bills as well as an SR 10 surcharge on patients using government health clinics and hospitals. A higher tariff was put in place, raising the fees on most imports from 7 percent to 12 percent, while a 20 percent tariff was imposed on cement and other goods that competed with similar Saudi products. The government also proposed an annual SR 200 road tax on all vehicles, as well as a 5 percent real estate transfer fee.[44]

The government also reinstituted an income tax on expatriates. A similar tax had been dropped during Faisal's reign in order to attract a foreign work force. This time, the Ministry of Finance and National Economy proposed a graduated scale with a top bracket of 30 percent. Besides income, all end-of-service awards, accommodation benefits, and air fare allowances were taxable as well. The tax, which would have raised SR 5 billion, had a second objective: the reduction of the expatriate work force. The gambit succeeded beyond expectations. Expatriates, who had already experienced salary cuts due to the recession, began resigning in the thousands. Work slowed to a crawl at hospitals and banks around the kingdom as workers waited in hour-long queues to quit. Fearing Libyan-style currency controls, millions of dollars from expatriate accounts were transferred overseas. Four days after it had been published, the expatriate income tax was withdrawn. Two weeks later, most of the other user fees were scrapped in the face of mounting domestic pressure.[45]

The government's second revenue-raising idea was more successful. During his budget speech, Fahd announced the creation of "development bonds," the Kingdom's first public borrowing in twenty-five years. Fahd added that the government would issue up to SR 30 billion worth of the bonds in the first year, with all proceeds being used to cover the budget deficit. To sidestep the issue of interest, always a bugbear in financial matters, Fahd said the bonds would be Islamic with their rates of return set to new, unspecified projects. The king's explanation was greeted with skepticism because most of the country's large projects had already been completed. There was also the matter that the yields, when announced to banks later that spring, seemed suspiciously similar to the rates on U.S. Treasury notes. Banks were slow to take the bonds despite their attractive yields, fearing another riyal devaluation, the long-term nature of the bonds, and the absence of a secondary market.[46] Their reluctance to take up the notes became so critical that SAMA began dropping none-too-subtle hints that failure to do so would lead to limits on their offshore deposits. That threat failed to yield the intended effect, and it was increasingly left to cash-rich government agencies such as the Public Investment Fund (PIF) and the General Organization for Social Insurance (GOSI) to take up the bulk of the bonds issued. In effect, the government was reduced to borrowing from itself.

By the end of 1988, SAMA Governor Hamad al-Sayyari claimed that more than SR 30 billion worth of the bonds had been placed, but gave no figures regarding the amount taken by commercial banks and that taken by government agencies. The government issued approximately SR 25 billion worth of the bonds in 1989 and up to SR 41 billion in 1990 and SR 50 billion in 1991.[47] However, it was recognized as early as 1989 that the bonds could not cover all of the deficit, when PIF borrowed $660 million from a consortium of Saudi banks. Although the agency claimed that the money was needed for new projects, the general feeling among bankers was that the agency used the money to purchase more bonds.[48]

The Impact of Operation Desert Storm

The Saudi economy's downward spiral bottomed out in 1986–1987. The economy in fact grew slightly in 1987, as oil revenues rose slightly for the first time in six years, and the government increased expenditures in a move to resuscitate the private sector. Also stimulating the economy was the government's release of several billion dollars to settle outstanding payment delays. The upturn, however, proved illusory; the following year oil revenues again slipped due to lower crude prices in the wake of the conclusion of the Iran–Iraq conflict, which led to the flooding of international oil markets with those two countries' pent-up productions. Saudi oil revenues fell from $17.49 billion to $16.64 billion, and government expenditures hit their lowest level of the decade. Although that was partially offset by an upsurge in capital repatriation after "Black October," the economy continued to stutter even as the cessation of hostilities improved investor confidence and signaled some hope that Saudi firms would participate in the rebuilding of Iraq. This optimism was fueled later in 1990 when the government issued its budget, which increased expenditures for the first time since 1981.

The Saudi economy returned to its "boom" footing following the Iraqi invasion of Kuwait. Saddam Hussein's tanks accomplished in twenty-four hours what Saudi oil policy had failed to achieve during the decade of the 1980s: they boosted prices *and* Saudi oil production. Spot prices hit $30 per barrel within hours of the invasion, and the Kingdom's production climbed to over 9 million bpd to make up the shortfall from Kuwait's oil fields as well as the oil embargo on Iraq. Although the price of crude subsequently fell back during the fall and winter after hitting a high of $40 per barrel in late September, Saudi Arabia, like all major oil producers, reaped a windfall and in fact initially contributed to the soaring price. Refusing to pump more oil until the end of August, when OPEC officially sanctioned its new quota, Saudi Arabia watched the price of oil climb to nearly $30 per barrel before it moved to meet the shortfall.[49] Saudi oil income for September 1990 more than doubled to $5.2 billion from $2.5 billion of the year before, and overall the Kingdom's 1990 oil revenues were officially put at $31.50 billion—more than 50 percent higher than 1989's $20.24 billion. Many believe that the government's inflow was even greater but was hidden to avoid antagonizing Western critics, who were eager to condemn Saudi profiteering.[50]

Offsetting higher oil revenues, however, were the Kingdom's new financial undertakings. Within days of the Iraqi invasion, the Saudi government was making the first of many new financial commitments. Besides pledging $15 billion to the U.S. government for its role in Desert Storm, the Kingdom extended credit and grants to other supporters in the West and the Arab world. The Kingdom issued a $1.5 billion wartime loan to the Soviet Union, $1.7 billion to Egypt, $1.6 billion to Syria, $1.2 billion to Turkey, and smaller amounts to Djibouti, Lebanon, Somalia, Bahrain, and Morocco. In addition, existing loans to Egypt and other Arab countries supporting the Kingdom were forgiven. Domestic expenditures also soared, as the government underwrote the costs of food and materials for the Allied forces. Overall, the Saudi government was estimated to have spent $64 billion on the war effort, with another $20 billion in cash grants or aid.[51] Such expenditures had a price; the Saudi budget deficit grew from $14.9 billion in 1990 to between $20 billion and $30 billion in 1991. Reaching a consensus on the figures is difficult because the Saudis themselves have issued contradictory numbers, further clouding the issue. That they were in some financial difficulty, at least in the short run, is irrefutable. The Saudis approached the Kuwaitis about tapping into their overseas investments and deposits to help defray Riyadh's share of Operation Desert Storm, but their request was rejected.[52] Other signs of short-term liquidity problems surfaced as well: payment delays again began occurring on a regular basis. In early 1992, the issue had become so serious that the U.S. government began pressuring Riyadh on the behalf of fourteen American companies, which were said to be owed $500 million.[53]

Although the Kingdom's financial situation worsened, the war brought a mini-boom to the economy. Consumer spending skyrocketed as more than 600,000 Allied troops arrived, needing a full range of materials and food. Also fueling the economic expansion was the sudden inflow of more than 300,000 Kuwaiti refugees, many of whom arrived with little beyond what they could cram into their cars or vans.[54] Their arrival fueled a tremendous increase in consumer spending as they settled into makeshift housing, including the "rush housing" units in Riyadh, Jeddah, and the Eastern Province, great multi-billion-dollar complexes that had remained empty since their construction during the boom. Pumping additional money into the economy was the rapid and unpredictable mass exodus of Saudis and expatriates alike that followed various Iraqi threats and SCUD attacks. During the height of the hostilities, more than 50 percent of the Eastern Province's population is said to have fled, while the figure for Riyadh was between 15 percent and 30 percent.[55] Not surprisingly, Jeddah's economy benefited from the influx of refugees.

Mirroring the boom period, profiteering was rife as few Saudi businessmen had qualms about price gouging. The head of the Saudi armed forces, Lt. General Prince Khalid bin Sultan bin Abdulaziz, begged his American counterparts not to buy anything on their own to avoid price inflation, as prices for non-Saudis were sometimes double those charged to Saudis.[56] The problem was widespread, and even affected rations for Allied troops. One of the more perplexing cases involved the Astra Corporation, which received a contract to supply the Allied troops with food. Astra, owned by several senior princes of the al-Saud, was said to have marked up prices so high that its profit margin was a hefty 100 percent. The company subsequently denied the allegation.[57]

Iraq's defeat did nothing to slow the economy, and the boom has continued, largely fueled by increased government expenditures. After failing to issue a budget for 1991, the government's 1992 and 1993 budgets contained steadily rising expenditures. Defense spending, with many items off-budget, has also grown. Further stoking the local economy were the massive expansion projects undertaken by Saudi ARAMCO, the Saudi Basic Industries Corporation (SABIC), the Saline Water Corporation (SWCC), and electricity companies. Overall, more than $50 billion worth of new construction projects are expected to be tendered by the end of the century, although this figure may be in jeopardy due to the downturn in oil prices that occurred in 1993.

Consumer spending is also expanding, partially due to the increase of subsidies in light of political pressure. In March 1992, Fahd announced lower prices for gasoline, water, electricity, and bottled gas. The changes, which were accompanied by lower port fees, which reduced the prices of imports, were expected to add at least $1 billion to the pockets of consumers. Another factor has been the decision by thousands of Kuwaitis to build homes in the Kingdom, in case the emirate is again invaded. The increase in construction has in turn fueled another real estate boom, with some pieces of property showing 20 percent increases every month. The sharp rise in construction also led the government in early 1993 to rescind the

20 percent duty it had earlier placed on cement imports. Construction wages have also nearly doubled.[58]

Consumer spending has become more and more important to the economy; Ministry of Finance and National Economy officials estimate that it now contributes between 45 percent and 50 percent of GNP, up from 25 percent to 30 percent in the 1970s.[59] Renewed consumer confidence coupled with the hope that Saudi firms would be given preferential treatment in the rebuilding of Kuwait suggests that the Saudi economy is positioned for several years of high growth. In fact, the Ministry of Planning estimates that for the period from 1990 to 1995, manufacturing will grow at an annual rate of 7.5 percent; petrochemicals, 8.0 percent; agriculture, 7 percent; oil refining, 5.4 percent; and oil and natural gas, 2.0 percent.[60]

The ministry's optimism seems well founded, but only if several problems are overlooked. Among them are growing government indebtedness, a dysfunctional banking system, the Kingdom's court system, and the unresponsive Saudi bureaucracy.

Key Economic Problems

Growing Government Indebtedness

Saudi Arabia's inability to balance its budget is beginning to alarm many, as public sector borrowing shows no sign of slowing down. Although Saudi Arabia released its first balanced budget in nine years in 1994 as expenditures were slashed 20 percent from the preceding year's levels, the budget revealed few details as to how the al-Saud are planning to achieve fiscal balance. In 1985 when the al-Saud issued their last previous balanced budget, the real deficit totaled SR 50.4 billion. Not surprisingly, few believe that 1994's budget will be adhered to, especially given the country's domestic unrest, which makes cost cutting unpopular (see Table 5.3).

The problem posed by budget deficits is a real one. Since 1983, the Kingdom has racked up eleven consecutive years of deficit spending, totaling more than SR 500 billion. The real figure may be substantially higher since Saudi budget figures are notoriously inaccurate and often serve as rough guidelines for spending. There are also large discrepancies between projected and actual figures; the latter are usually released the following year and purport to show real revenues and

Table 5.3

Saudi Government Budgets, Selected Years, 1971–1994

Year	Revenues (SR billion)		Expenditures (SR billion)		Surplus/Deficit (SR billion)	
1971	6.4	(7.9)	6.4	(5.8)	0.0	(+2.1)
1972	10.8	(11.1)	10.8	(7.3)	0.0	(+2.9)
1973	13.2	(15.4)	13.2	(9.2)	0.0	(+6.4)
1974	22.8	(41.3)	22.2	(16.5)	0.6	(+24.8)
1975	98.2	(101.4)	45.7	(30.3)	+42.5	(+71.3)
1980	261.5	(348.1)	245.0	(236.6)	+16.5	(+111.5)
1981	340.0	(368.0)	298.0	(284.6)	+42.0	(+83.4)
1982	313.4	(246.2)	313.4	(244.9)	00.0	(+1.3)
1983	225.0	(206.4)	260.0	(230.2)	–35.0	(–23.8)
1984	214.1	(171.5)	260.0	(216.4)	–45.9	(–44.9)
1985	200.0	(133.6)	200.0	(184.0)	00.0	(–50.4)
1986[a]	—	(76.5)	—	(137.4)	—	(–60.9)
1987	117.2	(103.8)	170.0	(173.5)	–52.8	(–69.7)
1988	105.3	(84.6)	141.2	(134.8)	–35.9	(–50.2)
1989	116.0	(114.6)	141.0	(149.5)	–25.0	(–34.9)
1990	118.0	(154.7)	143.0	(210.4)	–25.0	(–55.7)
1991[a]	—	—	—	(261.6)	—	(–77.0)
1992	151.0	—	181.0	—	–30.0	—
1993	169.2	—	197.0	—	–27.8	—
1994	160.0	—	160.0	—	00.0	—

Source: Ministry of Finance and National Economy.
Note: Actual revenues and expenditures given in parentheses.
[a] No budgets issued in 1986 and 1991. Estimates are IMF figures.

expenditures. However, many expenditures such as defense spending and payments to the royal family occur off-budget.

In recent years, Saudi budget deficits have been running from 6 percent to more than 17 percent of GDP. For example, the Kingdom's estimated 1993 budget deficit was the equivalent of 11.3 percent of GDP, an amount approximately double the comparable American figure. Nonetheless, the Kingdom's growing deficit was ignored throughout most of the 1980s and early 1990s for one simple reason: Saudi Arabia was funding deficit spending through a drawdown of its substantial overseas assets.

The latter were estimated at anywhere from $115 billion to $120 billion as of 1981 when their drawdown began. Today, liquid reserves are estimated at between $6 billion and $7 billion.[61] The remainder of the Kingdom's foreign assets are comprised of now worthless loans to

Iraq ($26 billion) and other Arab countries, which have in effect been written off. Given this reality, the Kingdom has had no choice but to borrow money to cover its needs.

Since 1988, the Kingdom's internal debt has risen from zero to approximately $60 billion, of which between one-quarter and one-third is in the form of short-term treasury notes to banks. More alarming has been the growth of medium- and long-term debt. Composition of the latter is intriguing because its exact size is unknown given the amount of government paper issued since 1988 and the advent of "development bonds." SAMA has never clarified how many development bonds have been issued, or what percentage has been placed with banks or with government agencies. This information has even been refused to the twelve domestic banks, which have been solicited and pressured to take the paper. Estimates vary wildly. If SAMA is to be believed, no more than SR 30 billion was placed in 1988, and another SR 25 billion in 1989. Amounts for 1990 and 1991 are less clear. Even before the Kuwaiti crisis, SAMA had told the IMF that it intended to issue SR 33.5 billion of bonds in 1990, SR 43.0 billion in 1991, and SR 48.5 billion in 1992.[62] At least another SR 30 billion of bonds seems to have been placed in 1993. If that is true, then SAMA had issued upward of SR 210 billion worth of bonds by the end of 1993, of which 30 percent, or roughly SR 70 billion, is estimated to have been placed with the Kingdom's twelve banks. The remainder has been placed with government agencies and is considered less pressing.

Other domestic debt is easier to identify. In July 1989, PIF borrowed $660 million from a consortium of domestic and GCC financial institutions for unspecified projects. The PIF loan was the first direct government loan to have been made in more than twenty-five years and was rightly regarded as a trial balloon as far as testing not only the lending environment but also the reaction of the country's powerful fundamentalist forces who oppose interest. PIF's loan, once approved, was followed in rapid succession by others. In June 1991, the Ministry of Finance borrowed $2.5 billion from the Kingdom's five largest banks, save the Al-Rajhi Investment Banking Corporation. Several of the lenders were told by the Ministry of Finance that their participation was mandatory. This information was subsequently leaked, undoubtedly to show the banks' pique at both the low rate of interest (below the benchmark London interbank rate [LIBOR]) and the ministry's heavy-handedness.[63]

Table 5.4

Saudi Budget Allocations, 1987–1993 (SR billion)

Category	1987	1988	1989	1990	1992	1993
Defense/security	60.8	50.3	—	51.9	54.3	61.6
Education/human resources	23.7	21.7	24.0	26.2	31.1	34.1
Health/social development	11.1	7.7	10.6	11.8	12.2	14.1
Transport/communications	11.9	10.1	8.3	9.2	8.3	9.1
Administration	10.3	6.4	—	—	—	—
Lending institutions	3.6	6.5	6.0	6.0	—	—
Economic development	8.4	7.5	5.0	4.8	8.0	8.9
Utilities	—	18.6	—	—	—	—
Domestic subsidies	6.8	—	5.3	7.2	7.1	9.2
Municipal services	8.1	7.7	5.4	6.9	6.3	7.0
Infrastructure	4.3	—	2.6	—	2.1	2.1
Agriculture/water	—	—	—	6.9	—	—
Other	21.0	4.1	73.9	12.1	51.6	50.9
Total	170.0	141.2	141.1	143.0	181.0	197.0

Source: Ministry of Finance and National Economy.
Notes: No budget was issued in 1991; budget categories change yearly. Many expenditures occur off-budget. The 1994 budget gave no breakdown.

Several para-statal concerns, mostly SABIC affiliates and utility companies, also tapped the domestic market in 1990–1992, with Hadeed, the SABIC steel concern, being the first with a loan of SR 500 million. It was followed by SCECO-West (the electricity company of the Western Province) for $1.2 billion; Vela (Saudi ARAMCO's tanker subsidiary) for $300 million in the spring of 1992; Ibn Zahr (a SABIC affiliate) for $500 million in April 1992; the Ministry of Finance for another SR 10 billion in May 1992 to cover part of the purchase of British Tornado jets; Ibn Sina (a SABIC affiliate) for $275 million in August 1992; and al-Sharq (a SABIC affiliate) for $300 million in late fall of 1992. Overall, Saudi loan obligations to domestic banks stood at SR 11.7 billion ($3.12 billion) in local currency and $4.535 billion in dollar-denominated debt by the end of 1992. These obligations continued to mount in 1993.

The Ministry of Finance, Saudi ARAMCO, and Vela all tapped international markets for additional funds after the Kuwaiti crisis. The largest was a $4.5 billion placement secured by the Ministry of Finance in May 1991 from a consortium of banks led by J.P. Morgan.

Saudi ARAMCO borrowed $2 billion in March 1992, and Vela borrowed another $900 million in the same month. Overall, Saudi commitments to international lenders totaled $7.4 billion by the end of 1992. This figure jumped substantially in 1994 as the Kingdom renegotiated more than $9 billion worth of arms debt and purchased more than $6 billion worth of civilian aircraft on credit.

The government has made no attempt to hide its increased borrowing or the payment of interest. Instead, Fahd justified government borrowing during his 1992 budget address, noting, "The difficult circumstances of the previous two years, which brought heavy financial burdens, forced the government to borrow large amounts of money from inside the country and abroad."[64] He added later in another interview,

> Our debts before Iraq's problem were limited. But during the following nine months, the Kingdom undertook a great spending program. It was spending, which was without any restriction. It is not strange for a country to resort to credit markets in exceptional circumstances.[65]

Another member of the government, Prince Abdullah bin Faisal bin Turki, tried to put an altruistic spin to the government's action. Abdullah, head of the Royal Commission for Jubail and Yanbu, said, "One of the reasons why the government is borrowing is to increase the confidence of the private sector."[66]

However, there are other obligations as well. In late 1991, SAMA introduced treasury bills in denominations of four, thirteen, twenty-six, and fifty-two weeks to replace its former Bankers Security Deposits Accounts' (BSDAs) zero-coupon bills. With an attractive yield, total uptake has been approximately U.S. $25 billion or SR 93.75 billion. Increased government borrowing seems likely as the Ministry of Finance and National Economy has told all state organizations that they are to be self-funding in the future.[67] As a result, several para-statal concerns could be coming to the market for additional funds. Among the potential borrowers are SABIC affiliates; Saudia, the national airline; the Saline Water Conversion Corporation (SWCC); and other electricity companies.

The Kingdom's increased indebtedness has not gone unnoticed. Since 1991, the Bank of England has questioned the country's creditworthiness, and British banks have avoided the Kingdom's line of

credit established by Morgan Guaranty in 1991. Several U.S. government credit agencies have also expressed alarm, and one almost downgraded the Kingdom's credit rating in March 1993 until the Clinton
administration applied pressure. The International Monetary Fund
(IMF) has also trumpeted warnings, advising the Kingdom's rulers to
curtail expenditures or increase revenues. Prior to the announcement of
the 1994 budget, the government had forestalled doing either. Instead,
it had increased spending and subsidies while coping with the effects
of falling oil prices. Not surprisingly, estimates of 1993's budget deficit as a percentage of GDP were more than 11 percent, compared to the
targeted amount of 3.3 percent.

Added pressures seem likely. Although the government's debt load
is presently manageable, much medium-term debt will begin coming
due in the mid-1990s, severely affecting the Kingdom's finances at
that time. By the year 1997, the IMF projects that interest payments on
the Kingdom's debt will cost SR 28 billion, or roughly 12 percent of
all budget expenditures (see Table 5.5). Overall debt is expected to
total more than U.S. $108 billion, or roughly one year's GDP. Much
will depend on the government's newfound fiscal responsibility. If
spending is indeed curtailed as the 1994 budget implies, and oil prices
remain stable, the government should be able to meet its obligations.
The country's current account deficit, however, suggests that may
prove to be difficult, despite some narrowing in recent years (see Table
5.6). However, if the price of oil declines further, Saudi Arabia's new
indebtedness could have telling results. To meet its obligations, the
Kingdom would have to either borrow additional monies, or forego
repayments—a scenario that is not as unlikely as it sounds given the
country's past record on payment delays. Additional drawdowns of the
country's foreign assets are no longer an alternative. Yet there is one
other option. The government could raise funds by selling its shares in
Saudi companies and by privatizing such state concerns as Saudia and
Saudi Telecom. As of 1986, the government owned more than half of
the available shares on the Saudi stock market; those issues could be
cashed in.[68] However, such a course seems unlikely.

There are other worries as well. Many of the para-statal concerns
going to market, such as the SABIC affiliates and Saudi ARAMCO,
have ample cash flows and good credit histories. Other borrowers—
such as Saudia, SWCC, and the electric companies—do not. The latter
are especially risky, given the fact that they are prohibited from charg-

Table 5.5

Saudi Budget Projections, 1994–1997 (SR billion)

Year	Budget			Interest payments	Total debt
	Revenues	Expenditures	Deficit		
1994	175.0	201.0	−26.0	20.0	299.0
1995	180.0	210.0	−30.0	22.0	329.0
1996	186.0	221.0	−35.0	25.0	364.0
1997	192.0	233.0	−41.0	28.0	405.0

Source: IMF, "Staff Report: Saudi Arabia," 1993.

Table 5.6

Saudi Current Account Balances, 1982–1993

Year	Balance (U.S. $ billion)	Year	Balance (U.S. $ billion)
1982	+7.58	1989	−7.30
1983	−17.14	1990	−9.20
1984	−18.40	1991	−27.73[a]
1985	−12.93	1992	−19.43[a]
1986	−11.94	1993	−11.10[a]
1987	−9.57		
1988	−9.80		

Source: SAMA Annual Reports.
[a] IMF estimates.

ing real prices for their products and rely on government support and subsidies to remain liquid. That risk element has so far been ignored by both domestic and international lenders. And finally, in the worst-case scenario, if the House of Saud were overthrown and replaced by an Islamic republic, most of the country's medium-term debt obligations would be unilaterally abrogated due to their inclusion of interest.

The government's lack of fiscal restraint has another down side as well. By tapping the domestic market for funds, the government is in fact competing with the private sector for available monies. Although continuing to stress the importance of the private sector in stimulating the Saudi economy, the government's action is guaranteeing that the Saudi private sector will remain starved for credit.[69] Unlike the public sector, which can draw on international sources of funding, such options are no longer open to private borrowers, especially in light of the banking crisis of the 1980s and an unresponsive legal system.

Banking

The Kingdom's banking system was one of the chief casualties of the country's recession. Although it has since staged a recovery, Saudi banks have increasingly abandoned true banking as the government borrows more and more from them. Banking has always held a tenuous position in the country. Usury remains illegal, as does interest. The latter is viewed as especially heinous by the Kingdom's fundamentalist wing because the Prophet Mohammed equated giving or taking interest with having an incestuous relationship with one's mother, or committing adultery thirty-six times.[70]

During the boom, the banks were showered with deposits, many of them interest-free demand deposits from religious Saudis. Flush with cash, the banks subsequently recycled their deposits to domestic concerns, often falling over themselves and their own regulations in efforts to find borrowers. Despite the ideological and legal dilemmas posed by interest, banks neatly sidestepped the issue by masking interest as "commissions," "service charges," or "bookkeeping fees." In the wild boom days of the late 1970s and early 1980s, loans and advances skyrocketed from a mere SR 1.8 billion in 1973 to SR 29.2 billion in 1980, SR 46.6 billion in 1982, and SR 59.09 billion in 1985 (see Table 5.7). New entrepreneurs with no business experience were given millions of dollars, while banks often accepted fraudulently overvalued pieces of property for collateral. Documentation was lacking, and it was not unusual for borrowers to pledge the same collateral to several banks at the same time. But bank profits soared and few worried about the lack of guarantees.

When the downturn occurred in 1982–1986, the results were just as "impressive." As the government curtailed spending and instituted payment delays, Saudi enterprises lost their ability to repay their loans. Bankruptcies increased and the banks suddenly found themselves on the receiving end as thousands of borrowers either missed payments or completely reneged on their loans. Contractors, realizing the futility of suing the government, instead appealed to the Islamic or Sharia courts for

Table 5.7

Saudi Commercial Bank Loans and Advances, 1973–1990

Year	Outstanding loans (SR billion)	Year	Outstanding loans (SR billion)
1973	1.80	1982	46.6
1974	3.06	1983	47.94
1975	5.29	1984	54.87
1976	8.29	1985	59.09
1977	7.95	1986	56.53
1978	10.61	1987	54.35
1979	18.99	1988	59.40
1980	29.2	1989	68.54
1981	39.48	1990	59.94

Source: SAMA Annual Reports.

debt relief, claiming that the banks' charging of interest was un-Islamic, thereby invalidating their obligations. The courts readily complied and sometimes deducted interest payments already made from the principal of outstanding loans. Banks had no choice but to make huge provisions to cover their losses, and four Saudi banks out of the then eleven—Saudi Cairo, Saudi Investment, United Saudi Commercial, and Bank al-Jazira—required government support to remain solvent.[71]

In the light of such massive arrears and fraud, the government limited its actions to a number of face-saving measures including the creation of a special committee to handle banking disputes. The efficacy of the committee was debatable, and the banks themselves enacted several measures of their own. First was the creation of a blacklist of problem debtors, which theoretically froze all banking services to those appearing on the list. Initially opposed by the Ministry of Finance and National Economy and SAMA, the list was no more effective than the special SAMA committee.

The banks' other weapon proved infallible against future loan losses: the banks simply quit the domestic market save for a handful of quality borrowers and the government. Although bank profitability has since improved and some Saudi banks, such as Saudi American, rank among the more profitable in the world, the Saudi banking system remains suspect.

Not surprisingly, the Iraqi invasion of Kuwait spurred a massive flight of capital. In the first few days of the invasion, more than $10 billion in private deposits were removed from Saudi Arabia, and only gradually returned. Faced with massive liquidity problems, SAMA rushed in and offered to buy back up to half of the banks' holdings in development bonds. But as the possibility of an Iraqi invasion lessened, investors began repatriating their funds. With the conclusion of hostilities, Saudi banks have for all intents and purposes become government and para-statal lenders as government borrowing has mushroomed. They have also largely abandoned true banking due to the Kingdom's ideological and regulatory climate.[72] The result has been that private sector borrowing is relatively rare. Such a development is not overly troubling as private sector liquidity remains high. However, transferring those funds to would-be entrepreneurs remains a problem and continues to stunt private sector economic development. Until the question of interest is resolved and banks are given some guarantee that the funds they advance will be repaid, large sections of the private sector will continue to have no access to funding, with substantial ramifications for the Saudi economy.

More worrisome is the increase in government indebtedness to banks. The government's debt to the Kingdom's commercial banks rose more than threefold during 1989–1993 and shows no sign of slaking. Overall, government debt with banks now comprises anywhere from 30 percent to 40 percent of their deposits, roughly double the percentage held by American banks. There is another danger as well: most government debt held by the banks is long-term, while most of their deposits are short-term. The resulting mismatch of assets and liabilities could result in serious liquidity problems for the Kingdom's financial system.

The Legal System

The Saudi legal system remains one of the major impediments to the Kingdom's future economic growth. As Prince Talal bin Abdulaziz said during his 1961 press conference in Beruit, "In our country there is no law that upholds the freedom and rights of the citizen."[73] Despite the legal reforms embodied in Faisal's Ten-Point Program launched in 1962 and Fahd's Basic Law of 1992, little has changed. The Saudi legal system remains a quagmire. Cases can be handled by Sharia courts, several quasi-legal bodies, or royal diktat. The legal system is also bedeviled by inconsistent enforcement by the ultimate legal card, the House of Saud. The princes and princesses of the House of Saud and their entourages remain above the law. Saudi Arabia remains a country where SAMA's closure of a financial institution charged with irregularities can be overruled by Prince Sultan bin Abdulaziz, the defense minister; where the pressure of Fahd can force the "resignation" of the chairman-elect of Saudi American Bank; and where Interior Minister Prince Naif bin Abdulaziz can overrule court decisions on a whim.[74]

The Saudi legal system is unique in the Arab world as it remains the only one based solely on the principles of Sharia, or Islamic law. The Koran, as Saudis from Fahd downward point out, is the country's constitution and forms the backbone of the country's legal system. That presents a number of problems, as no distinction is made between secular laws and religious convictions in Islam, which encompasses all aspects of life. Sharia is also not codified, leading to a variety of conflicting rulings depending not only on which school of jurisprudence is followed but on which of the commentaries a particular judge may use on a particular day.

Therein lies the problem: the Kingdom's legal system needs some updating to make it more compatible with the demands of a modern economy. Compromise has bedeviled all Saudi monarchs since Abdulaziz united the country in 1925. He had dealt with the issue by leaving the Hejaz's more advanced legal system in place, including the commercial courts, which had been introduced by the Ottoman Turks. In doing so, the Saudi monarch had hoped to ease the legal gap between his kingdom's two chief provinces. Abdulaziz first appealed to his ulema for help. They disappointed him, ruling in February 1927 that "if there be any of them (Ottoman laws) in the Hejaz, it will be immediately abolished, and nothing except the pure Sharia will be applied."[75] Not liking their decision, Abdulaziz chose to ignore it, allowing the Hejazi institutions to continue. However, the issue was a particularly prickly one, especially as the king's ulema viewed the law and legal system as their special bailiwick. This situation weakened attempts at changing the system and continued to plague Saud and Faisal.

The issue of reform of the judiciary was finally broached in 1962 by Faisal, who made the promulgation of a constitution and the creation of an independent legal system and Justice Ministry two of the ten points in his reform package. The promise of a constitution remained unfulfilled at the time of his death; the creation of the Justice Ministry was more successful; it took place after the death of Riyadh's Grand Mufti in 1970. Faisal then abolished the position, replacing it with the Justice Ministry, and appointing the chief *qadi* of Jeddah, Mohammed al-Harkan, the country's first justice minister. The functions of the Mufti's office were split into several departments. Besides creating the justice ministry, Faisal also created several quasi-legal committees under the Commerce Ministry to handle commercial issues. The first of these was the Committee for the Settlement of Commercial Disputes (CSCD), created in 1967. Empowered to hear all commercial disputes save for those dealing with land, the CSCD had courts in Jeddah, Riyadh, and Dammam. Each "court" had three judges—two schooled in Islamic law and the third a legal consultant from the Ministry of Commerce. The CSCD's work load grew quickly; in 1973 the Jeddah branch heard 36 cases with claims of approximately SR 2 million. Thirteen years later, the same body was ruling on anywhere from 700 to 800 cases each year, with total claims of SR 700 million. Despite its increased work load, the CSCD's staffing remained constant until it was phased out in 1987–1988 in favor of a Board of Grievances, which was considered part of the king's executive staff. Another body still in existence is the Negotiable Instruments Committee (NIC), which reviews written contractual obligations. Located in Riyadh, Jeddah, and Dammam, the NIC is staffed by three legal experts from the Ministry of Commerce.

In addition to these bodies, there are several other quasi-legal organizations. There are review boards that handle labor disputes, as well as the SAMA panel, which offers judgments in banking disputes. In fact, the creation of more and more quasi-legal bodies outside the pale of the cleric-dominated Ministry of Justice seems to be a long-term policy goal of the al-Saud in their quest for a more independent judiciary. Not surprisingly, the ministry has moved to protect its jurisdiction. As early as 1986, the ministry issued a circular saying that all legal disputes, including commercial disputes, were to be heard in Sharia courts if they occurred outside the three main population centers where the NIC and CSCD were based. Similar pronouncements were made in 1990–1993, when fundamentalists in tapes and leaflets called for the abolition of all legal committees and proposed that all cases, not only criminal ones, be heard in Sharia courts.[76] Such calls have been largely ignored, as have calls that all Saudis be given equal treatment before the law regardless of rank, social standing, or position.

If receiving judgments remains difficult in Saudi Arabia, the enforcement process is even more tortuous. Once a judgment is handed down by a Sharia court or commercial panel, the judgment is sent to the local governor who then sends it to the civil rights police who oversee its enforcement. The process is extremely venal; policemen are often paid to protect defendants fearing arrest or seizure of assets. In addition, Saudis with close ties to the governor or police can avoid arrest altogether, even though a court has issued a judgment. It is also not uncommon for members of the royal family to enter the judgment mechanism. One such intervention occurred in 1987 when Riyadh Governor Prince Salman bin Abdulaziz ordered Saudi American Bank to drop all proceedings against one of his friends, who owed the bank millions of dollars. The bank had no choice but to comply, and even offered its errant client fresh funds to smooth the prince's ruffled feathers.[77]

Foreign investors have also discovered another danger in doing business in the Kingdom: commercial hostage taking. Although rare, the issue has nonetheless seriously tarnished Saudi Arabia's overseas reputation. The risk is to foreign entities, that enter business partnerships with princes or high-ranking Saudis. When disputes arise, the Saudi partner sometimes takes his partner's employees hostage. The process is simple; all expatriates working in the Kingdom are given work documents upon surrendering their passports. Once the passport is in the hands of the Saudi partner, the employee is essentially at the employer's mercy. Although embassies can issue new passports, they can not issue the necessary exit–re-entry visa required to leave the Kingdom.

The problem of commercial hostage taking was so severe in 1987–1988 that a formal protest was lodged by the European Economic Community (EEC) missions in Riyadh with Foreign Minister Prince Saud bin Faisal bin Abdulaziz. No action was ever taken, and due to the magnitude of trade between most countries and the Saudis, foreign missions are reluctant to push the issue too hard for fear of hurting their business interests. The result is that some expatriates have been held against their will in the Kingdom for years—their only "crime" being the disagreement between their employer and the Saudi partner.

One of the more disturbing cases concerned Neville Norton, a British citizen who was held for sixteen years following several disputes with Prince Naif. During that time, Norton was arrested seventeen times and spent five years in Saudi prison.[78]

The Saudi Bureaucracy

Given the fact that a large percentage of Saudi Arabia's wealth is controlled by the government or public sector, the Kingdom's bureaucracy has been given an especially important role to play in the country's economic development. The bureaucracy has served as the government's chief vehicle for distributing oil wealth, as well as planning, coordinating, and fostering economic growth, especially given the private sector's unwillingness to take more than a short-term investment perspective. Unfortunately, studies suggest that the Saudi bureaucracy remains more of a hindrance than a help to economic growth.

Part of the reason is steeped in history. Prior to the ascension of King Saud, the Saudi bureaucracy was minuscule and largely consisted of Abdulaziz's coterie of followers. It was only in the mid-1950s that the foundations for the Saudi bureaucracy were laid, with the "importation" of hundreds of Egyptian technocrats who were brought in to streamline Saudi procedures and cleanse the bureaucracy of corruption. The system instituted by the Egyptians, however, was an amplification of the old Ottoman file system of countless signatures and counter-signatures. As a result, the new administration proved just as inefficient and venal as the one it replaced.[79]

Nor were the first men chosen to staff the new bureaucracy any better. Often they were plucked out of school (in some cases elementary schools) and given powerful positions in fields of which they only had a rudimentary understanding. The vast majority were also selected on the basis of family connection and loyalty to the al-Saud rather than inherent ability.[80] The boom brought with it other problems: not only was job turnover high as bureaucrats were likely to remain in the public sector only until they found a higher-paying position in the private sector, but the government and state apparatus were also used to provide jobs for Saudi university graduates unable to find positions elsewhere. The result is that the bureaucracy has been unable to provide leadership and has often acted more as an impediment rather than a catalyst to economic growth. Like government bodies the world over, many Saudi agencies and ministries have sought to protect their own little fiefdoms at the expense of national objectives. This problem is greater in the Kingdom, however, as the bureaucracy has more managerial powers than most.

The limitations of the Saudi bureaucracy are best illustrated by several surveys and studies. According to a study completed in 1988, 82 percent of the Saudi bureaucrats surveyed expressed their dislike of developing innovation compared to 70 percent of Egyptian bureaucrats and 68 percent of Sudanese bureaucrats.[81] Although this distrust of innovation is prevalent among most Arab bureaucracies, the percentage of Saudi dislike was especially high. Among Saudi respondents, 89.2 percent answered yes to the question, "Is it better to cancel programs that could cause social conflict?" while 94.9 percent expressed approval of the phrase, "Social change should not be instituted at the expense of traditional values." This conservatism was confirmed by another survey of 231 middle-level bureaucrats in 1985. Of the 123 who responded, only 12.8 percent said that more than half of their colleagues and subordinates were innovative. Just as importantly, 37.4 percent said that more than half of their subordinates were reluctant to take responsibility for their decisions. Equally damning were the conclusions that found favoritism, apathy, and lack of communication to be endemic to the Saudi bureaucracy.[82]

Another study commissioned by the Saudi Institute for Public Administration found that absenteeism among Saudi bureaucrats is rife, as are late arrivals and early departures in the workday. The study further found that many Saudi bureaucrats have outside jobs, which they put first.[83] All of this has led to complaints about the bureaucracy's inefficiency, lack of speed in handling documents, and inevitable corruption. In addition, many of the most able bureaucrats have left because the long tenure of many ministers has erased their chances for promotion. The move of many government bodies to Riyadh as well as the "Nejdization" of the bureaucracy have also led to the exodus of other qualified civil servants. Finally, the Saudi civil service protects all bureaucrats from firing, even when high rates of absenteeism and less than satisfactory performance justify termination. This latter fact is best illustrated by the example of two Saudia mechanics whose negligence nearly caused the crash of one of the airline's jets. Despite overwhelming evidence, and the strong backing of Defense Minister Sultan, it still took more than two years to have the offenders fired.[84]

Making the Saudi bureaucracy even more tortuous is the fact that the al-Saud have created more than sixty autonomous bodies and agencies outside established ministries.[85] Whether this has been done to negate the institutionalization of existing ministries, or to facilitate administration, is difficult to say. Some agencies, such as the Royal Commission for Jubail and Yanbu, are completely independent and funded separately. This has resulted in greater efficiency—the Royal Commission, for example, cut through the bureaucratic snarls surrounding the start-up of the industrial cities—but has also contributed to overlapping functions. Other agencies such as SAMA are considered independent but subservient to their corresponding ministries. Prior to the early 1980s, the heads of some of these agencies wielded as much power as the ministers to whom they were theoretically reporting. In fact, several such agency heads had been given minister-at-large portfolios in the cabinet.

Efforts at streamlining the Saudi bureaucracy have been few. In mid-1992, Fahd announced plans to simplify company start-ups. New companies no longer have to have their articles of association notarized, nor do they need royal decrees to commence operations.[86] Although this is a step in the right direction, the licensing and commercial registration process in the Kingdom remains time-consuming.

Sectoral Overview

The Saudi economy can presently be divided into four main sections: oil, petrochemicals, non-oil industry, and agriculture. This division necessarily excludes the government, even though the latter is intimately involved, either directly or indirectly, through subsidies in almost every endeavor.

Government participation has taken a toll as the Saudi non-oil economic sectors are inefficient. Government subsidies abound, allowing marginal concerns to survive. The danger in such a course is that the jobs such undertakings create will always be tenuous and reliant on government support.

Oil and Minerals

The basis of the Kingdom's oil industry is the ground on which it is built. The Kingdom stands over some of the world's richest oil fields,

Table 5.8

Saudi ARAMCO Proven Oil Reserves, 1971–1990 (million barrels)

Year	Reserves at beginning of year	Annual production	Reserves at end of year
1971	88,063	1,642	90,157
1972	90,157	2,098	92,992
1973	92,992	2,677	96,222
1974	96,222	2,997	103,480
1975	103,480	2,492	107,857
1976	107,857	3,054	110,187
1977	110,187	3,291	110,443
1978	110,443	2,961	113,284
1979	113,284	3,377	113,384
1980	113,384	3,525	113,491
1981	113,491	3,513	116,747
1982	116,747	2,310	165,459
1983	165,459	1,597	166,000
1984	166,000	1,435	166,300
1985	166,300	1,110	166,500
1986	166,500	1,712	167,000
1987	167,000	1,457	167,400
1988	167,400	1,804	252,384
1989	252,384	1,775	257,504
1990	257,504	2,284	257,900

Source: SAMA Annual Reports.

which, because they are relatively shallow and easy to drill, have well-head costs that are among the lowest in the world. The result has been the world's most profitable and, since the disintegration of the former Soviet Union, largest oil extraction industry. The country's proven oil reserves remain huge and have continued to grow despite accelerating production. As of 1990, Saudi ARAMCO's proven reserves totaled 257,900 million barrels, or approximately 26 percent of the world's total (see Table 5.8). That figure may be misleading as large sections of the country have never been charted or drilled.

New discoveries are constantly being made. One of the largest took place in 1988 near the town of al-Hawtah, 190 kilometers south of Riyadh—a field that boosted the Kingdom's known reserves by 20 percent. A few months later another field near Dilam, 47 kilometers southeast of Riyadh, was discovered. If the two fields are linked, it would be the world's largest on-shore field, even surpassing the Kingdom's Ghawar field.[87] The run of new discoveries continued through 1993 when geologists found oil, gas, and condensates near Mudeen, 180 kilometers west of Tabuk.[88]

Besides crude oil, the Kingdom has ample reserves of natural gas. Saudi natural gas reserves stand at 184.1 trillion cubic feet, putting the Kingdom third in the world behind the former Soviet Union and Iran. Other minerals abound. The most promising deposits are the gold mines at Mahd al-Dhahab and Sukhaybarat. The best-known of the pair is at Mahd al-Dhahab, said to be King Solomon's mine. There is evidence of intermittent mining activity for several thousand years. The mine has an estimated life of twelve to fifteen years, annually producing 2.8 tons of gold from 120,000 tons of ore. Sukhaybarat is now producing as well and is said to have a life span of thirteen years.[89] Other promising discoveries include large deposits of zinc, copper, bauxite, phosphates, and iron. One iron ore deposit at Wadi Sawain, about 340 miles northeast of Medina, is said to have upward of 300 million tons of low-grade iron ore, which could be used to supply the Saudi Iron and Steel Company (Hadeed) smelters in Jubail.[90] Although preliminary ore extraction has taken place, development of the site has slowed with the downturn in government revenues.

Coal has also been discovered in a wide arc from the Jordanian border, sweeping south through Buraidah, Riyadh, and the Empty Quarter. Exploitation of such deposits seems unlikely given the abundance of oil.[91] The Ghurayyah deposit near Wadi Sawain contains large amounts of tantalum, columbium, tin, and uranium, which could reportedly add 34 percent to the world's known deposits of tantalum and 8 percent to those of columbium.[92] One of the most promising mining areas lies on the floor of the Red Sea. Tests performed by the Jeddah-based Saudi-Sudanese Red Sea Joint Venture Commission have indicated that ocean-bed mud-pumping extraction could yield commercial quantities of copper, zinc, cobalt, and silver.[93] Stone quarrying is another possibility. Granite is quarried near Taif, Yanbu, and Medin, while limestone is quarried near Riyadh. Government policies specifying the use of local materials in construction have spurred the use of Saudi stone, but the Saudi preference for imported decorative stone has not helped that particular industry.

The Saudi budget crisis has seemingly ensured that the development of many minerals will be delayed for years if not decades. Saudi deposits tend to be either large with low-grade ore, or small with high-grade ore, making extraction costly and of questionable economic value at existing world prices. This is compounded by the fact that mining typically requires large amounts of water, which is in short supply.

History and Background

Interest in Saudi Arabia's oil potential began in the early 1920s when a British consortium was awarded an exploratory concession. They allowed the concession to expire unused, and in 1933, the concession was awarded to the Standard Oil Company of California (SOCAL). Five years later, the company had its first major strike, and the history of Saudi Arabia was forever altered.

Development of the American company's concession occurred slowly and nearly ground to a halt at the outbreak of World War II. However, as concerns intensified over America's oil-producing capabilities, interest in the Kingdom's oil fields intensified. The Arabian-American Oil Company (ARAMCO)—as SOCAL's joint venture came to be called—built a refinery and port complex at Ras Tanura using the labor of Italian prisoners of war, and soon was exporting large quantities of oil. Until the late 1960s, ARAMCO was given a relatively free hand in the development of the Kingdom's oil industry. Development generally meant the expansion of production facilities. Such a policy enabled Saudi Arabia to produce nearly 10 million bpd throughout the 1960s and 1970s. However, the emphasis on production meant that development of downstream facilities was neglected, leading to importing of many refined products. That reliance on foreign supplies, as well as the desire for higher profits from downstream ventures, led the Kingdom's technocrats to insist that the country's petroleum industry be developed, over the objections of ARAMCO's American partners. To that end, in 1962 the Saudis created Petromin, a wholly owned state company, to oversee their move into the downstream sector.

Petromin's first downstream project was the construction of fairly low-tech refineries in Jeddah and Riyadh. Rapid expansion followed. Under the leadership of Abdul Hadi Taher, Petromin handled all hydrocarbon-related industries until 1975 when the Saudi Basic Industries Corporation (SABIC) was created to oversee the country's petrochemical industry. By the end of 1987, Petromin consisted of over twenty firms, each of which operated independently. Petromin owned or had partial stakes in one lubricant base oil refinery, three domestic refineries, three joint venture export refineries, two joint venture lubricant blending plants, and one wholly owned lubricant blending operation. Petromin also sold crude oil, handling state-to-state deals as well as the odd private sale by members of the al-Saud. The company also handled liquefied petroleum gas (LPG) sales to foreigners and sales of gas to SABIC companies. Petromin's best profits, however, came from sending crude oil abroad for refining, and re-importing it for resale. Petromin's large size and unwieldy composition acted as detriments to its overall efficiency. Also having an impact was the government's decision to sell many of Petromin's products, including gasoline, at below cost.

The Kingdom's recession led to the reorganization of the Saudi petroleum industry as profitability became a major priority. With the fall of Yamani in 1986, his successor, Hisham Nazer, moved to undertake a reorganization. Armed with a study from Arthur D. Little, Nazer moved quickly to rationalize operations. His first act was to complete the nationalization of ARAMCO. Although the oil company had been "nationalized" in the seventies, the final paperwork had not been finished, and ARAMCO remained an American-registered company. Nazer scrapped the existing corporation and its vestiges of American ownership and transformed it into a Saudi entity called Saudi ARAMCO. However, Nazer's main focus was Petromin. In January 1989, Petromin was turned into a holding company and had the scope of its operations further reduced. Its crude sales division was passed to Saudi ARAMCO, and Petromin was then broken up into three divisions: Saudi Arabian Marketing and Refinery Corporation (SAMAREC), Petrolube (which produces greases and lubricants), and a vaguely defined Minerals Division.

The Kingdom's oil industry was altered in 1993 for the second time in less than four years when SAMAREC was scrapped and its operations, and those of Petromin, were merged with Saudi ARAMCO in a royal decree issued by Fahd on July 1.[94] Fahd's action made Saudi ARAMCO the largest state-owned integrated oil company in the world. The forced merger was undertaken for a number of reasons. First and foremost was the desire for greater efficiency. The creation of SAMAREC had failed to solve the problems it had inherited from

Petromin, including a bloated work force of 12,000. Saudi ARAMCO, it was felt, with its long history in the industry and with the vestiges of American management, could get SAMAREC into shape faster than any domestic management. Saudi ARAMCO was also conceded to have better technicians and training expertise.

A second reason for the merger was the expansion of the Kingdom's oil industry. Saudi ARAMCO's financial status was stronger than SAMAREC's, so the former was able to tap international and domestic markets for finance. SAMAREC, laboring under inefficient management as well as deficits acquired from selling its products below cost, was not. The third reason for the merger was that as Saudi Arabia pushed into downstream products, Saudi ARAMCO's marketing might was perceived as greater.[95]

The merger is expected to require months if not years to complete. Under terms of the agreement, Saudi ARAMCO took all of SAMAREC's assets in the three domestic refineries at Yanbu, Riyadh, and Jeddah, the domestic distribution network in the Kingdom, and SAMAREC's overseas marketing operations for refined products, sulfur, and LPG. Saudi ARAMCO also took the shares in the joint venture refineries that Petromin operated with Mobil, Shell, and Petrola, as well as Petrolube. All joint venture operations with foreign partners will continue to operate as before, but with their Saudi share of products now being marketed by Saudi ARAMCO. Existing SAMAREC contracts with customers will also be honored by Saudi ARAMCO.

Post–Desert Storm Saudi Oil Operations

Operation Desert Storm served as a catalyst for the rapid expansion of the Saudi oil industry. Since the conclusion of hostilities, the industry has launched a massive multi-billion-dollar program aimed at expanding production, increasing refining capabilities, and securing downstream markets. Overall, Saudi ARAMCO is expected to spend more than $35 billion over the next decade in its efforts; the former SAMAREC is expected to spend another $12 billion during the same period to upgrade its refineries.[96]

The first tine of the Saudi strategy is already bearing results. Saudi oil reserves have mushroomed, and Saudi ARAMCO has rapidly moved to exploit new fields. Besides increasing production, the Saudis want to improve their current slate of products, especially lead-free gasoline. By the end of the century, the former SAMAREC refineries plan to be exporting at least 350,000 bpd of unleaded fuel. The linchpin in this is the upgrading of the giant Saudi ARAMCO refinery at Ras Tanura, parts of which are more than fifty years old. The cost of the upgrade is an estimated $12 billion dollars over twelve years.[97] At the end of its overhaul, the refinery should be able to produce more than 1 million bpd from a full slate of products. Saudi ARAMCO is also planning to move ahead on the upgrade and expansion of the former SAMAREC's domestic refineries in a three-phase plan. Phase I will concern the Yanbu, Riyadh, and Jeddah refineries at a cost of $2 billion, but has been delayed due to the Kingdom's budget crunch.[98]

Saudi Arabia is also adding to its international distribution network. In 1988, Saudi ARAMCO made its first acquisition, picking up 50 percent of a joint venture with Texaco (Star Enterprises) in a controversial $812 million deal. In return, Saudi ARAMCO acquired three modern refineries, 1,400 Texaco stations, and 10,000 franchised stations in a twenty-three-state area. The deal is an insurance policy during periods of low oil demand as the Texaco outlets provide a permanent market for 600,000 bpd of crude.[99]

The Saudis have also pursued downstream markets in the Far East with differing degrees of success. In May 1991, Saudi ARAMCO signed a preliminary contract with Nippon Oil Company and Nikko Kyodo Company, both of Japan, as well as Caltex Petroleum Corporation of the United States. Under terms of the agreement, the Nissa Petroleum Project Company was created to undertake several refinery projects in both Japan and Saudi Arabia at a projected cost of U.S. $8 billion. Problems immediately arose: falling crude prices and the economic downturn in Japan plus a reevaluation of Saudi ARAMCO's budget forced the cancellation of the proposed Saudi refinery in mid-1993. Several months later the Japanese segment of the deal was canceled as well.[100] More successful has been Saudi ARAMCO's purchase of 35 percent of SsangYong Oil Refining Company, South Korea's third largest oil refiner and a major lubricants producer as well.[101]

To secure markets, Saudi ARAMCO has also sought other opportunities, including an oft-rumored joint venture deal with France's Total by which the Saudi company would acquire several refineries and petroleum stations in a deal conservatively estimated at $7 billion.[102] Such an acquisition, however, increasingly seems unlikely, especially given lower oil prices and Saudi ARAMCO's falling resources.

The expansion of the Kingdom's international markets underlines a profound shift in Saudi oil policy as the Kingdom's strategy has shifted to carving out market share. During the Gulf conflict, the Kingdom regained its former market share within the cartel, which it had conceded during its role as swing producer during the early 1980s. Today, Saudi Arabia seems unwilling to give up its newfound gains, refusing to produce less than 8.0 million bpd. Such a stance has contributed to the softening in the price of oil. The return of Kuwaiti crude exports has already pressured world markets, as has Iran's increasing production as well. When Iraq returns to OPEC, the impact on the worldwide price of crude could be substantial, knocking it to between $10 and $12 per barrel.

The problem for Saudi Arabia is that as the country sinks deeper into debt, a certain level of oil revenue is necessary to repay existing obligations, as well as to avoid the need to take out additional credits. To achieve that level, Saudi Arabia may very well have to scrap its OPEC membership—a policy consideration that seems less and less unlikely as the Kingdom seeks to preserve its newfound market share.

Petrochemicals

Mirroring the expansion of Saudi ARAMCO is the growth of the Kingdom's petrochemical industry. Saudi Arabia's production capacity of petrochemicals was expected to jump from 13 million tons to more than 20 million tons when a $6 billion growth program was completed in 1993.[103] Expansions were planned for eleven of SABIC's industries, especially in three product areas: ethylene, ammonia, and methanol. In addition to these products and their derivatives, SABIC is also moving into other products such as propylene and polypropylene, as well as MTBE, a lead-free octane booster for gasoline.[104]

Saudi Arabia's petrochemical industry owes part of its existence to Abdullah Tariki. Tariki, who became the country's first oil minister, was a young ARAMCO engineer when he began complaining about the process of flaring. Most Saudi oil is mixed with natural gas—in particular, ethane—in the ground. When it is pumped, the gas has to be separated from the oil, and for years the gas was flared, or burned, at the wellhead. At the height of the oil boom, flares illuminated the desert, and Tariki rightly complained that ARAMCO was wasting a precious natural resource. Tariki's complaints led to the Kingdom's

Master Gas System. Built at a cost of $20 billion, the Master Gas System collects the ethane and other gases at the wellhead for use as fuel and feedstock for the Kingdom's petrochemical industries. In 1976, SABIC was created to guide the Kingdom's first generation of petrochemical plants. Working closely in tandem with the Royal Commission for Jubail and Yanbu, SABIC created or took control of fifteen petrochemical and iron processing plants in the next decade.

The Saudi investment in resource-based industries (RBIs) proved enormous. Besides investing in the Master Gas System, and spending another $37 billion in infrastructural projects for the Jubail and Yanbu sites, billions more were spent on the plants themselves. Unlike other oil-rich countries, Saudi Arabia's venture into RBIs was characterized by its emphasis on securing international partners. This was partially due to the experiences of the Saudi Arabian Fertilizer Company (SAFCO), which had gone on line in 1970, and had proved less successful than had been projected. Because of that, SABIC pursued "50/50" joint venture agreements with international concerns, which gave it access to foreign technologies and managerial experience while spreading investment risk as well. More importantly, foreign partners were also responsible for marketing nearly three-quarters of the new companies' outputs.

The Kingdom's RBI operated under several advantages and disadvantages. Among the former were government incentives by which plants were made eligible for free land, heavily discounted energy and water, and concessionary financing. Tax holidays were also offered, and SABIC, like Petromin before it, offered oil entitlements with foreign investors being guaranteed a certain amount of oil at OPEC prices per every million dollars invested in the projects. Most important was the fact that the Kingdom priced its feedstocks substantially below world levels. In 1985, when most of the Kingdom's petrochemical complex was coming on line, the price of basic feedstocks—ethane and methane—was approximately $0.50 per BTU, compared to a price of $4–$4.50 in Europe, and the United States' $3.50–$3.75.[105] Making the deep discounts possible was the fact that these first plants were based on abundant supplies of ethane, a gas that can only be flared or shipped at great cost to export markets.

Discounted feedstock prices, however, were necessary to offset the Kingdom's vast disadvantages. Among the latter were its great distance from export markets, more expensive building costs, and the lack of a skilled work force. Subsidized feedstock prices were necessary from another view: since most European petrochemical plants are naphtha-based (naphtha is a by-product of the refining process), oil prices of less than $30 per barrel erase the Kingdom's normal price advantage as regards feedstock, necessitating price supports.

In recognition of those discounts, the Europeans, Americans, and Japanese erected tariff barriers against SABIC petrochemicals, plastics, fertilizers, and steel. The Saudis and their GCC brethren bitterly protested, since they allow foreign products to enter their countries virtually duty-free. The matter continues to drag on as GCC and EEC negotiators have been unable to reach agreement. The issue is a critical one for SABIC and its GCC counterparts, as the EEC already accounts for 25.6 percent of SABIC's overall output.[106] Given the impasse, SABIC has decided to locate future facilities in home markets, with overseas production projected to comprise 30 percent of the company's overall total in the future.[107]

The Saudi private sector's investment in petrochemicals has been mixed due to several factors. During the initial first generation of petrochemical plants, SABIC was awarded exclusive rights to manufacture most petrochemicals in the Kingdom. SABIC, critics noted, later refused to surrender dozens of unused licenses because, as senior SABIC officials explained, it considered the private sector incapable of handling such big jobs.

There were other reasons as well. First and foremost, the first-generation petrochemical plants were regarded as less profitable than their second-generation counterparts. SABIC officials were thus unwilling to give the private sector the fruits of their labors by allowing them access to second-generation licenses. This intransigence has been facilitated by the slow pace of SABIC's privatization. The government was supposed to sell upward of 70 percent of its shares to the private sector by 1985. Today, that figure stands at only 30 percent—in direct contravention of SABIC's charter. SABIC remains under government control, and the Saudi minister of industry remains the company's chairman. As such, licenses for secondary petrochemical plants have been regularly blocked or delayed by the minister's office. Another problem has been SABIC's insistence that local investors buy its products at international prices rather than the subsidized prices at which it sells to its own affiliates. Private sector investment has been lower than projected, despite boosts from groups such as Saudi Venture Capital

Group (SVCG) and Chemvest. Other firms are gradually entering the field, but most of their contributions are in export industries rather than in manufacturing because the former provide the most promising markets.

The difficulties facing the private sector were amply underlined in the summer of 1993 when the Council of Ministers refused to approve the country's first private sector petrochemical project. The project, a joint venture between Mobil and the Arabian Chemical Investment Company, called the Arabian American Chemical Company, would have produced upward of 830,000 tons of MTBE per year. At the time of the council's decision, the company had already secured funding from SIDF and a consortium of banks and was only awaiting commercial registration. The decision was all the more curious as Louay Nazer, the son of the Kingdom's oil minister, Hisham Nazer, is the president of the Arabian Chemical Investment Company. In rejecting the planned company, the council justified its decision because "of the need to have a clear policy by which investments are carried out in the petrochemical industry."[108] However, as many analysts noted, private sector investment in the petrochemical industry has been bandied about for years during which time the government was supposedly preparing its policy. What seems likely is that the government has decided to have some public sector participation in all petrochemical projects, through either Saudi ARAMCO or SABIC. This new course was reinforced later in November when another private sector petrochemical project between the United States' AMOCO Company and Arabian Chemical Investment Company was canceled as well.

Some officials concede that the government's approach to developing the Kingdom's petrochemical complex is all wrong. "They are doing it backwards," an analyst from the Saudi Industrial Development Fund (SIDF) told the authors. "They think that by supplying the material, such as basic plastics, they will generate the business. But if you look at the plastic industry, historically, it doesn't work that way. Plastics are used in substitution for other materials."

Non-Oil Industry

More than 1,900 companies comprise Saudi Arabia's non-oil industrial sector. Some are viable concerns, but others, perhaps the majority, are not. Typical of many is the Riyadh Wooden Door Company. Launched with great fanfare in the late 1980s, it was touted as another example of the Kingdom's growing industrial revolution. State-of-the-art machinery produced high-quality doors for the growing housing market, and the company was also making a profit. But beneath the veneer of success was another story. Save for one Saudi manager, all of the blue-collar work force was Thai, while the managers were American. In addition to the workers, all materials were imported, including the wood, glue, and, of course, machinery. Profitability was also dependent on subsidized electricity, subsidized water, and subsidized finance. Riyadh Wooden Door Company thus amply illustrates the shortcomings of the Kingdom's non-oil industrial enterprises, specifically their dependence on subsidies, foreign workers, and imported materials.

Although much effort and money have been spent on expanding the Kingdom's non-oil industrial base, the results have been uneven. Early Saudi industrialization was largely situated in al-Hasa, where ARAMCO established an office that gave loans and assistance to local entrepreneurs. The first wave of infrastructural projects in the 1950s also laid the foundations for the Kingdom's cement, building materials, and construction industries as low-tech companies were founded to churn out needed concrete, bricks, and cinderblocks. Development soared during the Kingdom's boom period. As with other endeavors, industrialization was accompanied by the introduction of investment incentives and other subsidies. Foreign companies were also encouraged to invest. Despite various incentives, industrial investment was less than expected. With construction costs ranging from 40 percent to 70 percent higher than the United States, a small domestic market, long distances from suppliers and markets, no protection for intellectual property rights, and the lack of a trained work force, Saudi Arabia presented limited investment opportunities. Still, for foreign companies wanting to curry favor with Riyadh or secure additional contracts, some investment was often necessary. The result was an increase in industrial projects, as the number licensed in the country grew from 400 to a little more than 1,900 during the boom.[109] The majority of industrial concerns were in building materials and food processing. Due to the boom, efficiency was often overlooked, especially as contracts to local concerns were often padded to aid their development.

The budding industrial revolution, however, was severely hurt by the recession that began in 1981. Many firms went bankrupt in the resulting shakeout of the economy; others drastically cut back their operations as government contracts and expenditures sharply decreased. The government tried several tactics to stimulate the local industrial sector. In its Third Five-Year Plan, which went into effect in 1985, the government challenged the private sector to become more assertive and active. Such pleas largely fell on deaf ears. Private sector investment, which rose 13.8 percent in 1981, fell 3.8 percent the next year, and 7.2 percent in 1983, a downward trend that continued throughout the recession. The number of industrial licenses issued by the Ministry of Industry and Electricity fell sharply as well. Overall, non-oil GDP rose at a paltry annual rate of 1.8 percent for the ten-year period of 1981 to 1991. However, even that growth was misleading, as much of the Kingdom's non-oil industrial sector was dependent on government or oil industry contracts.

To fight the recession, the Kingdom's planners hit upon several ideas. One was to pressure its main trade partners to encourage their companies to invest in the country. American, Japanese, German, French, British, and Italian firms were targeted with mixed results, especially as the Kingdom has refused to sign double taxation accords with most of its trade partners. Causing additional concerns was the issue of hostage taking, as well as the long delays prospective investors had in receiving Saudi visas. In addition, Saudi efforts occurred at the peak of the recession, which meant that Riyadh was dealing from a position of weakness. As its imports tumbled, the pressure it could bear on its main suppliers also fell. Among the projects most eagerly courted was that of a 60,000 unit per year light pickup truck assembly plant.[110] The plant's viability was always questionable because it would have depended on imported parts and labor, plus it could never have offered enough sales to provide simple economies of scale. Negotiations between the Saudis and Toyota, Nissan, and other Japanese automakers went on for years without success. Although the Saudis offered a full range of subsidies and incentives, as well as protective tariffs, the Japanese never rose to the bait, especially following the less than stunning successes achieved by the Kingdom's two existing automotive plants—one a bus factory, the other a heavy truck assembly plant. By 1986, hopes for the truck plant were dead.

Another tactic the Saudi government tried was the offset investment program, which has been tied to defense sales.[111] The program began in 1983 when the Saudi government informed bidders for a $3.94 billion military communications and control complex that they would have to invest a sum equal to 35 percent of the technical services, equipment, and technology component of the contract in Saudi-based, high-tech joint ventures. The offset program, the brainchild of Defense and Aviation Minister Prince Sultan bin Abdulaziz, had two priorities: the transfer of needed technology to Saudi industries and the training of a highly skilled Saudi work force.

The winning consortium, led by Boeing and Westinghouse, subsequently founded the Boeing Industrial Technology Group (BITG) to oversee industrial investment. BITG proposed ten projects. The first four were mostly aviation-oriented and included an airframe maintenance center, an avionics electronic maintenance center, an aircraft hydraulics and subsystems maintenance center, and a computer software center. General Electric, which won a radar supply contract, also proposed a jet engine overhaul company as its contribution to the offset program. All of the companies called for "50–50" equity sharing by BITG and other foreign investors, and their Saudi counterparts. Technical contractors were also appointed by each company to oversee the technology transfer.

The quintet encountered immediate problems. The Saudis insisted that the national airline, Saudia, be given equity participation, thus confronting the new companies with the prospect of having their largest potential customer on their board of directors. Other Saudi concerns were reluctant to invest; the Saudi Advanced Industries Company was created to provide smaller businessmen a vehicle for participating in the new companies, but the flotation had to be extended and considerable government pressure exerted before the SR 100 million offering was fully taken up. There were lengthy delays in garnering SIDF subsidized funding, industrial licenses, and commercial registration. The oft-promised high-tech industrial park was put on hold several times, forcing additional stoppages. Other problems came from the Saudi government's strange refusal to promise business to the offset ventures, even though air force contracts were essential to their success.

BITG had other problems as well. First and foremost was the realization that despite assurances to the contrary, there was virtually no pool of qualified Saudis to work in the new plants, especially in the electronic engineering field. Thus, it was necessary to recruit expatriates to do the work. In other cases, the Saudi Offset Committee insisted that the new companies perform tasks beyond their capabilities. The companies were way behind schedule when Boeing was removed from the Peace Shield Project by the Saudi government in 1991 and replaced by Hughes Aircraft. Following its dismissal, Boeing said it was free from further investment.[112] Its departure has left the fate of the first offset companies uncertain, especially as their economic viability has been questionable since their inception.

However, the troubles of the Boeing Peace Shield Offset Program have not deterred similar projects. As part of the al-Yamamah contract for the supply of Tornado aircraft in 1987, the British committed themselves to a similar program even though offset was not included in the actual contract to supply Riyadh with planes. Arm-twisting followed, and the British eventually agreed to invest. However, the failure of the BITG experience led the British to insist that their own investment program forego high-tech enterprises. As a result, British companies have undertaken more viable joint ventures in pharmaceuticals, food processing, and petrochemicals.[113] France has also begun an offset investment program in the country in anticipation of the Saudi purchase of three frigates. Paris has already committed itself to a gold-refining project with Thomson-CSF as part of its offset investment.[114] Overall, the U.S. Department of Commerce estimates that these offset projects could generate upward of $4 billion worth of fresh investment in the Kingdom.[115] The problem for investors is that the Saudis remain adamant that investment ventures that create few jobs for Saudis and require the import of trained expatriates to do the work, and are financially risky.

The future of Saudi Arabia's non-oil industrial sector remains uncertain. In some fields, such as food processing, opportunities abound, as do projects taking advantage of the Kingdom's low-cost petrochemicals. However, many of the Kingdom's entrepreneurs continue to concentrate their investments in huge, energy-dependent projects such as aluminum and copper smelters, paper pulp processing plants, and wire cable factories, whose economic viability will disappear if subsidies on water and electrical power are eventually lifted. The failure of the non-oil industry to contribute more fully to the country's economic development is best illustrated by the story of Savola, the Kingdom's leading cooking oil manufacturer. After receiving government approval to increase its capital in a public flotation, the company announced that the new monies would be used for starting projects in Egypt and Luxembourg rather than expanding local production. The company's policy earned it a public rebuke from Finance and National

Economy Minister Mohammed Abalkhail, who said that Saudi companies should focus their attention on the local market.[116] Given the size and peculiarities of the latter, that may be something few Saudi industries are willing to do.

A study of the Kingdom's manufacturing sector, including petrochemicals and oil refining, came up with some startling results. Despite the expenditure of billions of dollars, the degree of industrialization in the Kingdom per percentage of GDP is among the lowest in the Arab world. The study found that in 1989, the value of Saudi Arabia's manufactured goods (MVA) totaled $6.48 billion, which accounted for only 8.4 percent of the country's GDP.[117] Among its neighbors, only Oman, at 4.3 percent, was lower. The percentages of other countries were Bahrain, 10.8 percent; Kuwait, 14.5 percent; Jordan, 12.1 percent; North Yemen, 13.8 percent; the United Arab Emirates (UAE), 8.5 percent; and South Yemen, 10.9 percent. The Arab world's leader was Morocco with 26 percent. The study further reported that the Kingdom's manufacturing percentage of GDP actually fell during 1985–1989, rather than increasing. This feat was matched only by the UAE. Overall, the study said that Kuwait had the highest MVA growth rate for the four-year period, followed by Morocco, North Yemen, Qatar, Sudan, and Oman.

Agriculture

One of the anomalies of Saudi Arabia's economic development has been the fostering of its agricultural sector. The Kingdom's agricultural policy is based on the premise of self-sufficiency. Given the country's poor soils and even worse rainfalls, such a commitment seems almost ludicrous. Historically, the country's agriculture was limited to the Asir region, where rainfall allowed some farming of cereal crops, and along the oases. According to a study in 1970 and before the boom in agriculture, only 0.2 percent of Saudi Arabia's land was being farmed, and of that amount fully 80 percent was being irrigated.[118] Farm size was extremely small, averaging only eight hectares. Grains and alfalfa took up half of the acreage and were closely followed by vegetables, dates, and fruits.[119] Despite the low yields and meager resources, as late as the early 1950s, more than 90 percent of the Saudi population was said be employed in some sort of agricultural pursuit, including nomadic pastoralism.

It was left to the oil boom of 1973 to propel agriculture to the forefront. Under the auspices of the Ministry of Agriculture and Water, Saudi Arabia began encouraging large-scale agricultural projects with the creation of several incentives and subsidies. The government distributed free farmland to Saudi farmers, and interest-free loans were offered through the Saudi Agricultural Bank (SAAB). Loans covered the whole gamut of expenses, from annual needs such as fertilizers and seeds to long-term expenses such as pumps and machinery. The government also provided subsidies, which covered 50 percent of the costs of engines and pumps, and 30 percent of dairy and poultry equipment needs. Additional subsidies cut the costs of fertilizers and animal feed in half, and pesticides were largely given away. The government also covered the costs of importing dairy cattle from overseas and often provided seeds for free.[120]

The government pushed agriculture to promote self-sufficiency as a hedge against food embargoes, diversify the economy, distribute oil income to Saudis, and staunch the flow of rural Saudis to the cities. However, most of their motivations now seem flawed. Self-sufficiency has been accomplished in several products, most notably wheat, but the threat of a food embargo was always slight. Not only do the Saudis have large stockpiles of grains built up, but they also have the option of buying from a large variety of sources. The agricultural program has also done little to redistribute petro-wealth; instead, most of the farming subsidies have made their way to members of the al-Saud and other members of the Kingdom's elite who own or have invested in the largest agricultural companies. The renewed emphasis on agriculture has not kept rural Saudis at home. Instead, the urban rush continues, and many Saudi farmers have hired Egyptians and other expatriates to farm the fields while they live in the cities.

Given those reasons, the Kingdom's agricultural policy is criticized for costing billions in subsidies and seriously depleting the Kingdom's fossil water reservoirs for the spurious goal of growing unneeded wheat. The issue is a sensitive one. When former U.S. Agriculture Secretary John R. Block visited the Kingdom in May 1983, he created a diplomatic stir when he called Saudi self-sufficiency efforts "crazy," especially when the Kingdom could buy cheap agricultural products from the United States.[121] The Saudi response was predictable: "Is it crazy to make the desert bloom?" shrieked an editorial in the now defunct *Saudi Business* magazine. Those sentiments were echoed by

Table 5.9

Saudi Wheat Production, Selected Years 1978–1992

Year	Tons	Year	Tons
1978	3,297	1987	2,600,000[b]
1982	239,690	1988	3,300,000[c]
1983	674,631	1989	3,600,000
1984	1,346,930 [a]	1990	3,600,000
1985	1,700,000	1991	3,900,000
1986	2,000,000	1992	3,900,000[d]

Source: SAMA Annual Reports, industry estimates.
[a] Subsidy reduced.
[b] Barley subsidy introduced.
[c] Two-tiered subsidy introduced.
[d] Estimate.

Agriculture and Water Minister Dr. Abdulrahman al-Sheikh, who claimed that "farming is a most expressive means of patriotism. . . . The miracle has happened, and the arid desert has turned green, all within one decade."[122] However, the minister's position is somewhat colored given the fact that he is the chairman of the Kingdom's largest agricultural company, and has a vested interest in seeing that those subsidies remain.

Judged from certain statistics, the Kingdom's agricultural program has achieved a certain success—even though the country remains the third largest food importer in the world. Land under cultivation has jumped from 150,000 hectares in 1975 to more than 3 million in 1988. Today, the Kingdom is self-sufficient in wheat, eggs, poultry, yogurt, and milk, as well as a variety of vegetables. Imports made up 65 percent of Saudi food requirements in 1989, down from 85 percent in 1984. Agricultural products are now exported and in a bizarre twist are even used to cover the purchase of weapons.[123]

This "miracle" is best illustrated by wheat, the Kingdom's prestige crop. From less than 3,300 tons in 1978, Saudi wheat production grew to more than 3.9 million tons in 1991 (see Table 5.9). Formerly an importer of wheat, the Kingdom has become the world's sixth largest exporter. The government spurred production by instituting artificially high prices, guaranteeing SR 3,500, or U.S. $1,000, per metric ton of wheat. The government-supported purchase price was thus five times the world price of wheat. When the costs of other subsidies were added—such as electricity, diesel fuel for pumps (2.7 cents per liter), and low-cost loans—the Kingdom was paying upward of fifteen times the world price of wheat for its homegrown substitute. Agriculture and Water Minister al-Sheikh subsequently defended his ministry's price supports, noting,

> the incentive price we offered paid for many more things besides wheat production; it included the costs for land reclamation, construction of new facilities, training of farmers, and for the introduction of modern means of agriculture in place of the traditional ones. The incentive price we paid to farmers is actually a reinvestment of our income in the expansion of the agricultural sector and it is an improvement of the standards of living in rural areas.[124]

The incentives proved more than merely sufficient. Large pivot irrigation systems quickly sprouted, and farmers were soon producing harvests in excess of the estimated 1 million tons of wheat annually consumed by the country. The rich subsidies also attracted businessmen sensing quick profits. Large publicly held agricultural companies were formed, and by the mid-1980s six such firms controlled upward of 30 percent of the wheat market. Their shareholders often included influential princes, and their boards were sometimes headed by the governor of the province where the company was based, such as the case of Prince Miqren bin Abdulaziz, the governor of Hail and chairman of the Hail Agricultural Development Company. Privately held farms, in which princes were major shareholders, were said to account for another 20 percent of the production.

Harvests mushroomed, and the government was forced to construct huge storage complexes to hold the grain. The government reacted slowly to the burgeoning surplus. Leery of antagonizing the royal shareholders of the agricultural companies as well as anxious to protect its prestige product, the Ministry of Agriculture did nothing but send out circulars to the companies asking for reductions in their wheat acreage. As early as 1985, the ministry was threatening to purchase only 60 percent of the harvest from large producers. However, production continued to climb, and in 1986, the ministry lowered the wheat purchase price to SR 2,000 (U.S. $533) per ton. The lower price had no discernible effect as production still rose.

Table 5.10

Saudi Barley Production, 1984–1992

Year	Production (1,000 tons)	Year	Production (1,000 tons)
1984	7	1989	315
1985	3	1990	400
1986	13	1991	500
1987	136	1992[a]	500
1988	186		

Source: SAMA Annual Reports.
[a] Estimate.

The following year the ministry tried a more direct approach, ordering all publicly held companies to plant one-third of their acreage in barley, for which it created a price support of SR 1,000 (U.S. $266.66) per ton. Additional steps were taken as well. The ministry lowered the guaranteed purchase price of wheat for large producers to SR 1,500 (U.S. $400) in 1988, and in 1991 announced plans that it would only buy wheat from farmers who had been issued growing permits. Despite those steps, Saudi Arabia's wheat harvest topped 3.9 million tons in 1991, costing the government an estimated $2.12 billion.[125] As the mountain of wheat has continued to grow, the country has had no choice but to dump it on the world market at levels below the government's cost or to use it as foreign aid. As a result, agricultural products now make up 30 percent of the Kingdom's non-oil exports.[126]

The wheat program may have spurred production of the grain, but it also encouraged farmers to abandon other crops. Dairy farmers, given land to raise barley to feed their animals, instead planted wheat and collected the support price, which they then used to import barley while collecting a tidy profit on the entire transaction.[127] The lure of Saudi subsidies led to wheat smuggling along the Yemeni border as entrepreneurs on both sides of the border sought to buy wheat from aid agencies working in the Horn of Africa and resell it to the Grain Silo Organization.[128] Since the imposition of wheat subsidies, production of millet, sorghum, and corn have all decreased while barley production has lagged (see Table 5.10), despite the fact that the Kingdom's annual needs are in excess of 4 million tons a year.[129] The continued emphasis on wheat and other water-intensive crops has done irreparable damage to the Kingdom's underground reserves of fossil water. Various estimates say that it takes more than 3,000 tons of water to produce one ton of wheat in the country.[130]

Water usage remains a controversial issue in the Kingdom, especially given the country's low levels of rainfall. Since the start of the oil boom, Saudi planners have devoted billions of dollars to desalinating salt water and tapping large reservoirs of underground fossil water. The former today meets 15 percent of the country's annual water needs, largely being used for urban and industrial consumption. The remaining 85 percent of the annual need is for agriculture and is met by the country's fossil water supplies. Fossil water is rain that fell in the Arabian peninsula thousands of years ago when the region was a vast savannah. Percolating through the ground, the water collected into huge aquifers, which began to be tapped on a large-scale basis in the 1970s as the Kingdom began its massive agricultural programs. Hundreds of feet underground, these deposits are largely irreplaceable. Estimates as to fossil water's life expectancy vary widely. Saudi Ministry of Agriculture and Water experts claim groundwater supplies will last for 500 years if used at current rates, but most studies strongly dispute this.

A U.S. Department of Agriculture report, which predicts that Saudi Arabia will exhaust its groundwater supplies in the next ten to twenty years as consumption continues to grow at a yearly 10 percent clip.[131] Studies notwithstanding, water levels have dropped dramatically in the country. Well water levels at one large agricultural company farm near Tabuk fell 150 meters in its first year of operations. Water levels at the city of al-Khobar in the Eastern Province fell more than 90 meters in the last eleven years, 60 meters of which were in the two-year period of 1989 and 1990. And in the Saudi farming belt of Wadi al-Qassir, agricultural companies have had to erect water-cooling towers as they have been forced to drill deeper and deeper into the earth's core in search of fresh supplies.

The Ministry of Agriculture and Water has attempted to arrest the declines by limiting the number of wells drilled in recent years. In 1984, the Kingdom's wells numbered roughly 45,000 when the ministry enacted its moratorium on drilling. One year later, the ministry reported the number of wells in the country at 37,000. However, the moratorium was chiefly limited to small farmers and landowners, and not the Kingdom's large agricultural companies, which are the major users.[132]

To meet the Kingdom's water needs, which are expected to nearly double from 12 billion cubic meters in 1990 to more than 20 billion in 2010, the Agriculture and Water Ministry is exploring several options. For the Kingdom's urban areas, which use desalinated water, the ministry is constructing waste treatment plants, which they hope will recycle upward of 40 percent of the water used. At present, wastewater is dumped in the desert or used to irrigate trees and flowers. The ministry is also considering the construction of additional dams in the country to catch rainwater. As of 1988, the ministry had constructed 180 dams with a total storage capacity of 475 million cubic meters; 4 additional dams with a capacity of more than 335 million cubic meters are under construction. The ministry had also completed studies for 11 additional dams with a capacity of 1 billion cubic meters. Most of the dams are located in the southwestern end of the country, but construction has been delayed by the government's budget crisis.

Another option has been the much publicized "Peace Pipeline" offered by the late Turkish president Turgut Ozal. The proposal, which was initially made in 1987 but never accepted by the Kingdom, called for the construction of two $10 billion pipelines running from eastern Turkey through Syria, Jordan, and Saudi Arabia. One would have terminated near Mecca, while the other would have ended in the UAE. Project consultant Brown and Root planned a third pipeline as well, which would have carried 500,000 bpd of crude back to Turkey to pay for the water, a payment Turkish experts calculated would be only 20 percent of the cost of desalinated water. The plan has been beset by numerous obstacles, not the least of which has been the general political instability of the region and the poor relations between the major recipients. However, the plan received a boost in 1992 when Iran announced plans to pipe water to Qatar in a $1.5 billion deal.[133]

It seems likely that the Kingdom will eventually change its water policies. Surprisingly, this view was publicly voiced in the winter of 1992 by an academic at King Saud University. In a widely published study, Osama Bahanshal called for comprehensive actions to conserve water. He further charged that agricultural self-sufficiency was possible only at high economic and environmental costs.[134] The fact that Bahanshal's study was allowed to be published indicates that some members of the government are having doubts about the

Kingdom's agricultural policies. Increased concern about water is also one of the reasons why the country's proposed paper pulp plant has been delayed.

The Agriculture and Water Ministry continues to defend the Kingdom's agricultural policies, which have cost over SR 100 billion in price supports since 1972. As noted by al-Sheikh,

> Unfortunately we have become a target for attack, mainly from some countries that dismissed our experiment in agricultural development as unnecessary and too costly. My reply is that cost is a two-faceted phenomenon. What may be regarded as a cost from a commercial point of view may be simultaneously regarded as income or a return from a social and national point of view.[135]

Conclusion

Whether or not the Saudi economy will reach its full potential is difficult to predict. The Kingdom's economy is oil-based and dependent on government expenditures and will remain so for the foreseeable future.

Unfortunately, the Kingdom's economic planners have complicated matters by emphasizing high-profile, high-prestige projects that are heavily dependent on subsidized energy and water. While having the biggest and the best has satisfied certain normal human desires, the Kingdom's new state-of-the-art industries have done little to create jobs. Instead, most have required massive inflows of expatriates. They also remain tenuous undertakings, given their dependence on government largess to survive.

Present policies have a political as well as an economic cost. If the Saudi government is ever to free itself from subsidies and undue intervention in the marketplace, it needs to divorce itself from such intimate responsibility for the economy. Otherwise, it will be held responsible for forces utterly beyond its control, such as fluctuations in the oil market and natural business cycles.

Perhaps the government would have done better to have followed the example of ARAMCO, which encouraged business development in al-Hasa by offering funding and training to would-be entrepreneurs. Although their enterprises are smaller and less impressive, these small businessmen have proven more successful and have created jobs more grounded in economic reality.

Notes

1. *MEED: Middle East Business Weekly*, March 22, 1991.
2. Richard Nyrop et al., *Saudi Arabia: A Country Study*, p. 7.
3. Robert Lacey, *The Kingdom*, p. 228.
4. Ibid., p. 280.
5. David Edens, "The Anatomy of the Saudi Revolution."
6. Lacey, *The Kingdom*, p. 279.
7. Ibid.
8. Ibid., p. 301.
9. Saudi Press Agency, November 26, 1989.
10. T.R. McHale, "A Prospect of Saudi Arabia," pp. 128–49; and Ministry of Planning, "Fifth Five-Year Plan."
11. Ramon Knauerhause, "Saudi Arabia's Economy at the Beginning of the 1970s," p. 129. This problem remains in Saudi Arabia today. Overweight trucks continue to destroy the Kingdom's highways. It is also not unusual to see roads being torn up several times to lay different utility lines rather than coordinating such public work. The reason is simple: utility contracts are an important patronage tool, as well as a way of distributing oil wealth.
12. Ibid., pp. 126–27.
13. Ibid., pp. 128–29.
14. Ibid.
15. Ibid.
16. Robert E. Looney, *Saudi Arabia's Development Potential*, p. 167.
17. Arthur Young, *The Making of a Financial Giant*, p. 142.
18. Saudi Arabian Monetary Agency (SAMA), *Annual Report*, 1988.
19. In parts of the Tihama, these educational subsidies were the only income tribesmen earned.
20. Peter Beaumont, "Water and Development in Saudi Arabia," pp. 42–60.
21. U.S. Embassy, *Subsidy Study*, 1985.
22. Real Estate Development Fund (REDF) loans also led to overbuilding; in the mid-1980s, the Riyadh Development Authority estimated that 32.5 percent of all apartments in the city and 24.2 percent of other housing was vacant. Riyadh Development Study No. 5.0.
23. Lacey, *The Kingdom*, p. 422.
24. William Ochsenwald, "Saudi Arabia and the Islamic Revival," pp. 271–75.
25. Lacey, *The Kingdom*, p. 422.
26. Peter Wilson, *A Question of Interest: The Paralysis of Saudi Banking*, p. 9.
27. *Time*, January 21, 1991.
28. Richard Auty, "The Economic Stimulus from Resource-based Industry in Developing Countries," p. 216.
29. *Christian Science Monitor*, May 15, 1990.
30. Reza Islami and Rostam Kavoussi, *The Political Economy of Saudi Arabia*, p. 58.
31. Richard Auty, "The Economic Stimulus," pp. 216–17.
32. Richard Auty, "The Internal Determinants of Eight Oil-Exporting Countries' Resource-based Industry Performance," p. 359.
33. Nyrop, *Saudi Arabia*, p. 180.

34. IMF, "Saudi Arabia: Staff Report," 1989.

35. Saudi newspapers were expressly forbidden from referring to the Kingdom's downturn as a "recession" or "depression" due to the sensitivity of Finance and National Economy Minister Mohammed Abalkhail.

36. This policy was adopted over the strong dissent of Crown Prince Abdullah bin Abdulaziz. The exact figure of SAMA's overseas assets has long been a matter of controversy.

37. *Saudi Gazette,* May 7, 1984.

38. Saudi Press Agency, February 10, 1986.

39. Auty, "The Economic Stimulus," p. 217.

40. Ghassan Salame, "Political Power and the Saudi State," p. 84.

41. *MEED,* December 29, 1989.

42. *Saudi Gazette,* February 8, 1987. Barley, for example, cost between $95 and $100 per ton before the price war; afterward it cost between $60 and $70 per ton.

43. Knauerhause, "Saudi Arabia's Economy," p. 135.

44. *MEED,* February 13, 1988. For ordinary Saudis, the real estate tax would have been the largest bite on incomes.

45. *Saudi Gazette,* January 6, 1988.

46. Wilson, *A Question of Interest,* p. 173.

47. *MEED,* September 4, 1992.

48. Ibid., July 7, 1990.

49. Lawrence Freedman and Efraim Karsh, *The Gulf Conflict, 1990–1991: Diplomacy and War in the New World Order,* p. 182. Although Saudi Arabia's desire to obtain OPEC approval before pumping more oil may seem superfluous, the Kingdom was motivated to avoid charges from Iraq, Iran, and Libya that it was paying off American troops through a subservient oil policy.

50. *New York Times,* October 19, 1990.

51. *Washington Post,* April 3, 1991.

52. *BusinessWeek,* March 18, 1991.

53. *MEED,* June 5, 1992.

54. Kuwaiti refugees pumped hundreds of millions of dollars into the local Saudi economy through their purchases of houses, consumer goods, and food.

55. "Country Report: Saudi Arabia," *EIU,* no. 1, 1991.

56. General H. Norman Schwartzkopf with Peter Petre, *It Doesn't Take a Hero,* p. 364.

57. *BusinessWeek,* February 25, 1991.

58. *MEED,* August 6, 1993.

59. *MEED,* May 22, 1992.

60. Ministry of Planning, "Fifth Five-Year Plan," Riyadh.

61. IMF, "Saudi Arabia: Staff Report," 1991.

62. IMF, "Saudi Arabia: Staff Report," 1989.

63. *MEED,* June 21, 1991, and *Middle East Economic Survey (MEES),* April 20, 1992.

64. *MEED,* January 17, 1992.

65. Ibid.

66. *The Middle East,* April 1992.

67. *MEED,* May 22, 1992.

68. Wilson, *A Question of Interest,* p. 160.

69. *Hadith*, Abdallah bin Hanzallah, and *Hadith*, Abu Hurayah.
70. Wilson, *A Question of Interest*, ch. 6.
71. SAMA's help was largely confined to placing interest-free deposits with the banks.
72. "Country Report: Saudi Arabia," *EIU*, no. 2, 1992.
73. Lacey, *The Kingdom*, p. 341.
74. *MEED*, January 24, 1992.
75. Ayman al-Yassini, *Religion and State in the Kingdom of Saudi Arabia*, p. 74.
76. *Time*, June 17, 1991.
77. Wilson, *A Question of Interest*, p. 133.
78. *MEED*, August 23, 1991.
79. Lacey, *The Kingdom*, p. 311.
80. Islami and Kavoussi, *The Political Economy*, p. 17.
81. Monte Palmer, Abdelrahman al-Hegelan, Sayeed Yassin, and Ali Leila, "Bureaucratic Innovation and Economic Development in the Middle East," pp. 12–27.
82. Abdelrahman al-Hegelan and Monte Palmer, "Bureaucracy and Development," pp. 48–68.
83. This fact accounts for the high absenteeism rate among Saudi bureaucrats, besides engendering humerous conflicts of interest.
84. Wilson, *A Question of Interest*, p. 56.
85. Nyrop, *Saudi Arabia*, p. 212.
86. *MEED*, April 24, 1992.
87. *New York Times*, November 8, 1989.
88. Saudi Press Agency, March 15, 1993.
89. *American Metal Market*, July 24, 1991.
90. Saudi Basic Industries Corporation (SABIC), *1988 Annual Report*.
91. *South*, p. 100.
92. *Arab News*, November 12, 1988.
93. Ibid., June 8, 1986.
94. *MEES*, June 21, 1993; and *MEES*, July 5, 1993.
95. Ibid.
96. Ibid., October 14, 1991.
97. *BusinessWeek*, May 13, 1991.
98. Foster-Wheeler officials, who won the contract to upgrade SAMAREC's refineries, said in August 1993 that the project has been delayed indefinitely, presumably due to funding problems.
99. *Financial Times of London*, June 17, 1988; and *BusinessWeek*, April 2, 1990.
100. *Far Eastern Economic Review*, February 14, 1991.
101. *MEED*, July 31, 1992.
102. *MEES*, January 25, 1993.
103. "Saudi Arabia Special Report," *The Middle East*, February 1992.
104. SABIC, *1992 Annual Report*.
105. *Financial Times of London*, April 22, 1985.
106. "Saudi Arabia Special Report," *The Middle East*, February 1992.
107. *BusinessWeek*, September 17, 1990.

108. Reuters, July 17, 1993.
109. *Saudi Arabia* (newsletter of the Saudi embassy in Washington), February 1990.
110. *Saudi Gazette,* January 25, 1986.
111. Ibid., March 25, 1989.
112. *MEED,* March 22, 1991.
113. Ibid., August 14, 1992.
114. Ibid., January 17, 1992.
115. Ibid., August 7, 1992.
116. Ibid., July 10, 1992.
117. Ibid., June 29, 1990.
118. Looney, *Saudi Arabia's Development Potential,* p. 142.
119. Peter Beumont, "Water and Development in Saudi Arabia," pp. 42–60.
120. *The Economist,* April 6, 1985.
121. Ibid.
122. *MEED,* October 6, 1989.
123. *The Economist,* July 1, 1989.
124. *Arab News,* May 28, 1986.
125. *MEED,* January 24, 1992.
126. *Arab News,* June 10, 1988.
127. *The Economist,* April 6, 1985.
128. Ibid.
129. *MEED,* September 13, 1991.
130. "Country Report: Saudi Arabia," *EIU,* no. 1, 1993.
131. *The Economist,* July 15, 1989.
132. The water issue is just one example of the difficulty in reconciling national and royal interests: most of the large companies are owned by princes who are reluctant to see their water supplies, and in turn, their income from agricultural subsidies, reduced.
133. *MEED,* February 7, 1992.
134. Ibid., January 31, 1992.
135. Ibid., October 6, 1989.

6 SOCIAL ISSUES

Saudi society has changed dramatically in the last twenty years. Before the oil boom of 1973, Saudi society revolved around work and the mosque. People toiled hard and put in long hours in their struggle to survive. Outside the few settlements, life centered around herding and subsistence-level agriculture. Days passed in a monotonous routine: work till noonday prayer, followed by a siesta to escape the brutal midday heat. Work only resumed in the late afternoon and continued until evening prayer. Islam permeated all aspects of Saudi life and provided its followers with specific rules of conduct for their personal, public, and religious lives. Other facets of life were spartan. Education was strictly limited to boys, who might learn a few verses from the local imam. Girls married young, more often than not to first or second cousins, and bore many children. Large families were a necessity as infant mortality was high. Medicine was rudimentary, consisting of Koranic verses, herbs, camel urine, and heated branding irons. Recreation was simple if it existed; due to Unitarianism's sway, music and games were frowned upon if not disallowed.

Social life was simple: families visited one another or close friends. Since life was hard, these visits, which consisted of sitting and talking, became highly ritualized affairs, entertainment in and of themselves. Few Saudis had knowledge of the outside world, so boredom and dissatisfaction were relatively unknown as there was little with which people could compare their lives. In any case, luxuries or other forms of entertainment were unknown or costly and given the region's poverty, unattainable.[1]

The boom in oil prices abruptly ended the traditional way of life. Affluence transformed a feudal tribal society into a modern nation-state. Per capita income jumped from U.S. $412 in 1962–1963 to more than U.S. $7,200 in 1992.[2] Generous government programs made education and health care free and available to all. Subsidies covered the cost of most necessities, and the Kingdom's work ethic dissipated in the first flush of oil riches. The family suffered as well; government lending agencies such as the Real Estate Development Fund (REDF) made it possible for young married couples to have their own housing, breaking up the extended family unit. Money also enabled many Saudis to travel abroad where their Unitarian values were confronted with different values and attitudes. For some, the resulting clash culminated in reborn religiosity; for others, it brought greater tolerance and support for change.

The government has attempted to adapt Unitarianism's eighteenth-century austerity and prohibition of innovations to oil riches. The al-Saud have instructed their imams to preach that Islam and material wealth are not incompatible and that Islam is a religion of tolerance. However, such attempts have largely failed, and the inability to reconcile austere Unitarianism with modernism has resulted in a wide divergence in public and private mores. The Kingdom's rulers and ulema may forbid the opening of movie theaters, but the Kingdom's video stores offer a wide variety of uncensored and definitely un-Wahhabi-like fare. Alcohol and tobacco may be condemned in the mosque, but private use abounds behind closed doors, and there is a thriving black market in Johnny Walker whiskey and the local home brew, *siddiqui,* or "friend." Photography may be shunned by some because it depicts the human image, but camera stores abound.[3]

The divisions in Saudi society have only deepened in the wake of Operation Desert Storm. The arrival of hundreds of thousands of Allied troops and fleeing Kuwaiti civilians was bound to have an impact. Today, the conflict between those wanting additional changes and those supporting a return to traditional values has heightened rather than diminished.

Social Trends

Saudi population data is clear on one point: the Kingdom's population is increasingly urban. The change is startling. In 1902, less than 10 percent of the Kingdom's inhabitants lived in cities. Settlements were clustered along the Hejaz and at a few scattered oases in the Nejd and al-Hasa. Mecca, Jeddah, Riyadh, and Medina were the largest urban centers. As late as 1948, Riyadh was estimated to hold 25,000 souls. Mecca's population was put at 40,000, while Medina's was 20,000.[4]

The catalyst behind urbanization was Abdulaziz bin Saud's effort to build a nation-state. Abdulaziz recognized that until the tribes were settled, his political power would remain tenuous. City and town dwellers were easier to control, and bin Saud, committed to building his Kingdom, was nothing if not practical. He instituted a number of laws aimed at settling the tribes, and the number of city dwellers slowly grew (see Chapter 1). Oil revenues led to increased royal expenditures, which in turned spurred the urban economy. Trade and construction jobs were initially created, attracting tribesmen.[5] Still, only 30 percent of the Kingdom's population was said to be urban in the early 1960s.[6]

That quickly changed with the spurt in oil prices after 1973. Increased petrodollars accelerated the development process and the rush to the cities. Also having an effect was the late King Faisal bin Abdulaziz's emphasis on electrification, which made air conditioning possible. The advent of the latter changed the rhythm of Saudi life, which heretofore had been based on midday inactivity due to the unbearable heat. Petrodollars paid for the construction of thousands of apartments and villas, as well as making loans available for the Kingdom's burgeoning middle and upper classes. Oil money allowed the government to offer massive subsidies and to create thousands of jobs in its own bureaucracy.

The government was so successful in its inducements that the rush to the cities became overwhelming during the boom. Urban dwellers were said to comprise 66 percent of the Saudi population by 1980, and 75 percent by 1990, a proportion far outstripping such neighbors as Iraq and Iran, but still the lowest among the six members of the Gulf Cooperation Council (GCC).[7] The Kingdom's urban population was also increasingly concentrated. Riyadh, Jeddah, and Mecca contained more than half of the country's urban population as of 1990. This contrasts markedly with many of the Kingdom's neighbors, however, where city life is often concentrated in one huge capital megapolis. By comparison, Saudi Arabia's cities are more evenly matched.

Most Saudis prefer city life today. Despite efforts by the government to stem the flow to the cities by improving rural services and introducing farming subsidies, tremendous gaps between city life and rural life remain. A study published by the United Nations Development Program in 1992 compared several sectors of rural and urban society. Using a base of 100 for urban life, rural health care scored an 88, water resources, 74, and sanitation only 30.[8]

Urbanization has not been achieved without a price. Traditional values associated with tribal life suffered, especially when confronted by rapidly growing affluence and modernization. The confusion was often palpable as the government sought to bridge the gap between twentieth-century conveniences and a mentality that had not changed for centuries. For example, many of the government's public housing units contained instructions on how to use basic appliances and facilities, and it was not uncommon during the 1980s for the lavatories on the national carrier's jets to feature diagrams illustrating how to use the toilet and washbasin.[9]

Urbanization and affluence brought other changes. Consumer spending burgeoned as if to make up for the centuries of involuntary abstinence. Imports swelled, and Rolls-Royce, Rolex, and Cartier became the new status symbols, replacing goats and camels. Consumption soared and a cult of waste reigned. Brand-new cars often littered the Kingdom's highways, abandoned when they experienced minor problems; for many Saudis it was easier to buy a new car rather than repair the old. Japanese exporters were soon claiming that the Kingdom had more VCRs per capita than any other country in the world. Obesity and dental problems soared as sugar, meat, and fat consumption skyrocketed. Thousands of foreign servants were "imported" to work in Saudi homes, causing additional friction. "These maids are now seen in almost every flat and villa . . . in the markets and shops; . . . they are moved by a Western mentality and lifestyle and will destroy our children and family," lamented an unnamed Saudi in a letter to the editor at *al-Muslimoon,* an Islamic newspaper.[10] Although Saudi women suddenly had time to shop and visit one another, the cultural repercussions have sometimes been shocking: some Saudi children grow up speaking Arabic as a second language.

Urbanization saw other changes. Crime, divorce, and alcoholism soared during the first years of the boom. A breakdown in the crime rate is revealing; murder linked to honor and feuds rose 94 percent during 1971 to 1975. Other crimes increased as well; economic and financial crimes jumped 154 percent, while fraud jumped 318 percent.[11] Moral crimes (or those with a sexual element) increased 150 percent during the same period. The largest increase occurred in drug and alcohol crimes, which mushroomed 1,400 percent. Although the increase in the number of foreigners was partially to blame, the Ministry of Interior conceded that 60 percent of the culprits were Saudis. The number of crimes jumped by 169 percent for the next five-year period as well, with alcohol and drug offenses increasing another 150 percent.

That trend continued into the 1980s. The Ministry of Interior, which releases sporadic statistics, reported that 16,343 crimes were committed in 1984, the last year for which comprehensive statistics are available. Of that number, alcohol-related crimes accounted for 3,319, or nearly 20 percent of all offenses. Theft comprised 33.6 percent of all crimes reported to the police, and of that number, car thefts accounted for a hefty quarter. Immorality offenses accounted for 11.8 percent of all crimes. The ministry added that 523 capital crimes were committed during the year, of which 115 were murders (up from 1983's total of 44). Attempted murder accounted for 161 cases, while murder threats numbered 105.

The ministry noted that there were 4,100 prisoners in 1984, of whom 2,905 were Saudis. Only 50 prisoners were women. According to the data, Saudis were 67 percent more likely than foreigners to be in jail for theft, 25 percent more likely to be incarcerated for murder, twice as likely to be imprisoned for drugs, alcohol, or immorality charges, but less likely for vehicle accidents.[12] The sudden overload in the Saudi penal system led to experimentation with a number of innovative measures. In the late 1980s, King Fahd decreed that all prisoners memorizing the Koran would have their jail sentences cut in half.[13]

Crime has continued to grow, especially with the rise of unemployment among young Saudis. Western embassies noted in 1989 that the number of executions throughout the country—which are readily announced every Saturday by the Saudi Press Agency—topped more than 100 that year, an abrupt rise from the year before. The number of floggings and public amputations for theft also rose.[14] Capital crimes continue to be a problem; for the twelve-month period between May 1992 and May 1993, 105 convicted murderers were publicly beheaded, leading Amnesty International to protest.[15]

Alcohol and drug abuse continue, exacerbated by the lack of recreational activities. "If you're young here, you turn either to drugs or to religion," noted one young Saudi in 1993.[16] The incidence of drug use had risen so much that in 1987 the ulema issued a *fatwa* prescribing the death penalty for drug dealers. Since the penalty was announced, more than 100 dealers have been arrested, and more than 50—the majority of them Pakistanis—have been publicly beheaded.[17] Since implementation of the new policy, the Ministry of Interior announced that the number of addicts in the country had declined 60 percent. The ministry further estimated that casual drug use had dropped 26 percent.[18]

Rapid development has led to other problems, including those linked to mental health. In a 1988 survey of 280 students at Riyadh's King Saud University, 51 percent of the respondents expressed anxiety over the pace of copying Western habits in their country; 46 percent mentioned concern over the rise in the use of illegal drugs; 45 percent said they were upset by an upsurge in traffic accidents; and 37 percent expressed concern over the neglect of younger children.[19] The survey also discovered a high level of depression among young Saudis. "Psychopathological and depressive symptoms were reported by extremely higher proportions of Saudis than usually reported in other societies," the authors noted.[20]

Emerging from more than twenty years of easy oil money, Saudi youths have different ideas, values, and attitudes than their parents. Born into an easy subsidized life-style, many see no reason to work. Others, who have seen different ways of life during their travels or via satellite dish, have grown increasingly restive by the limited options they see in the country. Social life still clings to old values that no longer ring true: religion, work, and a minimal level of education. Unitarianism has meant that the government has had limited success in introducing alternative outlets for the young. There are no cinemas and no theaters. Television and radio are heavily censored; newspapers and magazines are tightly controlled as well. The Saudi Ministry of Information was created in 1962 to serve as a watchdog on the press, and two years later it was given the right to shutter newspapers and scrutinize all editors. Given the country's high illiteracy and only recent reading tradition, newspapers and magazines are not popular. Outside influences are suspect; the Kingdom only decided in 1993 to license Mickey Mouse products.[21] Clubs are suspect due to their possibility for subversion; gatherings of three or more people are prohibited; and health and sports facilities have caught on slowly. The failure of alternative recreational outlets is no better illustrated than with the case of the $114 million, gold-leafed cultural palace that the al-Saud built a short distance from Riyadh. Larger than the New York Met, the building can stage plays, concerts, operas, and ballets. Yet despite the patronage of the king's son, Prince Faisal bin Fahd, the structure remains empty and unused.[22] Parks and recreational outlets are segregated; Riyadh's zoo was segregated following complaints by local *mutawaeen* that it was being used as a trysting place.[23] Tighter restrictions have also been placed on Saudi youth for traveling abroad; passports are no longer issued to Saudis younger than twenty-one years of age.[24] The sole place where young Saudis can meet and talk unimpeded is the mosque, where disaffected youths are easily swayed by fundamentalists opposed to the regime.

The government has tried to use sports as an outlet. Soccer is especially popular, and more than forty stadia have been erected throughout the country. Millions of riyals are spent each year on the teams in the Kingdom's premier league, which features clubs supported by different princes. The results have been mixed. Although soccer has served as a means to unify the country and develop a national psyche, it has led to an upsurge of scandals, outbursts, and unruliness. Soccer has also come under fire from fundamentalists as most matches take place on Friday. Fundamentalists also claim that team uniforms are immodest. The failure to introduce additional recreational outlets means that many young Saudis have no place to turn. Youths resort to driving around aimlessly, or making anonymous phone calls, hoping to meet members of the opposite sex. "It is the boredom in my leisure time that forces me to take a drive after midnight," Nabeeh Ribh told one newspaper. "I feel like running away from home after remaining inside for so long. I stop my car by the side of a telephone booth and begin to dial indiscriminately in search of someone who will answer."[25]

The recession of the mid-1980s and the Iraqi invasion of Kuwait convinced many Saudis that the Kingdom's problems were the result of their straying from God and the true tenets of Unitarianism. Not surprisingly, there has been a rebirth in religiosity and fundamentalism, both of which oppose the Western innovations that have been introduced.

The Status of Women

Saudi Arabia remains a country comprised of two societies: one for men, the other for women. The two have little interaction, and the latter is completely dependent on the former for decisions affecting it.[26] The differences between the sexes are taught at an early age. Honor is paramount to the Saudi male, and is especially centered on his women, whether they be his sisters, daughters, or wives. According to one al-Saud princess,

> Convinced that women have no control over their own sexual desires, it then becomes essential that the dominant male carefully guard the sexuality of the female. This absolute control over the female has nothing to do with love, only with fear of the male's tarnished honor. The authority of a Saudi male is unlimited; his wife and children survive only if he desires. In our home, he is the state. This complex situation begins with the rearing of our young boys. From an early age, the male child is taught that women are of little value: they exist only for his comfort and convenience. The child witnesses the disdain shown his mother and sisters by his father; this open contempt leads to his scorn of all females, and makes it impossible for him to enjoy friendship with anyone of the opposite sex. Taught only the role of master to slave, it is little wonder that by the time he is old enough to take a mate, he considers her his chattel, not his partner.[27]

Social restrictions on Saudi women are immense, and the Saudi government defends those restrictions as being part of Islam's creed. There is some truth to that claim; the Koran teaches that women are secondary to men just as the Bible authorizes men to rule over women. The difference is that in Saudi Arabia, Islamic proscriptions are followed literally. Rigid sexual segregation is practiced, adversely affecting occupational and educational opportunities for women. Saudi women cannot drive, are seldom allowed to marry non-Saudis, and may never marry non-Muslims. Saudi men can do all three. Divorce is another issue. Although men can divorce their wives easily, simply by saying the words "I divorce you" three times, women can only attain a divorce by undertaking a long legal process, which is seldom successful. Even if they win, women never receive child custody if contested by their ex-spouses. Saudi women are prohibited from borrowing money in their own names and from opening their own businesses without their husbands' or fathers' approval. They cannot obtain home loans or land grants from the government. Employment in a few sanctioned professions is also prohibited unless the woman's family agrees. Travel abroad is again dependent on family permission and must be in the company of a male relative.

There is also the matter of dress. An overwhelming majority of Saudi women are veiled, a practice that begins when a girl reaches puberty. The veil, contrary to some assumptions, is not an Arab invention. It was borrowed from the Ottoman Turks. Although the Prophet Mohammed said that a woman only had to cover her hair, many Saudi women are forced or opt to wear a full veil, covering the entire face.[28] They also wear *abbayat,* black outer garments made of silk or nylon. Some women wear black gloves as well, in order to cover all exposed parts of their bodies.[29] Failure to dress in what is deemed an appropriate manner can result in a switch from a *mutawa* or worse.[30]

Women have made limited gains in the past four decades, especially in education and family life. As regards the former, education for women was prohibited prior to the 1950s. The first school for women was introduced—albeit quietly—by King Saud for his daughters in the mid-1950s and was followed by a similar institution opened by his half-brother Faisal and his progressive wife, Iffat. The latter was called Dar al-Hanan, or House of Affection, and it opened in Jeddah in 1956. The school was created under stealth, and its ambiguous name was adopted to throw off suspicious fundamentalists. Persuading families to send their daughters was difficult, with even slaves and servants of the royal family expressing reluctance.[31] Despite those initial misgivings, Dar al-Hanan proved successful, and in 1957–1958, Faisal and Iffat, with Saud's strong support, planned to make it national.

A royal commission, including members of the ulema, was created in 1960 to facilitate the introduction of women's education in the country. Iffat also founded a women's teaching college to prepare a core of Saudi women teachers to staff the new schools. Despite such royal support, women's education was introduced grudgingly. The schools came under the control of the ulema, who insisted that a curriculum heavily based on Koranic memorization be implemented. Nonetheless, there were still many protests from religious fundamentalists opposed to educating women. In such Unitarian strongholds as Buraidah, the opening of women's schools occurred only with royal troops dispersing protesters.

Subsequent numerical results have been impressive (see Table 6.1). The number of women's institutions grew from zero in the 1950s to 16 in 1960, and to 155 ten years later.[32] The number of women students also mushroomed from 5,180 in 1960 to 40,566 in 1970, and to 639,056 in 1980. As a result, illiteracy among the Kingdom's women

Table 6.1

Saudi Education Statistics by Sex, 1990

Category	Male	Female
	Number of Students	
Primary	919,949	768,934
Intermediate	279,770	216,594
Secondary	127,042	114,231
University	73,166	57,132[a]
	Number of Teachers	
Primary	55,381	45,321
Intermediate	20,559	15,159
Secondary	8,195	8,058
University	7,386	2,386[a]
	Number of Institutions	
Primary	4,806	3,574
Intermediate	1,766	1,057
Secondary	581	486
University	67	11[a]

Source: SAMA 1990 *Annual Report*.
[a] Including girls' colleges and girls' sections at universities.

has substantially declined. One 1988 study of over 200 Saudi women in the Eastern Province revealed that only 3 percent of the survey's older respondents—those fifty-five years or older—had completed the equivalent of a third-to-fifth-grade education; 16 percent had received some instruction in the Koran; and 81 percent were illiterate. Among the survey's second generation—those women thirty-five years or younger—23 percent had a university degree, 45 percent had completed secondary education, 19 percent had completed elementary education, and the remaining 13 percent had completed the equivalent of third-to-fifth-grade education.[33] None of the younger women were illiterate or had only been schooled in the Koran.

Educational achievements by Saudi women have been made despite substantial obstacles being placed in their way. The government's policy of strict sexual segregation has saddled women with facilities substantially inferior to those available to their male counterparts. For example, women students usually have access to libraries once a week, compared to six times a week for men. Class sizes for women are larger. Teachers for men are better trained, with more than 34 percent of the professors at the men's universities holding doctorates as compared with only 3 percent of their counterparts at women's universities.[34] Overall, budget appropriations for women's education total only 18 percent of that expended on men's education.[35] Part of the reason for that discrepancy is administrative. While the male educational system is under the jurisdiction of the ministries of Education and Higher Education, women's education is under the General Presidency for Girls' Education, an autonomous agency heavily staffed by clerics. The Presidency's attitude toward women's education is best summed up by former Superintendent General Mohammed bin Adwdah: "It is essential that female students be steered toward feminine disciplines," he explained. "There is no need for women to compete with men in disciplines that are not suited to their nature."[36] As a result, the curriculum for women has less emphasis on academic subjects, and greater emphasis on the Koran and Islamic studies. Women are also prohibited from studying certain disciplines such as architecture, engineering, and pharmacy studies. "The goal of the Presidency of Girls' Education is to produce a religious housewife, one Saudi woman told the authors. "If you do that twelve years, do you expect she will come out with lots of ambition?"

The educational differences increased with the recession of the 1980s. Women's education suffered larger budget cuts than its male counterpart. Book subsidies for women were reduced in the mid-1980s, and at some universities, teachers had to photocopy textbooks, paying for their own copy paper as well. Despite the blatant discrimination, few Saudi women complain. One former teacher noted, "They [Saudi women students] do not perceive any disadvantage, and are not aware of the fact that they have lesser facilities. They don't care about the discrepancy. . . . It [studying] gives them something to do. They get a smaller allowance than men but it is still a nice part-time job."[37] Despite those handicaps, Saudi women consistently do better on standardized tests and grade promotion than their male counterparts—a fact that the Ministry of Education is hard-pressed to explain. Studies in 1990 showed that it took the average Saudi boy 11.34 years to finish his primary education, while the average Saudi girl required only 8.67 years.[38]

Educating the Kingdom's women has had certain ramifications. First and foremost has been increased pressure to admit them to all areas of the work force. Their ban from certain occupations seems to be more social and legal rather than religious. For example, the Koran states that all believers should work, and does not discriminate against women.[39] Members of the Saudi elite have occasionally made statements seeming to support equal employment opportunities, and Saudi Arabia has signed several international agreements, including the International Labor Organization Convention No. 111, pledging to end occupational discrimination.[40]

Prior to the liberalization of education for women, employment opportunities were limited. Besides helping their husbands in the tending of livestock and farming (especially in the Asir, where it is still common to see men and women working together in the fields), the only job opportunities for Saudi women were sewing, selling foodstuffs, and working as domestics. The oil boom brought an abrupt end to those professions, especially as the economy developed.[41] Alternatives have been slow to emerge, and what progress had been made was abruptly terminated in the aftermath of the overthrow of the shah of Iran in 1979 and the Mecca uprising a few months later. The government quickly assured the ulema that mixed workplaces would not be tolerated. The next year, an interministerial committee was created to explore job opportunities for women within the context of Islam. Following alleged intense pressure from religious elements, no report was ever issued. As a result, educated Saudi women have been steered toward careers in education or health. There are problems with both. As regards the former, most available teaching jobs have already been filled. Health care presents limited options as well, because few Saudi women are interested given the relatively low social status of such work.[42]

Few women can work in the private sector due to Islamic rules on segregation, which have discouraged most businesses from hiring women. There have been some exceptions to this rule. Attitudes toward employed women are most relaxed outside the Nejd. Saudi ARAMCO initially hired women as secretaries and geologists but has been forced by religious pressure to scale back such efforts. The Jeddah-based Saudi Cable Company floated an idea in the mid-1980s to establish a women-only electronics company where male foremen would communicate with their charges via telephone and camera. The idea has yet to be approved. Some banks have opened women-only branches for their customers. This idea has met only half-hearted success; the branches offer some but not all services, and as a result, most women prefer to open accounts with male relatives at full-service branches. There have also been some women-only shopping centers opened in Riyadh and Jeddah, providing employment for Saudi and expatriate women. Although the opening of the centers was lauded by the religious authorities, they have had limited financial success because few Saudi women like to shop without their husbands.

Jobs and independence for women are influenced by other factors as well. Since women are not allowed to drive, transportation is a tremendous logistical problem. Few Saudis allow their wives to use public transport even though buses are segregated. The only alternatives are to hire a driver, use taxis, or have male family members provide transportation, all either costly or time-consuming propositions. A second consideration is the lack of day-care facilities. A growing number of Saudi women marry early, divorce early, and are then faced with raising their children on their own. The lack of day-care facilities has meant that few such women are able to work, even if they can find positions. Societal attitudes are also stacked against working women; many Saudi men refuse to marry a woman who is educated, let alone employed. Some men fear that the women will not want to give up their careers, while others seem intimidated by the idea of having an educated wife.

These ideas are easy to understand given societal norms that still place the woman's first duty to her husband and family. As former liberal Prince Nawwaf bin Abdulaziz noted, "Therefore the university graduate girl who works outside her home and family and takes more interest in her work than her home is unworthy. . . ."[43] Prince Nawwaf is not alone; his condemnation of working women was echoed by Dr. Ahmad Jamal, a Saudi professor of Islamic culture and author of the book, *Our Girls and the Right Path*. In his book, Dr. Jamal writes, "For any female, marriage represents her first need and her fundamental obligation."[44] Many Saudi men agree, and have sought wives from rural areas in Egypt, Syria, and India to avoid the problem with Saudi women, as well as to take advantage of cheaper dowries.[45]

The recession of the 1980s, however, led to renewed calls for women to enter the workplace. Liberalizing work attitudes would not only staunch the outflow of remittances and thus improve the country's current account deficit, but also trim the expatriate work force, which is viewed as a destabilizing presence, and inject billions of dollars into the Saudi economy from their earnings. Such arguments are fervently rejected by Saudi fundamentalists, who view any change of the country's segregated labor laws as un-Islamic. The effect of fundamentalists on the work force is undeniable. In 1990, the Ministry of Planning estimated that of the 1.923 million Saudis employed, only 168,900 were women. Overall, only 5.3 percent of all Saudi women of working age had jobs.[46] Even that number is deemed unacceptable by some religious conservatives. In May 1993, fundamentalists called for the suspension of all women, both expatriate and Saudi, from working in the Kingdom.[47]

Despite mixed results in expanding their employment opportunities, Saudi women have made marked progress on the home front. The Saudi family has changed tremendously in the space of two generations. Today, far fewer Saudi women live with their in-laws than in the past. According to a 1988 survey of women in the Eastern Province, fully 68 percent of the older respondents—those over age fifty-five—lived in extended families. Among respondents under the age of thirty-five, the number was just 6 percent.[48]

Other changes are just as vast. Of the older women, fully 94 percent said their marriages had been arranged, while the remainder said they had been semi-arranged. Of the younger women, 45 percent said their marriages had been arranged; 36 percent said they had been semi-arranged, and 19 percent said they were unarranged. Older women were also more likely to be involved in polygamous marriages than were their younger counterparts. Sixty-one percent of the older women said they had polygamous marriages, while only 10 percent of younger women said the same. The issue is a sensitive one, especially as unmarried Saudi women increase in numbers, victims of higher dowries, divorce, and their own education. Attitudes toward polygamy are still fluid; in one poll among university women, 36 percent said they would support their husband if he wanted a second wife, while 32 percent said they would not.[49]

Family attitudes have changed in other ways. Saudi women are marrying later in life. The average age at marriage for the older women was fourteen, with some marrying as early as twelve or thirteen. For the younger women, marriages occurred between the ages of sixteen and twenty-five.[50] However, marriages still occur between prepubscent girls and older men; an Islamic advice columnist in *Arab News* counseled one questioner, the father of a nine-year-old girl, to wait a few years before giving her in marriage to a twenty-year-old man. Nonetheless, the columnist concluded that the father had the right to do with his daughter as he liked.

Consanguineous marriage remains common for Saudi women despite an abnormally high rate of birth defects in the Saudi population.[51] Pressure to marry within the family is immense, especially to preserve the bloodline, save dowries, and keep family resources intact. In one survey of nearly 4,500 Saudi women, 54.3 percent said they were involved in consanguineous marriages. That number is similar to studies of Kuwaiti women, but is far higher than figures for Egypt and other Arab countries. Approximately 31.4 percent of the Saudi respondents said they were married to first cousins, while 22.9 percent were married to second cousins.[52] The study showed that better educated women and women from higher social and economic classes were less likely to marry within their families. For example, the study revealed that 64.8 percent of the illiterate women had entered into consanguineous marriages; that number declined to 44.7 percent of women who had secondary educations, and to 35.5 percent for women with college degrees.[53]

Women and Operation Desert Storm

Iraq's invasion of Kuwait, and the threat against Saudi Arabia, threatened to overturn not only the Kingdom's political order but its social order as well. Iraqi troops were stopped at al-Khafji, but thousands of female "invaders" arrived, either as American GIs or as fairly "liberated" Kuwaiti refugees, and they had an instant impact on their Saudi sisters. The influx of these foreign women served to galvanize some of their Saudi counterparts, who hoped that the Kuwaiti conflict would bring them the same opportunities that World War II had opened to American women. Initially, those hopes seemed well founded. Approximately one month after the Iraqi invasion of Kuwait, Fahd asked Saudi women to volunteer for a Ministry of Health program aimed at providing medical and humanitarian assistance to those affected by the war. Although Fahd stressed that women would perform "Islamically correct" tasks, his call to arms marked the first time in Saudi history that an appeal to women had been made.[54] Fahd's new line found a receptive audience among some Saudis. In early October, the Jeddah-based *Arab News,* which is partially owned by Riyadh Governor Prince Salman bin Abdulaziz and as such is often used to float government ideas, published an article written by Rabaa al-Khateeb. In it, al-Khateeb promoted equal work opportunities for women: "More and more women will, I believe, join the work force and those who have been waiting on the sidelines will have to join in," al-Khateeb wrote. "This will come as a result of our inevitable rethinking of the so far unchallenged view that women should play only a limited role in society. Asking one half of its small population to remain idle is a luxury that Saudi Arabia simply cannot afford. Least of all now."[55] Such rhetoric, plus the sight of American women GIs working in T-shirts and fatigues, driving, or carrying their rifles while shopping, spurred Saudi women to other action.

Just three months after the fall of Kuwait, forty-seven Saudi women protested the government's ban on women driving by taking to the streets of Riyadh in an unauthorized motorcade (see Chapter 2). The women could not have chosen a more controversial issue on which to pin their movement for greater rights. Although not prohibited by the Koran, driving rights for women have been bitterly opposed by the ulema and fundamentalists even though Bedouin women are commonly seen driving in the countryside. Fundamentalist opposition to women's driving is tied to several issues. First and foremost, opposition is centered around the argument that giving women the right to drive would lead to chance encounters between unrelated men and women, encounters that they conceded would often be initiated by the men. The fear is a real one, as the Bahraini government learned after the opening of the Saudi-Bahraini Causeway. As the tiny island-country was flooded by Saudis, some Bahraini women were deliberately rear-ended by Saudis attempting to meet them.[56] Another concern is that in order to drive, women would have to doff their veils. A third reason for religious opposition is the fundamentalist fear that driving would be the first step toward an overall re-evaluation of the role of women in Saudi Arabia, including sexual segregation and the right of women to work. That view is upheld by Saudi women. "The issue is not driving," noted one Saudi woman after the protest. "It is that here in Saudi Arabia, I exist as a person from the bellybutton to the knees."[57]

The sight of women driving through Riyadh, however, caused an immediate fundamentalist backlash. The *mutawaeen* again stepped up their persecution of women they considered immodestly dressed, and they also forced the state airline, Saudia, to lower the hems on its stewardesses' uniforms. The stewardesses, who are all non-Saudi as Saudi women are prohibited from such jobs, also had to cover their heads with veils.[58] Saudia's decision was reportedly made following a melee that occurred aboard one of its Riyadh-to-Jeddah flights. The flight was booked heavily by fundamentalists, who rose up once the plane had taken off, mistreating the hostesses and herding them to the back of the plane. The pilot subsequently returned to Riyadh.[59] The fundamentalists' victory was significant, because Saudia's patron is the liberal Defense Minister Prince Sultan bin Abdulaziz, the number three man in the Saudi government.

Undeterred, progressives petitioned Fahd in February 1991 for greater political freedoms, including broader freedoms for women: "While the noblest vocation of the Muslim woman is the raising of her children, she should not be excluded from having a public voice and enjoying the basic legal and social rights accorded to all citizens, as long as this is within an Islamic context," noted the petition.[60] The fundamentalist response was not long in coming; when religious conservatives presented their own petition to Fahd the next month, they called for the continuation of the status quo for women, and in later pronouncements, advocated even stricter punishment for the women who had participated in the earlier driving protest. Fundamentalists also attacked Riyadh's Saudi Women's Renaissance Association, an organization that helps Saudi women help themselves. Although the association counts a number of high-ranking princesses among its members, fundamentalists angrily attacked the group and its members, calling them "prostitutes" and "whores."[61] More serious was the arrest in mid-1991 of a leader of the feminist movement, who was subsequently tortured.[62] Despite having a broken leg, the woman was nonetheless made to stand in a crowded cell for an unspecified length of time. She also received twenty injections of an unknown substance. Another woman, Fawzia al-Bakr, was also imprisoned for four months, her crime being the submission of an article to a Saudi newspaper in which she criticized the al-Saud.[63]

The backlash has continued. In 1993, fundamentalists proposed a complete ban on women working in the Kingdom. In the face of growing fundamentalist ire, the government has done little except to allow the *mutawaeen* greater leeway in their harassment of women. Unfortunately, women and the curtailment of their rights are often used by the al-Saud to prop up their Islamic credentials. Thus, women continue to serve as convenient scapegoats for the regime.

Human Rights

Saudi Arabia's record on human rights has long been a matter of controversy. Basic human rights are often ignored, and slavery was abolished only in 1962.[64] Still, the Kingdom's human rights record is not as abysmal as that of Iraq, Iran, and Syria. Making the protection of human rights difficult in the country is the lack of a constitution and bill of rights. Although Fahd's Basic Law contains some guarantees (see Chapter 2), it by no means covers all rights. Opportunities for abuse are widespread, especially given the arbitrariness and inefficiency of the Saudi legal system (and in particular, the civil and religious courts), as well as official policies discriminating against Shia, women, and expatriates.

Faisal is generally regarded as the king who began the transformation of the Kingdom into a police state. Confronted by Nasserites, Baathists, communists, and repeated coup attempts, Faisal had no compulsion about throwing hundreds of his opponents into jail, where they were often beaten and mistreated, although few were killed. With Faisal's death in 1975, his successor, Khalid, freed many of the prisoners.

Police surveillance in the Kingdom has grown since the events of 1979, with particular emphasis on the country's large Shiite community. This supervision intensified after the 1987 Mecca riots when relations with Iran deteriorated. The Shiites' position in Saudi Arabia has always been problematic. When al-Hasa was first conquered by Abdulaziz, he was petitioned by his more fundamentalist allies for permission to cleanse the area of the Shia, who were viewed as heretics. Abdulaziz demurred, but similar requests have continued to the present day. Despite Abdulaziz's protection, the Shia languished under the rule of the al-Hasa governor, Abdullah bin Jiluwi, whose more than fifty-year governorship was marked by brutality and discrimination. The Shia's position improved with the arrival of ARAMCO, which had no qualms about hiring them. Still, life for the Shia was difficult.

Not only were government expenditures on basic services far less in their communities than in the rest of the country, but they were also discriminated against as regards government employment opportunities.[65] It is noteworthy that the government only opened its first modern hospital in the Shiite stronghold of al-Qatif in 1987.

Shiite quiescence, however, changed in 1979 with the triumph of Iran's Ayatollah Khomeini, who preached that Shiite minorities in the Gulf should claim equal rights. Troubles came to a head in November 1979, when the Shia in al-Qatif held their traditional celebration to commemorate the death of Hussein, grandson of the Prophet Mohammed. Their procession had traditionally been banned by the Saudi authorities lest the sight of self-flagellating adherents inflame Wahhabi sensitivities. But reflecting Khomeini's urgings as well as the fact that the Kingdom's police forces were still confronting the uprising in Mecca, Shiites held their procession. When government security forces attempted to stop it, fighting broke out and National Guard units fired on the marchers, killing several. Rioting spread to other Shia cities in the province, with at least twenty-one reported deaths.[66]

The ramifications of the 1979 al-Qatif riots and similar disturbances in February 1980 were widespread. Although the government began spending more money on infrastructure and facilities in Shiite areas, it also increased police surveillance and persecution. ARAMCO reevaluated its employment of Shia and in fact, fired some who were considered politically unreliable. The government also instituted tougher penalties for people arrested with Shiite books, tape cassettes, or pictures of Khomeini. One widely reported case concerned Zahra al-Nasser, a Shiite woman who was found to have a picture of Khomeini and a Shiite prayer book in 1989. Arrested by police on the Jordanian-Saudi border, she was subsequently tortured and died three days later in a Saudi jail.[67] Other Shiites suffered arbitrary arrests, beatings, sleep deprivation, and torture with electrical devices.

Shia continue to be treated as second-class citizens in the Kingdom. Saudi Shiites are not allowed to build new mosques or religious community centers. They are prohibited from visiting Shiite shrines in Iran and Iraq, an especially grievous ban since Shiite religious schools are only located in those countries. Saudi treatment of the Shia mirrors Iranian-Saudi relations. Following the 1987 Iranian riots in Mecca, the authorities again tightened security in the Eastern Province, but not enough to prevent two explosions in the Jubail petrochemical complex.

The incident was later traced to Shia dissidents, four of whom were subsequently beheaded. ARAMCO then froze all hiring of Shiites, further contributing to the area's already high joblessness. Although conditions have since improved with the appointment of Prince Mohammed bin Fahd bin Abdulaziz as Eastern Province governor, routine discrimination continues. Unemployment among Shia continues to be high, estimated at 30 percent.[68] Although Shiite Iran excoriated the U.S. effort during Desert Storm, Saudi Shia hoped that the Gulf conflict and arrival of American troops would force the Saudi government at least to guarantee them freedom of worship in the oft-promised "constitution."[69] Such hopes were dashed when Fahd released his reform package. However, the status of Saudi Shia might improve if the al-Saud enact promises made in Fahd's unofficial agreement with Shiite dissidents in October 1993 (see Chapter 2).

The Iraqi invasion of Kuwait led to an upsurge in human rights abuses, especially against expatriates from countries whose governments supported Baghdad. This occurred despite a promise from the Ministry of Interior in mid-August 1990 that "no Arab or foreigner hosted by us would be held accountable for the negative positions taken by his state or government against the Kingdom of Saudi Arabia."[70] The ministry's promise lasted one month. On September 19, the Saudi government announced changes in the labor code regarding Yemenis, who had been given special employment rights in the Kingdom with the Treaty of Taif in 1934.[71] Those guarantees were arbitrarily overturned, and Yemenis were given one month to find Saudi sponsors or leave. Of the 1.5 million Yemenis in the country, the vast majority could not and were forced to flee, often leaving their possessions, and in some cases their money, behind. Among Yemeni entrepreneurs in the Kingdom, the losses were just as bad, as they had to find Saudi partners or buyers for their concerns. Many could not, and had to take steep financial losses. Hundreds of Yemenis were also arrested by the Saudi police, and Amnesty International charged that more than 800 were tortured.[72] Jordanian, Palestinian, and Sudanese workers suffered similar discrimination.

Another human rights issue is the fate of more than 45,000 Iraqi refugees being held in several camps along the Iraqi border. On March 9, 1993, rioting broke out in the Rahfa refugee camp, and nine refugees and four Saudi security men were killed in the resulting melee. The cause of the rioting was inmates' demands that the Saudi-Iraqi border be opened to allow more refugees to cross over. Officials have been leery about doing that, given the fact that most of the refugees are Iraqi Shiites from the south.[73]

Since the conclusion of the war, the Kingdom's human rights record has come under renewed fire from Saudi progressives and fundamentalists alike. The former made their first plea in February 1991, when they petitioned Fahd for a legal system in which all Saudi citizens would be equal "regardless of race, tribe, social status or gender."[74] Fundamentalists also demanded the same when they presented their own petition the following month, stressing that the state should guarantee human rights and respect freedom of press and expression. Conservatives also requested that a separate and independent court be organized to investigate and try government officials suspected of corruption.

The House of Saud's response has been to continue its assertion that it respects human rights. In February 1992, Fahd categorically refuted claims of the existence of prisoners of conscience, noting that there is "not a single political prisoner in the Kingdom."[75] However, his denial must be tempered with the fact that Fahd, who was interior minister under Faisal, coordinated the arrests of hundreds of the late king's political opponents during the 1960s and early 1970s. Despite denials, most human rights organizations as well as Saudi opposition newspapers claim that the Kingdom's jails hold scores of political prisoners who are often subjected to routine beatings and torture.[76] One of the best known of these prisoners is Mohammed Fassi, who was spirited from the Hotel Intercontinental in Amman, Jordan, on October 2, 1991, and presumably turned over to Saudi authorities. Fassi, who is related to Fahd's full brother Prince Turki bin Abdulaziz by marriage, was allegedly arrested for making anti-Saudi broadcasts during Operation Desert Storm. Following his transfer to Saudi Arabia, Amnesty International charged that Fassi was being detained in a secret location in the Saudi capital and was in danger of being tortured.[77] Fassi has supposedly been joined by a number of Islamic fundamentalists, who have refused to temper their criticism of the regime.

The rumors of such abuses led fundamentalists to create the Kingdom's first human rights committee in early May 1993. The committee's founders, led by Abdallah al-Masari, announced their objective was "to alleviate injustice and defend the rights secured by Islamic law."[78] Ten days after the committee's creation, the government declared it dissolved and the members relieved of their jobs (see Chapter 2). The government's action occurred one day after the ulema issued a statement condemning the human rights committee as "superfluous" and "illegitimate." The head of the ulema, Abdulaziz bin Baz, went further, calling the committee "an illegal body that cannot be approved because Islamic law is already the law of the land in Saudi Arabia and religious courts abound, allowing all to submit any complaints." A few days later, the government went one step further and imprisoned the son of one of the committee's founders. However, whether the committee was truly interested in human rights, or in embarrassing the government in the eyes of the West, is open to debate. Among the founders were men who called for the exclusion of all women from the workplace and labeled the Shiites "apostates," an offense carrying the death penalty in the Kingdom.[79]

Labor Issues

One of the most pressing social problems facing Saudi Arabia today is that of labor. The issue is multifaceted: not only is there the question of millions of guest workers in the Kingdom and their maltreatment, but there is rising unemployment among Saudi workers as well. Since the start of the First Five-Year Plan in 1970, the Kingdom's work force has grown at an annual clip of 8 percent, adding 4.3 million workers during the twenty-year period ending in 1990. Most of the latter were foreigners, called in to build and then maintain the Kingdom's extensive infrastructure. The Saudi percentage of the Kingdom's work force has steadily contracted as a result. Saudis made up 72 percent of the Kingdom's work force in 1975, 40 percent in 1980, and an estimated 33 percent in 1990.[80] Some estimates place the Saudi content of the work force even lower. In a 1992 study of Jeddah's 600,418 workers, only 86,000, or roughly 14 percent, were found to be Saudis.[81] In the private sector, Saudis are said to comprise only 2 percent to 10 percent of all workers.[82] More than 1 million Saudi men are estimated to be unemployed or underemployed. The Ministry of Planning—whose figures are suspect due to their reliance on inflated population numbers—reported that of the 6.42 million Saudis of working age in 1990, only 29.9 percent had jobs. The breakdown according to sex was revealing: only 5.3 percent of the country's 3.2 million women of working age, and only 54.4 percent of the Kingdom's 3.22 million men, were em-

Table 6.2

Saudi Employment Projections, 1990–1995

Category	1990	1995
Overall employment in the Kingdom	5,771,000	5,985,300
Saudi employment	1,923,200	2,357,100
Men	1,754,300	2,142,100
Women	168,900	215,000
Expatriate employment	3,847,800	3,628,200
Public sector positions	624,800	633,500
Private sector positions	5,147,000	5,351,800

Source: Ministry of Planning 1990.

ployed.[83] The ministry further projected that there will be no notice-able change in those figures by the plan's completion in 1995, when employment among all working-age Saudis is expected to reach 30 percent. If the ministry's percentages are correct, they reveal either significant unemployment or government subsidies allowing Saudis of working age not to work.

There have been concerted efforts to reduce the Kingdom's expatriate work force. Not only are expatriates viewed as a destabilizing force, but their repatriation is thought necessary to open up jobs for Saudis. The Kingdom's Fourth Five-Year Plan, inaugurated in 1985, called for the reduction of the country's expatriate population by 600,000 by 1990. Instead, the expatriate work force increased. The recession and the Iraqi invasion of Kuwait have seriously altered the Kingdom's labor picture. First, the government no longer has the resources to continue creating public sector jobs; most ministries and agencies have instituted unofficial hiring freezes. From 1990 to 1995, government employment is expected to grow by only 8,700 positions. More than 574,800 Saudis are expected to join the labor force during the same period. The Ministry of Planning is hoping to absorb those numbers by natural attrition estimated at 140,900 positions, the creation of 204,800 new private sector jobs, and filling 220,400 positions presently held by non-Saudis with Saudis (see Table 6.2).

There are several flaws with this scenario. Unfortunately for the Planning Ministry's projections, many of the jobs that Saudis are expected to take from expatriates are in fields in which no Saudi wants to work. New jobs are also problematic; according to the ministry's figures, most of the new positions being added to the Saudi economy by 1995 are in manufacturing, agriculture, construction, social services, and trade, which, except for the latter, are largely unacceptable professions. The government has made the situation worse by investing in capital-intensive and high-tech industries such as petrochemicals, which have minimal labor needs.

Saudi attitudes remain a major obstacle. As former British ambassador Sir James Craig noted in his valedictory address about the Kingdom:

> [In the Kingdom there is] a disdain for any work which is not noble *(sharif)*. Most people shy away from work which they consider ignoble; Englishmen, for example, are reluctant to be waiters or dustmen. But the Saudi classification of jobs is extraordinarily strict. Not only do they reject all manual and menial work; they are also reluctant to undertake anything which is tedious or humdrum. Plumbing is manual and roadsweeping is menial; for these tasks they employ foreigners. But whereas taking decisions is noble, the work of preparing to take decisions is ignoble: so the collection of facts, the collation of statistics, the checking of references, the planning of timetables is skimped. The results are sometimes disastrous.[84]

One need not rely on a British ambassador's word; the issue of blue-collar workers has also been a steady topic of discussion among Saudis: "It is true that developing countries depend on skilled laborers who usually earn more money," lamented one woman to the newspaper *Okaz*. "Their skills ensure a secure and good life. Yet, I cannot marry one, lest my friends make a laughing stock out of me. Their views have not yet changed."[85] Part of the reason is rooted in the Kingdom's recent history of slavery, which existed as late as 1962. The most pernicious effect of slavery was that it made manual labor a thing done by "slaves" and not free men. Bedouin tradition reinforced this. Noble tribes herded camels and practiced military arts. Lesser tribes herded sheep or goats and earned more mundane livelihoods. The less manly townsfolk were artisans or traders, supplying necessary metal goods. Not surprisingly, blue-collar jobs and service sector employment are regarded as being fit only for expatriates.

Other problems abound. Of the 574,800 Saudis projected to enter the work force, many will have no skills or minimal educational training. The ministry projects that 15.7 percent, or 90,400, of the new entrants will not have completed elementary education. An additional 22.1 percent, or 127,000, will enter the work force with only an elementary degree. Secondary school graduates will number 60,500, or 10.5 percent. High school graduates, of both general and technical facilities, will number 148,500, or 25.8 percent. Students holding a post-secondary technical degree will number 7,400, or 1.3 percent. University graduates will number 68,600, or 12 percent, of which women will make up 44 percent. The remainder—12.6 percent, or 72,400—will have finished a short-term adult vocational training program.[86]

As those numbers suggest, the Saudi educational system is failing to train a skilled work force. The curriculum is still heavily slanted toward religious studies. As the Ministry of Education noted in 1978, the purpose of schooling is

> to teach Islam in a correct and comprehensive manner, to plant and spread the Islamic creed, to furnish the student with the values, teachings and ideals of Islam, to equip him with various skills and knowledge to develop his conduct in constructive directions, to develop society economically, socially and culturally, to prepare the individual to become a useful member in the building of his community.[87]

School curricula underline that emphasis. Long hours are devoted to Koranic memorization, while relatively little time is spent on science or mathematics.

The Kingdom's educational tradition is also young and untested. The first secular boys' schools were only developed in 1925, while secular secondary schools were only founded in 1937–1938.[88] Saudi Arabia's universities are even younger. The first institution of higher learning, the Shariah Islamic Law College of Mecca, opened in 1949. It was followed by Shariah College and Arabic Language School in 1953. The first secular university was only opened in 1957.

Other factors enter the education picture as well. Education is not compulsory, even at the primary level. Attendance is often inconsistent, and as a result, promotion to higher grades lags. As a result, less than half of all primary students enter secondary school. City dwellers are more likely to attend school, while, unsurprisingly, attendance is poor in the countryside. In addition, many Saudis drop out of school as soon as they feel they have sufficient job skills. Similar habits are manifested by the Kingdom's university students, who are pampered. Not only are they given hefty stipends to attend classes, but tuition, room and board, and textbooks are free or heavily subsidized. Students feel no compulsion to study subjects in which they might make a living. Religious studies remain popular, even though few job openings exist. For 1990, religious study majors accounted for more than 15 percent of all Saudi graduates, outpaced only by social sciences majors.[89] Religious studies majors at the Kingdom's universities far outnumber health, economics and business, and computer science majors. Leery about tarnishing its religious credentials, the government has done nothing to correct the imbalance.

The government has also emphasized vocational training with mixed results. The Ministry of Labor established the General Organization for Technical Education and Vocational Training (GOTEVT) to develop manpower. GOTEVT runs twenty-six Vocational Training Centers, eight Pre-vocational Training Centers, and eight Technical Institutes. The Vocational Training Centers are for any men between eighteen and forty-five years of age with at least a fifth-grade education. Students receive a monthly allowance, which is raised if the student passes 50 percent of the courses. They also receive housing, transportation, materials, and allowances for food and clothing. Graduates receive cash bonuses with extra for excellent grades, plus a bonus after completing six months on a job. Once a worker spends some time in his field, the Saudi Credit Bank gives him loans to start a business.

The technical schools are the equivalent of high school or secondary school. They offer courses in auto mechanics, electricity, machine trades, and architectural drawing. The Polytechnical Institutes are comparable to two-year colleges. Again, the students are paid and get other allowances. Pre-vocational Training Centers cater to school dropouts; graduates can then enter Vocational Training Centers. "Before our training schools did not attract people," noted the secretary general of the Greater Manpower Council, Dr. Hussein Mansour. "Now the number of people coming to the training centers is greater than they can handle. The young Saudis are eager, and some of the schools have begun raising their admission standards, from graduation from general school, to graduation from high school. They have also started asking for higher grades."[90]

Despite those gains, the problem of unemployment among younger Saudis is worsening and is already recognized by the government: "It is becoming increasing important to improve linkage between the education and training system, and [for] potential private sector employers to achieve better coordination between producers and users of skills, and to influence the attitudes and expectations of students," claimed the Ministry of Planning.[91]

Creation of a Saudi work force is further harmed by wealthy parents who spoil their children (and destroy their work ethic), as well as the plethora of government subsidies, which enable many to survive without working. The creation of a well-skilled Saudi work force is still years, if not decades, away. This is no better illustrated than in the private sector, where studies have shown that Saudi employers often pass over Saudi applicants for jobs. There are several reasons: Saudis often insist on higher salaries; Saudi applicants are often unskilled; they have poor work habits; and employers find it difficult to fire them. Attendance among Saudi employees is often sketchy, as family and private business concerns take precedence. Saudi employers are also reluctant to hire Saudis outside their own families due to a fear that such employees will use their jobs to compile lists of potential customers in order to launch competing companies. The problem was aptly summed up by Saeed Musfir, a Saudi and owner of a water tank factory. "They are all foreigners," Musfir said, describing his work force. "I pay them reasonable wages and their work is satisfactorily good. Moreover, they are committed and dedicated, and unlike Saudi workers, they never look for excuses to absent themselves during work hours. I had experience with two Saudi workers. They were skilled but they used to absent themselves very frequently, were arrogant and never accepted directions, which they interpreted as insults."[92]

The Saudi government has tried several tactics to reverse this trend. As early as 1954, the government decreed that all businesses operating in the Kingdom had to have 75 percent Saudi composition of their work forces.[93] The regulation has never been enforced. Later, when the Kingdom's banking system was partially nationalized, banks were ordered to "Saudize" their work forces. The latter also has yet to occur. As a result, the government continues to issue Saudization orders on a regular basis, especially to banks and hotels.[94] To avoid government pressure, employers use a variety of ploys. Some hire Saudis, but then insist that they stay home and come in only to collect their pay. Others give their Saudi employees offices, but no tasks or responsibilities. Other send their Saudis to school for additional training.[95]

The government has belatedly begun shifting more emphasis on the unemployment problem. In December 1992, Interior Minister Prince Naif, chairman of the Labor Council, said that the council would undertake a full review of the Kingdom's labor situation, with the aim of increasing employment opportunities for Saudis. The government also appointed former GOTEVT head Abdulwahab bin Abdul-Salam Attar as minister of planning. The Saudi government may eventually have no choice but to adopt some of the incentives being tried by the Bahraini government. To encourage the hiring of Bahraini nationals, the Manama government instituted grants for those companies offering jobs to Bahrainis. The grants range from U.S. $3,500 to U.S. $14,000. The government of Bahrain has also offered to halve electricity bills of Bahraini enterprises, which emphasize the employment of nationals.[96]

There is another downside to the Saudi labor picture as abuses against foreign workers have steadily grown. Besides the problem of commercial hostage taking (see Chapter 5), other problems abound. One of the most common is that of contract substitution, in which expatriate workers are forced to sign new contracts with lower wages. Failure to do so often results in threats of job loss, deportation, or the refusal of the Saudi sponsor to yield the employee's passport. Many expatriate workers—especially those from the Indian subcontinent, the Philippines, and southeast Asia—pay bribes to obtain Saudi work visas, so most accept pay cuts without protest. As a result, some expatriates work for as little as $30 per month in jobs that have eighty-hour workweeks.[97] Payment delays are also common; there are cases in which workers have waited months, if not years, for back wages. In some cases, they are never paid when their employer vanishes, and the police refuse to act.

Few complaints are filed with the Saudi Labor Court system. The filing procedure is difficult and fraught with danger. All complaints must be made in Arabic, a language that many expatriates do not know. Few Saudi labor officials, even if they know other languages, deign to speak them, and few labor offices provide interpreters. In addition, filing complaints often results in the employer's confiscating his workers' *dafatir al iqama,* or work permits. Without the latter, workers can be arrested by the Saudi police and deported. In fact, police brutality against expatriate workers, especially those from de-

veloping countries, is common and widespread.[98] Other problems
abound. As former Bangladeshi ambassador to the Kingdom Hedayet
Ahmad charged:

> The labor market in the Kingdom has developed into a vicious circle. . . .
> The workers will pay sometimes as much as $2,500 to an agent for his
> work permit and visa. After he arrives in the Kingdom on a multi-year
> contract, he is permitted to work only one year before being fired by the
> employer. The employer and labor agent then fleece another
> Bangladeshi worker while the other man flies home with barely enough
> money to cover the bribes paid to the agent and Saudi sponsor.[99]

Despite this, competition among supplier countries to send workers
to Saudi Arabia is intense and often open to underhanded tactics. In
1988, the Saudi Ministry of Labor put a temporary ban on Bangladeshi
workers, following a spate of reports that most Bangladeshis working
in the Kingdom were Shiites, or members of a radical Islamic sect. The
issue became so heated that former Bangladeshi President Mohammed
Ershad was forced to hold talks with Saudi officials to dispel the rumors. The Bangladeshi embassy later charged the stories were started
by their competitors at the Indian and Pakistani legations.

The worst labor abuses, however, are heaped on Saudi domestic
servants. According to a report written by the Philippine labor attaché
in Riyadh,

> [Women] who are going to Saudi Arabia as domestic helpers have no
> protection whatsoever. . . . It was our experience that female domestic
> helpers are helpless and subject to abuses because of the culture being
> practiced in the Kingdom. The Kingdom's concept of domestic helpers
> is still that of slaves, having no rights whatsoever. They can be given
> away as presents.[100]

Rape, physical abuse, and nonpayment of wages are common. The
situation is so bad that some countries have taken steps to limit their
export of domestics. In January 1988, the Philippines banned all
women from working as domestic helpers in the Kingdom. The ban
was lifted several months later, after Saudi Arabia refused to issue any
more work permits for Filipinos and' threatened to cut off oil sales to
Manila. Many other countries refuse to allow their women nationals to
work as domestic helpers in the Kingdom.[101]

The Gulf War only exacerbated the situation. There were repeated instances of expatriate workers being forbidden to leave the Eastern Province, including American employees of Saudi ARAMCO. The latter charged that they were threatened with the loss of their jobs and benefits if they departed during the fighting.[102] Other expatriates were forced to continue working in war zones without gas masks or other protective devices. Some embassies also reported cases in which their nationals, who were employed as drivers or laborers, were coerced into ferrying military supplies to the border with Kuwait, in violation of their contracts.[103]

Few countries, however, complain about the treatment of their nationals. Third World embassies are reluctant to anger the Saudis because their economies depend on worker remittances. For example, Bangladesh's second largest source of hard currency is remittances. In addition, some ambassadors are in the labor-exporting business themselves, and turn a blind eye to infractions. One of the more blatant examples concerned former Filipino ambassador Dr. Mauyag Mohammed Tamano, whose relatives own labor export agencies. He claimed that reports of maid abuse were fabrications of the press. "They were attacking our Arab brothers in the Manila press. There were allegations of ill-treatment of Filipino domestics. Then I had to appear on the radio and television to refute those allegations."[104]

Notes

1. *The Economist,* February 12, 1986.
2. Ramon Knauerhase, "Saudi Arabia's Economy at the Beginning of the 1970s," pp. 126–29; and *Middle East Economic Review,* December 1992.
3. Ayman al-Yassini, "Islamic Revival and National Development in the Arab World," pp. 108–10.
4. Raymond Mikesell and Hollis Chenery, *Arabian Oil,* p. 75.
5. Bedouin were especially keen to take jobs driving taxis or trucks, as transportation positions were not considered menial, and it also gave the former nomads a sense of mobility and freedom.
6. A. Reza S. Islami and Rostam Kavoussi, *The Political Economy of Saudi Arabia,* pp. 44–45.
7. *Gulf Economic and Financial Report,* December 1988.
8. *MEED: Middle East Business Weekly,* July 17, 1992.
9. Instructions were seen as late as 1985.
10. *Arab News,* December 12, 1988.
11. Ayman al-Yassini, *Religion and State in the Kingdom of Saudi Arabia,* p. 115.
12. Ministry of Interior, *1984 Annual Report,* Riyadh.

13. It takes the average person two and a half years to memorize the Koran.

14. "Country Report: Saudi Arabia," *Economist Intelligence Unit (EIU)*, no. 1, 1990.

15. Associated Press, July 13, 1993.

16. *BusinessWeek*, February 15, 1993.

17. Associated Press, February 20, 1993.

18. *Arab News*, March 18, 1989.

19. Abdel-Sattar Ibrahim and Abdulla Alnafie, "Perception of and Concern about Sociocultural Change and General Psychopathology in Saudi Arabian Students," pp. 179–87.

20. Ibid.

21. Associated Press, June 13, 1993.

22. *South*, October 1989.

23. Especially concerning the *mutawaeen* was the reptile house, which was dimly lit. The zoo eventually had to institute family days, women's days, and men's days.

24. "Country Report: Saudi Arabia," *EIU*, no. 1, 1990.

25. *Okaz*, June 22, 1989.

26. Louay Bahry, "The New Saudi Woman: Modernizing in an Islamic Framework."

27. Jean Sassoon, *Princess: A True Story of Life behind the Veil in Saudi Arabia*, p. 22.

28. Aside from some Saudi women, only women from Qatar, which is the only other Unitarian country in the world, follow such a severe veiling.

29. Women from al-Hasa and Hejaz are sometimes unveiled. The veil is such an ingrained habit among Saudi women that some exhibit no compunction about disrobing for medical examinations as long as they are not required to uncover their faces.

30. The *mutawaeen* sometimes do more than switch; in early 1987, they caused the wife of the Tunisian ambassador to miscarry her pregnancy after they pushed her because she had left her hair uncovered. The woman lost her balance and fell.

31. Robert Lacey, *The Kingdom*, p. 365.

32. Siham A. Alsuwaigh, "Women in Transition: The Case of Saudi Arabia," pp. 67–78.

33. Ibid.

34. Minnesota Lawyers, *Shame in the House of Saud*, p. 87.

35. Alsuwaigh, "Women in Transition," pp. 67–78.

36. Richard Nyrop et al., *Saudi Arabia*, p. 125.

37. All Saudi students receive stipends to study; however, most women receive lower stipends.

38. Robert E. Looney, "Patterns of Human Resource Development in Saudi Arabia," p. 675.

39. Minnesota Lawyers, *Shame in the House of Saud*, p. 92.

40. Ibid.

41. Alsuwaigh, "Women in Transition," pp. 67–78.

42. Saudi society views nursing as a "servant" position, and one that has no social prestige.

43. *Saudi Gazette,* January 29, 1987.

44. Ibid., February 24, 1986.

45. Saudi men, like other Arab men, are expected to pay a dowry for the bride, which is used as a sort of divorce insurance for the woman in case the marriage fails. Oil wealth has dramatically inflated dowries. In Alsuwaigh's survey, "Women in Transition," the average dowry for older women was $57; for younger women, the figure was $14,285.

46. Ministry of Planning, "Fifth Five-Year Plan," Riyadh.

47. *New York Times,* May 14, 1993.

48. Alsuwaigh, "Women in Transition," pp. 67–78.

49. *Al-Riyadh,* January 29, 1988. To combat the growing number of unmarried women, several anti-spinster societies have been formed. Members visit Saudi wives, asking them to persuade their husbands to take a second wife.

50. Alsuwaigh, "Women in Transition," pp. 67–78.

51. The issue is a controversial one; the Ministry of Health occasionally finds American and European doctors to lecture in the Kingdom about why in-breeding does not cause birth defects.

52. Simin Saedi-Wong, Abdul Rahman al-Frayh, and Henry Y.H. Wong, "Socio-Economic Epidemiology of Consanguineous Matings in the Saudi Arabian Population," pp. 247–52.

53. Ibid.

54. *New York Times,* September 25, 1990.

55. *MEED: Middle East Business Weekly,* October 19, 1990.

56. This was confirmed to the authors by several Saudi government officials.

57. *New York Times,* March 26, 1991.

58. Ibid., November 11, 1991.

59. This account was told to the authors by Western diplomats.

60. *New York Times,* July 5, 1991.

61. Ibid., December 31, 1991.

62. Minnesota Lawyers, *Shame in the House of Saud,* p. 46.

63. Ibid.

64. The abolition of slavery was part of King Faisal's Ten-Point Program.

65. As of 1989, only two of Saudi Arabia's deputy ministers were Shiites.

66. Joseph Kechichian, "Islamic Revivalism and Change in Saudi Arabia," p. 5.

67. Minnesota Lawyers, *Shame in the House of Saud,* p. 46.

68. *Time,* September 24, 1990.

69. *Wall Street Journal,* November 16, 1990.

70. *New York Times,* July 5, 1991.

71. Ibid., February 15, 1992.

72. Minnesota Lawyers, *Shame in the House of Saud,* pp. 33–51.

73. *New York Times,* February 15, 1992.

74. Ibid., May 14, 1993.

75. Ibid.

76. "Country Report: Saudi Arabia," *EIU,* no. 4, 1990.

77. *Washington Post,* January 22, 1992.

78. *MEES,* May 17, 1993.

79. Saudi Press Agency, May 22, 1993.

80. *Middle East Executive Report (MEER),* February 1989.

81. *MEED*, August 14, 1992.

82. This was told to the authors by officials from the General Organization for Vocational Training and Technical Education.

83. Ministry of Planning, "Fifth Five-Year Plan," Riyadh.

84. Sir James Craig, "Valedictory Number 2: The Saudi Arabians."

85. *Okaz*, April 16, 1987.

86. Ministry of Planning, "Fifth Five-Year Plan," Riyadh.

87. Soliman M. al-Jabr, "Social Education in Saudi Arabia," pp. 109–10.

88. Nyrop, *Saudi Arabia*, p. 119.

89. Ministry of Planning, "Fifth Five-Year Plan," 1990.

90. This is taken from the authors' interview with Dr. Mansour.

91. Ministry of Planning, "Fifth Five-Year Plan," Riyadh.

92. *Okaz*, October 16, 1987.

93. Ghassan Salame, "Political Power and the Saudi State," in *Power and Stability in the Middle East*, p. 89.

94. *MEED*, February 7, 1992; and *Arab News*, December 6, 1991.

95. *MEER*, February 1989.

96. "Country Report: Bahrain and Qatar," *EIU*, no. 2, 1993.

97. *The Nation*, March 18, 1991.

98. Minnesota Lawyers, *Shame in the House of Saud*, p. 49.

99. *Saudi Gazette*, September 17, 1985.

100. Minnesota Lawyers, *Shame in the House of Saud*, p. 72.

101. To lessen the chance of sexual abuse, the Kingdom enacted regulations that forbid women below the age of forty from working as maids. The measure has proven ineffective. The problem is a common one throughout the Gulf.

102. *MEED*, February 8, 1991.

103. *Far Eastern Economic Review*, January 31, 1991.

104. *Arab News*, June 8, 1987.

CONCLUSIONS

It is almost mandatory to end any profile of the Kingdom of Saudi Arabia with dire warnings for the House of Saud. Since the creation of the Saudi state, obituaries of its imminent demise have been written many times. The years of interfamily strife between kings Saud bin Abdulaziz and Faisal bin Abdulaziz, the threat of Nasserite Egypt, the abortive 1979 Mecca Uprising, and Operation Desert Storm all seriously threatened the country's stability as well as the continuance of the ruling family. But in each case, the al-Saud survived and triumphed, a tribute to their political skills and acumen.

Today, they are facing new problems and challenges, many of which are intertwined. Most are also of their own making. For sixty-plus years, the al-Saud have failed to broaden their political legitimacy, instead relying on their link with Unitarianism. Abdulaziz and his sons have co-opted or subverted all institutions and groups that posed real or potential threats to their rule. The Ikhwan were destroyed; the ulema and the religious establishment have been compromised by becoming government employees; the military has been neutralized; and technocrats have been reduced to serving as glorified clerks of the ruling house. Public discussion of issues is strictly suppressed, and the Kingdom's press is controlled. The result is that there are only two forums in which the Saudi masses can freely express themselves: one is the *majlis,* which is more adapted to asking for favors than arguing policy; the other is the mosque, which is easily manipulated by religious forces opposed to the royal family. Whether the new Consultative Assembly will offer any real alternative has yet to be seen. However, given the body's composition and limitations, its docility seems assured.

The al-Saud have also made other mistakes besides failing to broaden their support. They have mistakenly purchased billions of dollars of weapons, which have contributed little to security and much to national debt. They have invested hundreds of billions of dollars in unwise development schemes, which have paid minimal returns. The Saudi state has sparkling new industrial complexes and a state-of-the-art infrastructure. The Kingdom's economy has grown rapidly but its real productivity is questionable. Agriculture may indeed contribute a sizable percentage to the Kingdom's GDP, but that must be reconciled with the fact that Saudi wheat still costs the government five times world prices. The Saudi non-oil industry may have 2,000 different enterprises, but most employ expatriates and rely on expensive government subsidies to survive. Most importantly, the Kingdom's economy has failed at one of its most important tasks: the generation of jobs for Saudis.

The al-Saud have also erred badly in allowing the unfettered growth of Islamic institutions in their country. Not learning from the mistakes of 1979, the Saudi elite have blindly funded religious organizations as a means of bolstering their religious credentials. They have subsidized religious training at universities even though the Saudi economy cannot absorb these religious scholars who are then easily turned against the state. Just as dangerous has been the Kingdom's past support of foreign fundamentalist groups who now have no qualms in supporting their Saudi counterparts.

Growing criticism of the ruling family exposes the great weakness of the al-Saud monarchy. The crux of the al-Saud's dilemma is this: neither fundamentalists nor modernists specifically need the monarchy's existence to achieve their goals and aspirations. Consequently, the al-Saud have to prove to different political and social elements in Saudi society that the monarchy is the best guarantor of their rights and privileges. Progressives are urged to trust the monarchy to defend them against rabid fundamentalism, while religious conservatives are encouraged to look to the al-Saud as a bulwark against Westernization. All are taught to depend on the royal family for the "good life." Unfortunately, this image is fraying.

The great difficulty besetting the al-Saud is that since the death of Faisal, the royal family has avoided hard decisions. Because Khalid and, more importantly, Fahd have tried to smooth over problems and rule by consensus, too many concessions have been made to hard-line fundamentalists. The latter, for example, have been allowed to express their views in hundreds of mosques and schools, while Saudi progressives and modernists have been muzzled so as not to provoke further religious discord. In doing this, the al-Saud have inadvertently strengthened their own opponents.

Today, Saudi Arabia is increasingly resembling the shah's Iran. The parallels are many: the ruling family is perceived as being corrupt and tied to the United States; foreign policy is pegged to a strong American presence in the Gulf, with indirect ties to Israel; and oil policies are not based on national considerations.

While the House of Saud grapples with its dilemma, the West should avoid repeating the mistakes it made during the Iranian Revolution. The United States in particular should adopt a low profile in the ongoing conflict and resist the urge to make public statements of support. The West should refrain from pressing the Saudi elite to recognize Israel or to sign on to the Israeli-PLO accord. The West should also exercise restraint in meeting Saudi fundamentalists who dress themselves in "human rights" clothing to make their opposition to the al-Saud more palatable. Washington and European capitals should make no mistake: a fundamentalist victory would be disastrous for Western interests in the Kingdom.

The al-Saud are by no means condemned to defeat. Although the present regime is unpopular, its problems are not insurmountable. However, the situation calls for prompt and decisive action. Whether Fahd or his successor will find the vision and will to guide the country forward is the question whose answer no survey can predict.

BIBLIOGRAPHY

Official Documents

Saudi Arabia

Ministry of Agriculture and Water. *Annual Agricultural Report.* Riyadh, 1985–1990.
Ministry of Interior. *Statistical Review.* Riyadh, 1984.
Ministry of Interior. *1984 Annual Report.* Riyadh.
Ministry of Labor and Social Affairs. *Labor and Workmen Law and Attached Procedures.* Riyadh, 1986.
Ministry of Planning. Third, Fourth, and Fifth Five-Year Plans. Riyadh, 1980, 1985, 1990.
Saudi Arabia (newsletter of the Saudi embassy in Washington), February 1990.
Saudi Arabian Monetary Agency (SAMA). *Annual Report.* Riyadh, 1985–1992.
———. *Statistical Review.* Riyadh, 1985–1992.

United Kingdom

Sir James Craig, "Valedictory Number Two: The Saudi Arabians." Foreign and Commonwealth Office, 1984.

United States

U.S. Embassy. *Saudi Arabian Investment Perspective.* Riyadh, 1988.
U.S. Embassy. *Subsidy Study.* Riyadh, 1985.

Books

Abdeen, Adnan M., and Dale N. Shook. *The Saudi Financial System.* Chichester, England: John Wiley and Sons, 1984.
Almana, Mohammed. *Arabia Unified: A Portrait of Ibn Saud.* London: Hutchinson Benhan, 1980.
Armstrong, H.C. *Lord of Arabia.* London: Arthur Baker, 1934.
Beling, Willard A., ed. *King Faisal and the Modernization of Saudi Arabia.* London: Croom Helm, 1980.

Bligh, Alexander. *From Prince to King: Royal Succession in the House of Saud in the Twentieth Century.* New York: New York University Press, 1984.

Chapra, M. Umer. *Towards a Just Monetary System.* Leicester, England: The Islamic Foundation, 1985.

Cole, Donald Powell. *Nomad of the Nomads: The al-Murrah Bedouin of the Empty Quarter.* Cambridge, MA: AHD, 1975.

DeGaury, Gerald. *Faisal: King of Saudi Arabia.* New York and Washington: Praeger, 1966.

Dunnigan, James F., and Austin Bay. *From Shield to Storm.* New York: William Morrow, 1992.

El Mallakh, Ragaei. *Saudi Arabia: Rush to Development.* Baltimore, MD: Johns Hopkins University Press, 1982.

El Mallakh, Ragaei, and Dorothea H. El Mallakh, eds. *Saudi Arabia: Energy, Developmental Planning and Industrialization.* Lexington, MA: Lexington Books, 1982.

Emerson, Steven. *The American House of Saud: The Secret Petrodollar Connection.* New York: Franklin Watts, 1985.

al-Farsy, Fouad. *Saudi Arabia: A Case Study in Development.* London: KPI Ltd., 1986.

Field, Michael. *The Merchants: The Big Business Families of Saudi Arabia and the Gulf.* New York: Overlook Press, 1985.

Freedman, Lawrence, and Efraim Karsh. *The Gulf Conflict, 1990–1991: Diplomacy and War in the New World Order.* Princeton, NJ: Princeton University Press, 1991.

Golub, David. *When Oil and Politics Mix: Saudi Oil Policy, 1975–1985.* Cambridge, MA: Harvard Center for Middle East Studies, 1985.

Habib, John S. *Ibn Saud's Warriors of Islam.* Leiden, The Netherlands: E.J. Brill, 1978.

Hafiz, Faisal, and Murshid Samir, eds. *Who's Who in Saudi Arabia, 1983–1984.* Jeddah: Tihama for Advertising, Public and Marketing Research, 1984.

Halliday, Fred. *Arabia Without Sultans.* New York: Vintage Books. 1975.

Hameed, Mazher A. *Arabia Imperilled: The Security Imperatives of the Arab Gulf States.* Washington, D.C.: Middle East Assessment Group, 1986.

Helms, Christine Moss. *The Cohesion of Saudi Arabia: Evolution of Political Identity.* London: Croom Helm, 1981.

Helms, Robert F. II, and Robert H. Dorff, eds. *The Persian Gulf Crisis: Power in the Post–Cold War World.* Westport, CT: Praeger, 1993.

Hitti, Philip K. *History of the Arabs: From the Earliest Times to the Present.* New York: St. Martin's, 1960.

Holden, David, and Richard Johns. *The House of Saud.* London: Sidgwick and Jackson, 1981.

Hopwood, Derek. "The Ideological Basis: Ibn Abd al-Wahhab's Muslim Revivalism." In *State, Society and Economy in Saudi Arabia,* ed. Tim Niblock. New York: St. Martin's, 1982.

Howarth, David. *The Desert King: Ibn Saud and His Arabia.* New York: McGraw-Hill, 1964.

Hudson, Michael. *Arab Politics: The Search for Legitimacy.* New Haven, CT: Yale University Press, 1977.

Huyette, Summer Scott. *Political Adaptation in Saudi Arabia: A Case Study of the Council of Ministers.* Boulder, CO: Westview Press, 1985.

Islami, A. Reza S., and Rostam Mehraban Kavoussi. *The Political Economy of Saudi Arabia.* Seattle and London: University of Washington Press, 1984.

Johany, Ali D., Michel Berne, and J. Wilson Mixon, Jr. *The Saudi Arabian Economy.* Baltimore, MD: Johns Hopkins University Press, 1986.

Kissinger, Henry. *White House Years.* Boston: Little, Brown, 1979.

Knauerhause, Ramon. *The Saudi Arabian Economy.* New York: Praeger, 1975.

Lacey, Robert. *The Kingdom: Arabia and the House of Saud.* London: Hutchinson, 1981.

Longrigg, Stephen H. "The Economics of Oil in the Middle East." In *Modernization of the Arab World,* ed. J.H. Thompson and R.D. Rieschauer. Princeton, NJ: D. Van Nostrand, 1966.

Looney, Robert E. *Saudi Arabia's Development Potential.* Lexington, MA: Lexington Books, 1982.

Mackey, Sandra. *The Saudis: Inside the Desert Kingdom.* Boston: Houghton Mifflin, 1987.

Mansfield, Peter. *The New Arabians.* Chicago: J.G. Publishing Company; New York: Doubleday, 1981.

Mattione, Richard P. *OPEC's Investment and the International Financial System.* Washington, D.C.: Brookings Institution, 1985.

Mikesell, Raymond F., and Hollis B. Chenery. *Arabian Oil.* Chapel Hill: University of North Carolina Press, 1949.

Munif, Abdulrahman. *Cities of Salt.* Trans. Peter Theroux. New York: Random House, 1988.

———. *The Trench.* Trans. Peter Theroux. New York: Pantheon, 1991.

Niblock, Tim, ed. *State, Society and Economy in Saudi Arabia.* New York: St. Martin's, 1982.

Nonneman, Gerd. *Iraq, the Gulf States and the War: A Changing Relationship: 1980–1986 and Beyond.* London: Ithaca Press, 1986

Nyrop, Richard F., et al. *Saudi Arabia: A Country Study.* Washington, D.C.: American University Press, 1984.

Philby, H. St. John B. *A Pilgrim in Arabia.* London: Robert Hale, 1943.

———. *Arabian Days.* London: Robert Hale, 1948.

———. *Arabian Jubilee.* London: Ernest Ben, 1955.

Polk, William R. *The Arab World.* Cambridge, MA: Harvard University Press, 1980.

Presley, John R. *A Guide to the Saudi Arabian Economy.* New York: Macmillan, 1984.

Quandt, William B. *Saudi Arabia in the 1980s.* Washington, D.C.: Brookings Institution, 1981.

Rashid, Dr. Nasser Ibrahim, and Dr. Esber Ibrahim Shaheen. *King Fahd and Saudi Arabia's Great Evolution.* Joplin, MO: International Institute of Technology, 1987.

Robinson, Jeffrey. *Yamani: The Inside Story.* New York: Atlantic Monthly Press, 1988.

Safran, Nadav. *Saudi Arabia: The Ceaseless Quest for Security.* Cambridge, MA: Belknap Press of Harvard University Press, 1985.

Salame, Ghassan. "Political Power and the Saudi State." In *Power and Stability in the Middle East,* ed. Berch Berberoglu, 70–89. London: Zed Books, 1988.

Sampson, Anthony. *The Arms Bazaar.* London: Hodder and Stoughton, 1977.

———. *The Seven Sisters.* London: Hodder and Stoughton, 1975.

Sasson, Jean P. *Princess: A True Story of Life behind the Veil in Saudi Arabia.* New York: William Morrow, 1992.

Schwartzkopf, General H. Norman, with Peter Petre. *It Doesn't Take a Hero.* New York: Bantam, 1992.

Shawcross, William. *The Shah's Last Ride—The Fate of an Ally.* New York: Simon and Schuster, 1988.

Sonn, Tamara. *Between Qur'an and Crown: The Challenges of Political Legitimacy in the Arab World.* Boulder, CO: Westview Press, 1990.

Stookey, Robert W., ed. *The Arabian Peninsula: Zone of Ferment.* Stanford, CA: Hoover Institution Press, 1984.

Taheri, Amir. *Holy Terror: Inside the World of Islamic Terrorism.* Bethesda, MD: Adler and Adler, 1987.

van der Meulen, D. *The Wells of Ibn Sa'ud.* New York: Praeger, 1957.

Wells, Donald A. *Saudi Arabian Developmental Strategy.* Washington, D.C.: American Enterprise Institute for Public Policy Research, 1976.

Wilson, Peter. *A Question of Interest: The Paralysis of Saudi Banking.* Boulder, CO: Westview Press, 1991.

Woodward, Bob. *Veil: The Secret Wars of the CIA, 1981–1987.* New York: Simon and Schuster, 1987.

Yant, Martin. *Desert Mirage: The True Story of the Gulf War.* Buffalo, NY: Prometheus Books, 1991.

al-Yassini, Ayman. *Religion and State in the Kingdom of Saudi Arabia.* Boulder, CO: Westview Press, 1985.

Young, Arthur. *The Making of a Financial Giant.* New York: New York University Press, 1955.

Zwemmer, Reverend S.M. *Arabia: The Cradle of Islam.* London: Darf, 1900.

Monographs and Dissertations

Amnesty International. *Saudi Arabia: Detention Without Trial of Suspected Political Prisoners.* New York: Amnesty International, January 1990.

Bseisu, Adnan N. "Monetary Organization in Saudi Arabia." Master's thesis, American University of Beirut, 1958.

International Monetary Fund. *Saudi Arabia: Staff Report for the 1988 Article IV Consultation.* Washington, D.C., 1989.

———. *Saudi Arabia: Staff Report.* Washington, D.C., 1991.

———. *Saudi Arabia: Staff Report.* Washington, D.C., 1993.

Minnesota Lawyers International Human Rights Committee. *Shame in the House of Saud: Contempt for Human Rights in the Kingdom of Saudi Arabia.* Minneapolis: Minnesota Lawyers, 1992.

Saudi Basic Industries (SABIC). *Annual Report.* Riyadh, 1985–1992.

al-Solaim, Soliman. "Constitutional and Judicial Organization in Saudi Arabia." Ph.D. diss., Johns Hopkins University, 1970.

Journals, Magazines, and Newspapers

Abboud, Joseph B. "Gold Output Up at Second Saudi Mine." *American Metal Market,* July 24, 1991, 5.

Abdallah, Mushin. "Using the War as a Pretext." *World Marxist Review* 31, no. 3 (March 1988): 137.

Abdallah, Taisir M. "Self-Esteem and Locus of Control of College Men in Saudi Arabia." *Psychological Reports* 65, nos. 3–2 (December 1989): 1323–27.

Ahmad, Eqbal. "A Tug of War for Muslims' Allegiance." *World Press Review* 38, no. 11 (November 1991): 24–25.

Alsuwaigh, Siham A. "Women in Transition: The Case of Saudi Arabia." *Journal of Comparative Family Studies* 20, no. 1 (Spring 1989): 67–78.

Altorki, Soraya. "Family Organization and Womens' Power in Urban Saudi Arabian Society." *Journal of Anthropological Research* 33, no. 3 (Fall 1977): 277–87.

Amos, Deborah. "Sheik to Chic." *Mother Jones* (January–February 1991): 28–29.

al-Amri, Sa'ad. "Stop the Terror, End the Despotism." *World Marxist Review* 39, no. 2 (February 1987): 89–90.

Arab Banking and Finance. Various issues. London.

Arab News. Various issues. Jeddah.

Arabian Monitor. Various issues. Washington, D.C.

Armstrong, Scott. "Eye of the Storm." *Mother Jones* (November–December 1991): 30–37.

———. "Iraqnophobia: What the Media Neglected to Tell Us about the Iraq Crisis." *Mother Jones* (November–December 1990): 24–27.

Asharq al-Awsat. Various issues. London.

Associated Press. Manama.

Auty, Richard M. "The Economic Stimulus from Resource-based Industry in Developing Countries: Saudi Arabia and Bahrain." *Economic Geography* 64, no. 3 (July 1988): 109–25.

———. "The Internal Determinants of Eight Oil-Exporting Countries' Resource-based Industry Performance." *Journal of Development Studies* 25, no. 3 (April 1989): 354–72.

Bahry, Louay. "The New Saudi Woman: Modernizing in an Islamic Framework." *Middle East Journal* (Autumn 1982): 502–15.

Banker. Various issues. London.

Beaumont, Peter. "Water and Development in Saudi Arabia." *Geographical Journal* 143, no. 4 (March 1977): 42–60.

Bligh, Alexander. "The Saudi Religious Elite (Ulama) as Participant in the Political System of the Kingdom." *International Journal of Middle East Studies* 17, no. 1 (February 1985): 37–49.

BusinessWeek. Various issues. New York.

Butler, Kirt C., and S.J. Malaikah. "Efficiency and Inefficiency in Thinly Traded Stock Markets: Kuwait and Saudi Arabia." *Journal of Banking and Finance* 16, no. 1 (February 1992): 197–210.

Cain, Michael, and Kais S. al-Badri. "An Assessment of the Trade and Restructuring Effects of the Gulf Co-operation Council." *International Journal of Middle East Studies* 21, no. 1 (February 1989): 57–70.

Christian Science Monitor. Various issues. Boston.

Cole, Donald P. "Bedouin and Social Change in Saudi Arabia." *Journal of Asian and African Studies* 16, nos. 1–2 (January 1981): 128–49.

Crawford, M.J. "Civil War, Foreign Intervention and the Question of Political Legitimacy: A 19th Century Saudi Qadi's Dilemma." *International Journal of Middle East Studies* 14, no. 2 (1984): 227–48.

Dawisha, Adeed I. "Internal Values and External Threats: The Making of Saudi Foreign Policy." *Orbis* 23, no. 1 (Spring 1979): 129–43.

Dubovsky, Steven L. "Psychiatry in Saudi Arabia." *American Journal of Psychiatry* (November 1983): 1455–59.

The Economist. Various issues. London.

Economist Intelligence Unit (EIU). Various issues. London.

Edens, David G. "The Anatomy of the Saudi Revolution." *International Journal of Middle East Studies* 5, no. 1 (January 1974): 50–64.

Euromoney. Various issues. London.

Far Eastern Economic Review. Various issues. Hong Kong.

Field, Michael. "Merchants and Rulers of Arabia." *Euromoney,* July 1981, 30.

Financial Times of London. Various issues. London.

Gallagher, Eugene B. "Medical Education in Saudi Arabia." *Journal of Asian and African Studies* 20, nos. 1–2 (January 1985): 1–12.

Gulf Economic and Financial Report. Gulf International Bank. Various issues. Manama, Bahrain.

al-Hegelan, Abdelrahman, and Monte Palmer. "Bureaucracy and Development in Saudi Arabia." *Middle East Journal* (Winter 1985): 48–68.

Hidore, John, and Yahya Albokhair. "Sand Encroachment in al-Hasa Oasis, Saudi Arabia." *Geographical Review* 72, no. 3 (July 1982): 350–56.

Hirst, David, and Michael Field. "The House of Saud on Shifting Sands: Will the Persian Gulf Crisis Transform the Kingdom?" *World Press Review* 38, no. 2 (February 1991): 20–22.

Humphreys, R. Stephen. "Islam and Political Values in Saudi Arabia, Egypt and Syria." *Middle East Journal* 33, no. 1 (Winter 1979): 1–19.

Ibrahim, Abdel-Sattar, and Abdulla Alnafie. "Perception of and Concern about Sociocultural Change and General Psychopathology in Saudi Arabian Students." *Journal of Social Psychology* 131, no. 2 (April 1991): 179–87.

al-Jabr, Soliman M. "Social Education in Saudi Arabia." *Social Education* 54, no. 2 (February 1990): 109–10.

Jenish, D'Arcy. "Islam and the Gulf War: Why Many Moslems Support Iraq." *Macleans,* February 11, 1991, 34–37.

Jenkins, Jolyon. "Shifting Sands: Why Kuwait Is So Small." *New Statesman and Society* 4, no. 137 (February 8, 1991): 12–13.

Kechichian, Joseph A. "Islamic Revivalism and Change in Saudi Arabia: Juhayman al-'Utaybi's 'Letters' to the Saudi People." *Muslim World* 80, no. 1 (January 1990): 1–17.

———. "The Role of the Ulama in the Politics of an Islamic State: The Case of Saudi Arabia." *International Journal of Middle East Studies* 18, no. 1 (Winter 1986): 53–66.

Kelidar, A.R. "The Problem of Succession in Saudi Arabia." *Asian Affairs* 9, no. 1 (February 1978): 23–30.

Knauerhause, Ramon. "Saudi Arabia's Economy at the Beginning of the 1970s." *Middle East Journal* 28, no. 2 (Spring 1974): 126–38.

Kraft, Joseph. "Letter from Arabia." *New Yorker,* October 20, 1973.

Kuniholm, Bruce R. "What the Saudis Really Want: A Primer for the Reagan Administration." *Orbis* 25, no. 1 (Spring 1981): 107–13.

Lewis, Bernard. "The Roots of Muslim Rage." *Atlantic.* September 1990, 47–57.

Long, David E. "Stability in Saudi Arabia." *Current History* 90, no. 552 (January 1991): 9–14.

Looney, Robert E. "Patterns of Human Resource Development in Saudi Arabia." *Middle Eastern Studies* 27, no. 4 (October 1991): 668–79.

———. "Saudi Arabian Budgetary Dilemmas." *Middle Eastern Studies* 26, no. 1 (January 1990): 76–87.

Los Angeles Times. Various issues. Los Angeles.

Maclean's. Various issues. Toronto.

McHale, T.R. "A Prospect of Saudi Arabia." *International Affairs* 56, no. 4 (Autumn 1980): 622–47.

MEED: Middle East Business Weekly. Various issues. London.

The Middle East. Various issues. London.

Middle East Economic Survey (MEES). Various issues. Nicosia, Cyprus.

Middle East Executive Report (MEER). Various issues. Washington, D.C.

Middle East International. Various issues. London.

Middle East Report. July–August 1992.

Middle East Money. Various issues. London.

Middle East Monitor. Various issues.

Mideast Mirror. Various issues. London.

Moon, Chung In. "Korean Contractors in Saudi Arabia: Their Rise and Fall." *Middle East Journal* 40, no. 4 (Autumn 1986): 614–33.

The Nation. Various issues. New York.

New York Times. Various issues. New York.

Newsweek. Various issues. New York.

Ochsenwald, William. "Saudi Arabia and the Islamic Revival." *International Journal of Middle East Studies* 13, no. 2 (August 1981): 271–86.

Okaz. Various issues. Jeddah.

Palmer, Monte, Abdelrahman al-Hegelan, Mohammed Bushara, and Ali Leila el-Sayeed Yassin. "Bureaucratic Innovation and Economic Development in the Middle East: A Study of Egypt, Saudi Arabia, and the Sudan." *Journal of Asian and African Studies* 24, nos. 1–2 (January–April 1989): 12–27.

Platt's Oilgram News. Various issues. New York.

Qatari News Agency. Doha.

al-Quds al-Arabi. Various issues. London.

"Reinventing the Wheel." *Ms.* Magazine, March–April, 1991, 14–15.

Reuters. London.

al-Riyadh. Various issues. Riyadh.

Riyadh Daily. Various issues. Riyadh.

Robinson, Walter V. "Saudi Society at Odds with Itself." *Journal of Commerce and Commercial,* August 28, 1990.

Rugh, William. "Emergence of a New Middle Class in Saudi Arabia." *Middle East Journal* 27, no. 1 (Winter 1973): 7–20.

Saedi-Wong, Simin, Abdul Rahman al-Frayh, and Henry Y.H. Wong. "Socio-Economic Epidemiology of Consanguineous Matings in the Saudi Arabian Population." *Journal of Asian and African Studies* 24, nos. 3–4 (July–October 1989): 247–52.

Saleh, Nassir A. "Geography in Saudi Arabia." *Professional Geographer* 54, no. 3 (May 1985): 216–18.

"Saudi Arabia." *Business America* 118, no. 18 (September 11, 1989): 21–23.

Saudi Business. Various issues. Jeddah.

Saudi Gazette. Various issues. Jeddah.

Saudi Press Agency. Riyadh.

South. Various issues. London.

Thesiger, Wilfred. "A Retrospect." *Asian Affairs* 21, no. 3 (October 1990): 259–67.

Time. Various issues. New York.

Turner, Louis, and James Bedore. "Saudi Arabia: The Power of the Purse-Strings." *International Affairs* 54, no. 3 (July 1978): 405–20.

————. "The Trade Politics of Middle Eastern Industrialization." *Foreign Affairs* 57, no. 2 (Winter 1978–1979): 306–22.

Umm al-Qura. Various issues. Mecca.

U.S. News and World Report. Various issues. Washington, D.C.

Utne Reader. Various issues. Minneapolis, MN.

Van Hollen, Christopher. "Don't Engulf the Gulf." *Foreign Affairs* 59, no. 5 (Summer 1981): 1064–78.

Walker, Richard Leigh. "In the Heartland of Islam." *Christianity Today* 35, no. 4 (April 8, 1991): 56–57.

Wall Street Journal. Various issues. New York.

Washington Post. Various issues. Washington.

al-Yassini, Ayman. "Islamic Revival and National Development in the Arab World." *Journal of Asian and African Studies* 21, nos. 1–2 (January–April 1986): 104–21.

INDEX

A

Abalkhail, Mohammed, 221
Abdulaziz bin Saud (King), 6, 17,
    19–20, 22, 23, 38, 235
    early political institutions, 41–42
    and economy, 173–75
    and foreign relations, 88–91
    and Ikhwan, 45–46
    last years of, 46–48
    and legal system, 201
    and military, 142–45
    and *mutawaeen*, 26
    and religious repression, 27
    and rise of modern state, 39–41
    and Franklin Roosevelt, 93
and Shiites, 250
    and tribes, 30
Abdullah bin Abdulaziz (Crown
    Prince), 20–21, 29, 60, 113, 133,
    165
    control of National Guard, 158
    foreign policy, 101–02
Abdullah bin Faisal bin Turki (Prince),
    195
Abdullilah bin Abdulaziz (Prince),
    74–75
Abdulrahman bin Abdulaziz (Prince),
    21, 113
Absenteeism, 205
Abu Musa, 119
Accountability, 77, 86*n.116*
ACC. *See* Arab Cooperation Council
Advances, 198, 199

Adwdah, Mohammed bin, 243
Agriculture, 176, 185, 221–28
Agriculture and Water Ministry, 222,
    224, 226–28
Ahmad, Hedayet, 261
Ahmad bin Abdulaziz (Prince), 21, 158
Airborne Warning and Control System
    (AWACS), 152
Air conditioning, 235
Air Force. *See* Royal Saudi Air Force
Al-Aqsa Mosque (Jerusalem), 99
Al-Awfi, Fayyad Mohammed, 59
Al-Badr, Mohammed, 97
Al-Bakr, Fawzia, 249
Al-Bashir, Omar Hassan, 120
Al-Buraiymi Oasis, 8, 94, 95, 137*n.21*
Alcoholism, 236–38
Al-Dahna Desert, 10
Al-Dilam, Battle of, 143
Al-Fahd (family), 21
Al-Faisal (family), 20
Algeria, 114
Al-Ghosaibi, Ghazi, 25
Al-Hakim, Ayatollah Mohammed Baqr,
    121
Al-Harkin, Mohammed, 202
Al-Hasa (Saudi Arabia), 10–11, 15, 173,
    176
Al-Hassan, Hani, 134
Al-Hawali, Safar, 63–64
Al-Hawtah (Saudi Arabia), 207
Ali, Mohammed, 39
Alireza, Hajji Abdullah, 23
Al-Kabeer, Saud, 20

ABOUT THE AUTHORS

Both authors are journalists. **Peter W. Wilson** lived in Saudi Arabia for four years. He was a writer for the *Saudi Gazette* newspaper and a frequent contributor to other publications. Wilson's first book on the Kingdom, *A Question of Interest: The Paralysis of Saudi Banking,* was published in 1991.

Douglas F. Graham lived in Saudi Arabia for nearly seven years. He was a writer for the *Arab News* newspaper and a frequent contributor to other publications. Graham's first book on the Kingdom, *Saudi Arabia Unveiled,* was published in 1991.